THE APPRENTICESHIP OF SIN:

A JOURNEY FROM PROMISE,

THROUGH PRISON

TO PURPOSE

By

Pili C. Greenfield, Sr.

This book is written from the experiences of the author and is nonfiction {refers to literature based in fact, the real world}. He has tried to recreate events, locales and conversations from his memories of them. In order to maintain their anonymity in some instances he has changed the names of individuals and places. He may have changed some identifying characteristics and details such as physical properties, occupations and places of residence.

GreeneHouse Publishing Company
PO Box 58
Loganville, PA 17342-0058
www.greenehousebooks.com

Cover Illustration by 99designs
Cover and Book design by GreeneHouse Publishing, Inc.
Editing by GreeneHouse Publishing
Author photograph by Justin Featherstone of OLOT Photography

ISBN 13: 978-1-947953-01-7
ISBN # for eBook: pending
LCCN: 2017954696

First Edition September 2017
Manufactured in the USA

Printed in the USA by Lulu, Inc. of Raleigh, NC 27607

Table of Contents

Introduction

"The Apprenticeship of Sin: A Journey from Promise, Through Prison to Purpose" Todd Clark

I have known Pili for the better part of twenty years. I first met him at his church around 1995, in Northeast Washington, D.C., when I was conducting a workshop there.

A few months later, I asked him to participate in a Youth Internship Project that I had developed, which revolved around the making of a documentary about the Lincoln Theatre, an historically renown theater, primarily known for being the only performance venue available for pre-eminent African American singers and performers in Washington, D.C. during the musically prolific decades of the 1930's and 40's.

He enthusiastically participated, along with ten other D.C. area High School students. They conducted research on the theater's unique history, special contribution and strong connection to nationally celebrated African American performers, as well as its role and value later on to the primarily Black residents and visitors to the nation's capital, during the heavy and challenging times of racial segregation.

I was familiar with Pili at that time for being an extremely gifted musician and a brilliant composer. Several years after the internship had concluded, I hired him to compose many of the music soundtracks for various video programming that I was producing in the late 1990's. The original music he composed was an important part of several professional video spots, including several that celebrated the professional legacy of select recipients of the annual, prestigious, Adam Smith Award.

Pili was a natural musical genius, able to quickly craft just the right soundtracks for this lofty gala awards event.

So impressed was the organization's leader, that he extended an invitation for Pili to attend, which he did- and I watched Pili adroitly handle himself at the event-engaging in conversations with Fortune 500 CEO's and a select group of nationally elected politicians.

Pili comfortably held forth on any issue that came up during the evening and for years after that night, (up until even today), he still refers to that experience as a significant turning point in his expanding awareness of the free enterprise system and his own deterministic thinking about wanting to bring financial literacy to needful African-American youth who resided in the disenfranchised, inner-city neighborhoods around Washington, D.C. that he knew so very well.

These were also the places that Pili had grown up in- and where he in turn, had made some extremely unwise decisions as a young man. A few weeks ago, Pili spoke to the congregants of a local D.C. church at their recently held revival weekend, whose theme was entitled, "Let Your Light Shine".

He read from *"The Apprenticeship of Sin: A Journey from Promise, Through Prison to Purpose"*. The book, he told the congregation that night was one of the resulting consequences of having been incarcerated due to his pursuit of criminal activities in his younger life. The congregation became respectfully quiet and enthusiastically urged him to continue his message.

 In his remarks that night, as he does so very well in this ambitious, introspective and necessary work, Pili spoke directly and passionately about what had occurred in his life; growing up as a young teenager in D.C., carefully dissecting the sociological and personal influences that he identifies as having led to his 10 year sentence in a Federal penitentiary.

Pili wrote this book in order to chronicle his spiritual growth during his incarceration, but more importantly, through the writing of this book he has also been able to comprehensively analyze and interpret the events of his life journey, coming to age as a young African American male in a rough part of the nation's capitol, and then interpret the impact of many of those key events on our society as a whole.

The important and unique value of Pili's keenly analytical and detail-driven writing is that it provides an unusually candid window to the events and influences that occurred before he served his time and in doing so it offers a prescient warning to the political leaders, non-profit organizations, law enforcement personal, church congregations and neighborhood teachers of today-who often struggle to understand how to stop the overlapping and never-ending cycles of generational violence and disrupted growth that not only hold back- but ruthlessly decimate- entire generations of African-American families and friends.

In the intentional, non-traditionally ordered chapters, he eloquently shows how the recurring influences of {Poverty, Hate, Sex, Hypocrisy and Dysfunction} repeat themselves with greater and greater – and more devastating impact, and he relates how those cycles of destructive behavior and thinking led to his own stages of "growth" … as a precocious teenager who then becomes a seasoned young adult pimp.

In each chapter, Pili writes with passionate exposition and brutal honesty about what he sees are the universal influences and all too familiar factors that occurred within him, and around him, leading to his criminal life.

With this work, Pili has carefully, and in the end I believe, successfully, given measured consideration to all of the pertinent psychological, familial and peer influences that eventually led to his ten year sentence. In writing this book, and in sharing his deeply personal journey, Pili has the fervent hope that the destructive patterns that he meticulously highlights, (and which are still at work today creating the pimps of tomorrow), can be disrupted and made ineffectual.

On the night of the revival this past fall, Pili began his remarks by drawing from Matthew, 5:15 and 5:16 which read: Neither do men light a candle, and put it under a bushel, but on a candlestick; and it giveth light unto all that are in the house. Let your light so shine before men, that they may see your good works, and glorify your Father which is in heaven.

Through his book- and because of his current life focus, which he specifically acknowledges in his public speaking, he is the light that he sees himself able to offer- and he challenges others to bring forth their own light to rescue those in need. Pili's desire is to be a guide and a resource for anyone working with those who are involved with, and negatively affected by trafficking, and those who may still see it as a criminal business opportunity. Over the years, I have also had the opportunity to develop educational video programming for several anti-trafficking organizations.

With each of those projects, I gained a thorough understanding of the primary means of pimp control, and I was able to fully appreciate the negative impact and vicious trauma visited upon the lives of the young women who become trapped in that brutal world.

What makes Pili's book so unique and valuable is that there is now a clear way to better understand how an individual- in this case, a young African American male growing up in a twenty-first century urban environment- can be influenced to make the kind of devastating decisions that can lead to becoming the practitioner of trafficking.

Although his "pimp control" methodology did not mirror the violent brutality I saw in many of the programs I edited, it was none-the-less criminal in nature, and it remains devastating in terms of its negative impact on all of those involved.

But-as a result of writing this book, Pili has begun a journey towards becoming an engaging and powerful public speaker- with a desire to educate, challenge and inform.

This book has thus become an important and crucial first step in his ongoing redemption- leading to his desire to create opportunities to share with those most in need of hearing it, his insightful, challenging and hopeful message about what took place over his life: ending up in prison at a young age but emerging as a gifted writer and social justice advocate in his later years.

Because of his profound and revolutionary spiritual journey, and a determination to expand his knowledge through legal studies, he has transformed his entire outlook and re-established a fundamentally different value system.

This book tells that story with rare wisdom, informed hindsight and eloquent analysis.

In the end, Pili's book is an extremely revealing, eloquently written, brutally truthful expose and a perceptive analysis of not only his exposure and involvement to the world of trafficking and pimp control, but also an extremely insightful analysis of how he, himself, a young Black male, growing up in the rough neighborhoods of Washington, D.C. (and also in the suburban comforts of Prince Georges County), eventually got to a point in his life, step by step, where he was found guilty of the crime of human trafficking.

The book, and Pili himself, are indeed unusual in this regard because he has been able to effectively describe in intimate and personal detail what he actually thought and did as a young man (and a soon to be pimp) and we as his readers can see how those very same influences continue to persist and negatively impact the lives and families of many inner city black males today.

Pili's life journey now is in sharing how his "Apprenticeship" took place, in recounting what he saw and witnessed, in describing what he felt and experienced along the way: from the time he was a young inner city black male trying to fit in with his peers and fighting unsuccessfully back against a multitude of negative temptations; coming to terms with the violent surroundings and disfunctional community he was forced to maneuver through; to the dichotomy of the middle class comforts and aspirations he also grew up with.

His story will resonate with concerned teachers, clergy, social workers, police departments and any family that has been tragically impacted by the scourge of trafficking.

Pili's writing is extremely focused, seriously earnest, and profoundly honest.

Pili is now the proud father of three children and is currently striving to support his family, including the development of entrepreneurial business ideas that engage the community in dialogue and understanding.

I know he is looking forward to bringing his voice and presence towards helping to eradicate the persistence of trafficking, and instead bring a deeper understanding as to how individuals like him got involved.

I salute and thank Pili for wanting to share his story and for trying his best to make a positive difference, and for working hard to be a transformative influence for the better, in so many lives.

Todd Clark
March 15, 2017

Preface

Writing this book is among the top three most frightening experiences of my life. I say that because I realize that there is a great deal of honesty and introspection required in order to bring forth the message I felt led to convey. For a lot of people, reading this may not present much of a challenge, especially when you consider the target demographic I wrote this book for.

But for me, this undertaking has been no easy feat, especially in light of my current situation: at the time of this writing, I'm a black man in his late thirties who is approaching the end of a ten-year federal prison sentence. I was convicted of sex trafficking of a minor in connection with my role as a "pimp" who managed prostitutes under the guise of an online escort service. This was my second felony conviction and subsequent federal prison sentence; the first was a five-year, despite the fact that it was my first offense as an adult sentence, for selling crack cocaine.

A large part of my thought process was whether or not I should wait to write this book until after my release, so I could begin to share my story in conjunction with future endeavors I hoped to be a part of. I still question if I have accomplished enough.

My career in crime wasn't lucrative enough or ruthless enough to elevate my name to the status of infamy that is revered in American culture (especially among minorities), and-no matter how much I believe in my plans and purpose for the future-I have yet to achieve the fairy tale-like happy ending that often makes this type of literature appealing and inspirational to mainstream audiences.

I don't have a graduate degree to lend credibility to my observations, and I have a limited number of statistics and reports from experts that I use to support some of my conclusions. However, through the unending benevolence of my parents, I managed to earn an Associate's Degree in Paralegal Studies, and I have also completed a Certificate Program in Entrepreneurship that Kent State University provided "free of charge" to a select group of inmates at one of the prisons that I traveled through. Still, none of that makes me "qualified" to write this type of book.

Although I consider myself a Christian, I belong to the Unitarian Universalist Association. I'll explain my spiritual journey in greater detail throughout this book, but I wanted to make that point now for those who were expecting a certain type of book because of the title.

Anyway, through the UUA's prison outreach program, I got a chance to read a lot of literature that the UUA publishes, and there is always a lot of talk about their desire for multiculturalism and diversity. In considering this, I feel the need to address some of the issues involved in the work of building an inclusive culture in this "post-Obama era" that many communities of faith and social outreach claim to seek.

In searching to understand my role in this journey, I decided to take an honest look at my past, and that caused me to examine some of the things and places that I've experienced along the way.

Although this process has resulted in my writing becoming much more autobiographical than I intended, I certainly don't want to give the impression that I believe any of my former activities are praiseworthy.

I've read quite a few autobiographies that seemed to focus more on the insanity of the past than on the solutions of the future. Rather, I sought to understand what psychologists, anthropologists, preachers, teachers, and the like have sought to understand about the human condition since the beginning of civilization: what motivates a person to make some of the choices they make? I began to take a thorough assessment of all my decisions, my shortcomings, my mistakes, my character flaws and my fears.

It was through this process that I came to understand this methodology, this process, this system that I have titled "The Apprenticeship of Sin." I'm fully aware that the word "sin" may be a bit troublesome for some.

Most of the "mainstream" religious practices have very rigid, narrow definitions of what constitutes sin, and I know that there are those who suffer with self-esteem issues due to some of the practitioners of these teachings.

The working definition of sin that I have come to accept is any action contrary to your particular belief system, whether based on some sacred writing or book, your personal understanding of a higher power or, for me as a UU, the seven principles.

I really had no desire to write a book, but I received some inspiration from a few different sources that made me desire to speak out.

I am currently enrolled in the Life Connections Program (LCP), a faith based program here at the prison that is open to all faith traditions and is designed to help inmates like myself understand and explore their spiritual journeys. During a group discussion, we began tossing around the idea of sin with our group spiritual guide, Mrs. Judy, who happened to be an older, white, Catholic woman.

The discussion was based around the scenario of a four or five-year-old that tells a lie about some bad deed, such as breaking a lamp or writing on the wall. We began to debate whether this "sin" was an innate response to consequences, versus a learned behavior. Again, I'm sure that there have been numerous studies done on this issue by people with much more expertise in this area, but for me this discussion began to bring into focus the catalyst for my own sins, apart from the demonic influence that was taught to me during my Christian upbringing.

One day, the LCP chaplain organized a seminar led by a man named Azim Khamisa. Mr. Khamisa told the tragic story of how his son, Tariq Khamisa, was murdered in 1995 while delivering pizzas, by a then fourteen-year-old boy. He spoke of his subsequent journey in trying to deal with his son's murder, which included forgiving the young man who perpetrated the crime and working to end the conditions that cause young men all over the country to behave with such brutality. I listened with empathy for his loss, yet, I couldn't help but realize how little he and those involved in the work of "restorative justice" understand about what creates this type of savagery.

After reading Khamisa's book, `From Murder to Forgiveness`, I knew I needed to contribute my voice to this conversation. In his book, Khamisa speaks of the Tibetan Buddhist concept of transition known as a "bardo", a state of moving towards enlightenment for those who have prepared. I don't know much about enlightenment, but I knew that I had been doing the work to prepare for a transition from what I had been to what I had been called to be.

I believe that my "sinful nature" was taught to me; some lessons were learned involuntarily, and quite a few others were learned willingly, but all were taught, practiced, and mastered with the same diligence and perseverance required of any discipline.

It is from this perspective I desire to examine sin—from its inception during my childhood until it was fully formed amid my life as an adult, and now through my struggle to live up to the ideals and principles I have adopted on my road to redemption. I believe this insight has the power to transform lives; not through some magical spiritual awakening or supernatural power, but through real community building founded on honest discourse.

I won't pretend that my intentions are entirely altruistic; as a black man in a capitalist country I desperately need to form relationships with people who are capable of helping me navigate various business endeavors, apart from the world of crime that I have been apprenticed into. I know part of the debt I owe to those who were negatively affected by my sin must be repaid by using my gifts to help them overcome some of the obstacles they face.

By acknowledging my own struggles, my own flaws;
I hope to inspire others to recognize destructive patterns and practices they support, knowingly or unknowingly.
I hope to replace my former evil patterns and practices with the good I desperately tried to destroy, in spite of how uncomfortable or culturally unacceptable it may be.
I want to save my children, my family, and my community from becoming an agent of this destructive lifestyle, this apprenticeship of sin.

Acknowledgements

I'm almost certain I'm going to forget someone, but please charge it to my head and not to my heart. First and foremost, I must thank God for giving me the strength to see this through to the end. To my parents, Mike and Jackie Greenfield, thank you for being my rock in spite of all of my bad decisions.

To my children—Zhane Greenfield, Pili Greenfield, Jr., and Zhalil Greenfield—know that your father loves you, and I pray you will become something far greater than anything I've ever been or will become.

To my brothers Kalil and Jamaal, and to two of my cousins who are just like brothers to me, Jearld Cross and Ronald Dews, no matter what happens in this thing we call life, we're in this together until the end.

To my cousin Courtney, I love you for being you; don't let anything stop you from becoming who God wants you to be. To my aunt Jacci, I love you as you are, no matter what. To all of my family, which is too large to name everyone individually, know my love is with you forever. To Rina T. Daniels and Remeca Mashack, thank you for loving me and accepting me into your family and for your support of my comeback.

Thank you to everyone who has helped me to bring this project to fruition; especially to Justin Featherstone of OLOT Photography for all of the dope pictures and video, and to Frozine Morrow (AKA the "that" police) for your attention to detail and keen eye for the things I couldn't or didn't want to deal with. To Karema Greene—my publisher, business partner, and friend—No eye has seen, no ear has heard, and no mind has imagined what God has prepared for those who love him. (1 Cor 2:9). To all of the chaplains, prison ministers, and clergy who I met along this journey; current and former chaplains at FCI Allenwood, FCI Elkton, and FCI Petersburg—especially to the mentors;

guest speakers and volunteers of the Life Connections Program: I want you to know I appreciate all of the words and support you have provided along the way.

I have to send a special "thank you" to Pastor Lisa Brown for all of your wise words and support.

To all of the good men I have met during my time incarcerated, I say to you the world is waiting on you. Know that with all of the plans, dreams, and goals you have, 60-70% of them will probably fail or not work out how you planned once you return to society. Keep grinding anyway, keep planning, and keep striving.

Real ones are a rare species.

To all of the creeps, haters, and especially to the abusive law enforcement officers who got through their day by making life miserable for me and for people like me, God bless you.

To all of my real friends and real homies, all the good men who stood outside with me and tried to make something out of nothing, I don't need to mention your names for you to know what it is. Hit my phone.

This book is dedicated to the love and life of my grandmother, Ella Elizabeth Rowe Greenfield. I pray that God gives me the strength to be the man you wanted me to be.

Chapter I
THE FOUNDATION

{POVERTY, HATE, SEX, HYPOCRISY, DISFUNCTION}

POVERTY

I was born on August 27, 1978 in Washington, D.C. My parents
were both raised in Northeast D.C., and my grandparents' houses
were only about two minutes away from each other. I am the
second of three boys and my parents were married in 1975, on
my mom's birthday, at the Catholic Church my family still
attends. My mom was pregnant with my older brother; I was
always taught that the Catholic Church had some very strict rules
about that type of stuff, but apparently, they figured it all out. My
dad worked for the Navy as a civilian employee of the
Department of Defense, and my mom worked as an EEG/EKG
technician for a small doctor's office. Together they managed to
save enough money to buy a house in Landover, Maryland, a
town about five minutes outside of D.C. and in the same
neighborhood as the stadium where the Washington Redskins

play football. This was the early 1980's, a time when more and more middle class Washingtonians would begin to trade in the confines of the inner city for the single-family homes and suburban life of neighboring Prince Georges County, Maryland. This exodus was overwhelmingly African-American. In fact, with an abundance of well-paying jobs in the federal government, Prince Georges County remains one of the wealthiest, predominately African American counties in the country. As a child, I spent countless hours running around in the backyard of our house with my brothers and cousins, while summers were spent in Northeast D.C. at my maternal grandmother's. Together we enjoyed long summer days riding our bikes around the neighborhood, swimming, playing basketball, and enjoying ourselves at the local recreation center. I spent most weekends at my dad's mother's house, where my grandmother lived with my Aunt Jacci. My Aunt Gwen owned the house next door, where she lived with my cousin Courtney. She is seven years older than me, and we always shared a special bond that is more like brother and sister than cousins. My father's father passed away when my dad was very young, and because my grandmother never remarried, we all enjoyed the extra abundance of time and generosity that she had for us. She spent years working in the federal government in one capacity or another, and because Newports, Pepsis, and lottery tickets were her only vices, she poured her all into her family. We weren't wealthy, but we certainly weren't poor by anyone's definition or standard. I always had nice clothes, plenty of food to eat (especially on Sundays at Grandma's house), a clean, safe house, and an overall nice life. When you add all this up, one might ask, "How does poverty apply to you?"

The 1980's were a time of huge transformation in the black community, largely due to drugs - crack cocaine in particular. Although I didn't understand it at the time, most of my early interactions in my community set the foundation for how I would view socioeconomic status and culture were influenced by the use and distribution of drugs.

Yes, I did live in a fairly decent home, but this house was also directly across the street from the neighborhood liquor store.

I have excellent memories of all the wonderful experiences my family tried to provide for me, but I also witnessed drug use, drug dealing, prostitution, and all the other side effects of poverty. Our house was burglarized on more than one occasion, and one of my chores was to clean the beer and liquor bottles from our front yard that had been discarded by liquor store patrons. The bus stop where I waited to go to elementary school was directly in the middle of a street where transvestite prostitutes would ply their trade; on more than one occasion I witnessed what I would now describe as "the early morning rush". Coincidentally, that Catholic Church where I grew up happens to be in the center of another prostitution strip for transsexuals, and several times I've run across prostitutes hard at work and/or enjoying the fruits of their labor via crack pipe underneath a covered, elevated staircase outside of the church. I started to grasp the socioeconomic differences between myself and some of my classmates in my first years at elementary school. Every day I would ride a bus from my neighborhood to New Carrollton, Maryland, a neighborhood that had once been overwhelmingly white. This neighborhood was in the throes of "white flight", the mass exodus of white residents of a community that usually happens when black families begin to move in around them. If I had to estimate, according to my juvenile perceptions, I would say that the demographics were probably evenly mixed racially as I was entering kindergarten, but by the time I got to sixth grade, I would estimate that the racial make-up was about 80-90% black. I remember one day in first or second grade, the teacher passed out forms that would determine whether we would be eligible for free or discounted breakfast and lunch meals at school. I took the form home, asked my parents to fill it out, and brought it back the next day as I was told to do. About a week later, the teacher called all the students' names that were eligible, and all the kids from my neighborhood got a free lunch ticket except for me. In fact, I remember out of the fifteen or so black students in my class, there were maybe two or three of us who didn't receive free lunch tickets. I was upset; no one could explain to me at the time that my parents earned too much money for me to qualify for the program. All I knew, and all my peers saw, was that I was different from all of the other black kids. They had already begun to look at me differently because my mom had read books with me ever since I was old enough to remember. As a result, my reading comprehension skills were more advanced than most of the other black kids, and a lot of the other white kids, too. I couldn't understand why I wasn't like everyone else who was black. To me, it seemed as if all the other black children received some benefit that I didn't, as if I was being punished for the success of my parents. Most of the kids in my neighborhood always had new shoes or the latest fashions. As for my family, my father made it clear we would always have what we needed, but not necessarily everything that we wanted. I felt cheated out of the items that I felt defined inclusion by my peers and my community. I felt like I was at a disadvantage, as if the kids in my neighborhood were somehow living a life far superior to mine. I didn't understand all the parameters involved or how it was going to happen, all I knew was I wanted in, I wanted to have what they had.

I began to form my views of this "street life" early on. Summers at my grandmother's house on my mother's side of the family were always an enjoyable time. As I said before, I spent most of my time with my brothers and my cousins in the neighborhood and at the local recreation center. My grandmother always had lots of love, but was also a strict disciplinarian. What is considered to be child abuse by today's standards was considered to be common, child-rearing techniques in the black community, and although I never felt abused or traumatized, everyone knew that Grandma Vivies didn't play.

Her house is located in a neighborhood of single family homes that until recently was entirely African-American. Most of the families knew each other, and I inherited an extended family of sorts by virtue of the community infrastructure. As a young adult, I heard lots of stories about this type of community being commonplace all across America at one point in time. Looking back at it now, I am thankful I was able to have even a brief exposure to that type of civility among black people. This neighborhood would begin to change, however. With its close proximity to two housing projects on both sides, and the rise of crack cocaine, this neighborhood slowly began to take on the characteristics of a lot of the neighborhoods in the city. In fact, it was in this neighborhood I first saw a dead body. On a morning like so many others, our little group was riding through the alleys and streets around the neighborhood when we came across him. He was lying face up, with his arm twisted in an unnatural position and a gunshot wound to the side of his head. His head was swollen, his skin had a grey, ashen pallor, and his eyes were bulging with an unmistakable gaze of death. I remember us examining him for a while, and one of the members of my group making a nervous comment about the brain matter that was scattered across the concrete before we rode off. I faintly remember watching the police arrive later that day and going through their routine. Even though it was the first time any of us had witnessed death that intimately, none of us acted disturbed or saddened. I really can't say if that was due to the ideas about masculinity and toughness taught to boys at a young age, or if we had already begun to become desensitized to the violence and death of our community. This was the height of the "murder capital" era in Washington, D.C., a time where multiple instances of violent crimes were beginning to become commonplace. In my own way, I had already begun to develop some of the indifference necessary to navigate in a criminal society, and to eventually engage in my own criminal behavior.

One of the incidents I remember as being a contributing factor to this progression occurred one day as I was riding my bike home from the recreation center. I was riding along on my usual route, thinking about whatever it is eight or nine year olds think about. All of a sudden, I noticed an oddly shaped package of shiny plastic lying in the grass. I stopped to investigate further, and I discovered a bunch of tiny vials containing what looked to me like little pieces of soap or candle wax. Although I had never seen crack cocaine before, I felt the need to confirm if this was in fact the drug I had heard so much about. Being the curious young explorer I was, I decided to take the rocks back to my grandmother's house so that she could help me solve the case of the mysterious package. Of course, when she saw what I had brought into her house, I received a prompt and thorough "beating", followed by an intense reprimand about touching things I find out in the street. I later learned the package had a street value of over two thousand dollars - a figure too valuable for my mind to comprehend at the time, especially for such a small, seemingly worthless item. A few days later, an older teen, who I saw regularly in the neighborhood, asked me if I had found anything lying around. He said if I had what he was looking for, then he would give me a nice reward. Of course, after the encounter I had with my grandmother a few days before, I knew better than to admit to anything and I explained I had no idea what it was he was looking for. About a week later, I saw an all-black BMW with tinted windows and nice rims pull up outside of this guy's house. There were three or four guys inside of the car, and one of the guys in the car began arguing with the teen from the neighborhood. Before I knew it, they were fighting in the middle of the street. There was a lot of talk about money that was owed. I didn't know if the drugs I found had anything to do with it, but in my mind, I felt like it was a real possibility.

My understanding of finances was shaped by experiences with other members of my family as well.

My father's mother is probably the most altruistic person I have ever met. Her kindness and generosity were a welcome relief for me as a child as it was rare for my grandmother to tell me "no" to anything I wanted. As I got older, it would be that same enabling spirit that allowed me, and other members of my family, to continue in our negative, self-destructive behaviors. My Aunt Jacci lived with my grandmother for as long as I can remember. She never had children, so my brothers and I spent a lot of time with her and my grandmother. I never understood her addiction to heroin, not in the way I understand it now. She never exposed me to that side of her life; all I can remember of her addiction is we always thought Aunt Jacci was sleepy. Despite any of that, she is a phenomenal hair stylist who always takes a lot of pride in her work. There were always women coming to my grandmothers' house, where my aunt had set up her home salon, in order to get the latest hairstyles. My aunt always had a steady stream of clientele, and I can still picture all the various chemicals and equipment she had around the house back then. This was my earliest exposure to entrepreneurship, but at the time I had no context to put it in. Thinking back on those days now as an adult, I wonder how successful she could have been if not for the combination of the disease of addiction and the limited access to capital. The opportunity was certainly there had she been willing or able to capitalize on it. Of course, as a child, none of that mattered to me. My aunt is a longtime participant in Narcotics Anonymous and as a child she would take me with her to N.A. meetings and introduce me as her son. It was there I met some of the funniest, most outgoing people I have ever known. It would also be my earliest exposure to the stories of people who lived lives similar to what I saw in and around my neighborhood. My aunt would take me all over town with her, and my brothers and I would enjoy outings that were highlighted by my aunt's unpredictable and often volatile personality.

On one of these outings, my aunt took my brothers and me to some shabby Chinese restaurant in Chinatown. Of course, as far as we were concerned, this was a gourmet dining establishment. We would order pots of steaming hot tea and attempt to make our version of sweet tea with all the available sugar that we could find on the tables. Of course, the few packs of sugar placed on the table for normal use was insufficient for this purpose, so we began to request the waiter bring us more sugar. At first our waitress obliged our request, but at some point the waitress made the mistake of questioning my brother about the wisdom of using so much sugar. My aunt became enraged, and wasted no time in cursing her out in front of the whole restaurant before we were asked to leave. Often, we would travel around town on the metro bus. The old buses had a long cable running down the length of the bus attached to a bell that was used to signal the driver to stop. Of course, I found great pleasure in pulling this cable, even when we had no intention of getting off the bus. This was partly due to my youthful energy, but it was also because I felt like I could get away with it. I remember, in particular, one instance when my aunt and I were on the bus returning from the methadone clinic. As always, I pulled the cable for the bell multiple times, so much so the driver began to ignore it. Most of the passengers said nothing, but one lady decided she had had enough and was going to put me in my place. The woman looked over at me and screamed "stop ringing the got damn bell!" My aunt jumped up and began cursing this lady out and threatening her with intensity I had never seen before. By the time my aunt finished, I was crying and begging her to stop. I also remember my aunt taking my brothers and me to the movies. This particular movie theatre was the dirtiest, most run-down movie theatre I have ever seen in my life. Thinking back on that place now, I don't see how it was allowed to be open, legally. It was well past midnight when the movie began and you'd probably assume I was the only eight-year-old in the whole place, but you'd be wrong. There were lots of children my age running through the lobby and in the aisles, as well as teenagers making out and people smoking what I thought were "funny-smelling cigarettes", all inside a tightly packed theatre. There were roaches and rats on the floor feeding on the remains of sticky soda and old popcorn, but that seemed to be par for the course of this "ghetto" experience, just like the people who talked over the movie the entire time. I had never seen so much chaos and filth in one place, but I enjoyed every single minute of it. I felt like I had finally found an authentic cultural experience and this is what it truly meant to be black. I thought this is how all my life experiences should be and this is what my life should reflect - not the smart, articulate child my parents were raising me to be, but one of these kids in this crowd. I fully believed my parents didn't understand anything about this world, and thus, they couldn't understand this side of me, the one I wanted the other black kids to see.

My cousin Courtney has always been like my big sister. She is intelligent, articulate, quick-witted, and fluent in both Spanish and sign language. I always felt she had the ability to accomplish whatever she put her mind to, but I know the apprenticeship of sin had an effect on her life as well. At the start of the crack cocaine explosion in D.C., she was an attractive, social high school teenager. My earliest experiences with drug dealers would come through Courtney. As an only child, being spoiled and having her way was a normal thing for her. Drug money, and the men associated with it, would only contribute to this further, in ways I think she probably couldn't see at that time. On the weekends that I spent at my grandmother's house, I would go next door to her house to hang out with her.

She was always up on the latest go-go music and I would listen as she chatted with her friends about all of the latest happenings with the drug dealing young men they knew from around town. They had all the same interests as any teenage girl - fashion, dating, and social events - but the abundance of drug money that had flooded the community made their love interest a capable source of readily available cash, capable of financing extravagant purchases well beyond the limits of what any after-school job could provide. Her group of friends were all attractive socialites, and with so much drug money floating around in the hands of young men, it was only natural these women would be the objects of their desire. I remember the first time I met one of her boyfriends. He had on the biggest gold rope chain I had ever seen, and was driving a new Suzuki Sidekick. He had a smooth style about him and always had money in his pocket, and I began to covet the admiration and respect he and all my cousin's other drug dealing friends commanded. From the "extra" dollars her friends would give me from time to time to the guy who used to drive his brand-new Lamborghini to the recreation center where I spent my summers, I knew I was hooked. One day, I too would be this picture of success, this shining example of wealth to all the people in my neighborhood. I would be respected, loved by women and admired by men. Drugs would be my vehicle to the acceptance I sought, and would define my self-worth. No matter how many of my cousin's friends I saw die over the years, and no matter how many trips she took me on to visit her friends at Lorton Correctional Complex, I knew drug dealing would be in my life someday. That is what truly successful men did, at least the ones I knew. Sure, I had my dad who had a house and worked every day. But Dad didn't have a gold chain and a Lamborghini, and if I was ever going to fill up shoeboxes with $100 bills, I had to learn some things my dad couldn't teach. I had to learn how to be a hustler.

HATE

I'm going to admit something publicly in this book that has taken me years to come to terms with - I'm a fairly nice person. I hate confrontation and I try to avoid it whenever I can. I especially hate useless confrontation, the meaningless arguments over trivial matters that usually escalate to combat in my community. For the most part, I have always tried to actively pursue an alternative to confrontation, specifically when violence was involved or implied. I'm sure to most people reading this that quality would be considered virtuous, and most would agree that this is necessary behavior in the maintenance of any civilized society. But for children in poor, black communities, this is a quality children are taught to suppress at all costs. It is downright dangerous to be perceived as unwilling to argue and fight at a moment's notice, especially as a child. I think it is important to highlight this point as I begin to explain my understanding of the progression of sin, because this part of African-American culture is a key component in understanding the self-imposed genocide we see all across America. I believe it to be equally important to begin this discussion while I'm currently incarcerated; although I'm not incarcerated for an act of "direct violence" such as assault or murder, I very well could have been (sex trafficking of a minor is considered a violent crime under federal law). I don't have the latest statistics available to quote here, but through my limited research I'm comfortable saying that in the majority of violent crimes that are prosecuted, the defendant will be African-American and the jury will be comprised of mostly whites. I'll discuss that point a little more in a later chapter, but I do want to examine one key question: How do terms like "right" and "wrong" retain their intrinsic value in a culture based on anti-social behavior that is designed to encourage and even reward sociopaths?

I have what most would consider a weird name. Pili means "second born" in some African language or culture, I was told.

I'm not sure, but after some research I have reason to believe it's actually a girl's name. Cinese, my middle name, is pronounced kin-ne-say according to my mom and I'm not sure what it is supposed to mean. I think she found my names in one of those books of so-called African names. Bless her heart. On the other hand, Greenfield is a Jewish name and at various times, especially during election season, my family would receive pamphlets in the mail inviting us to "reconnect with our people" from one of the many Jewish organizations. This blend of names, Pili Cinese Greenfield, is what was chosen for me as an identity (and now for my oldest son, as well) at a time when Richard Pryor, Redd Foxx, and Eddie Murphy were cultural icons in the black community, largely due to their ability to make fun of people and things. As a child, most white people would simply ask me to explain what my name means, then politely comment it is "interesting" or "different." For the black community, however, and for black children in particular, it was fuel. Some call it playing the dozens, ragging, or cracking; in D.C., it's known as joaning. Joaning is more intense than teasing, the light name-calling and joking that you see white kids do in the movies. Joaning is the equivalent of a Comedy Central roast, a no holds barred session of wordplay and punch lines designed to humiliate. My older brother wasn't into that sort of thing and so after countless hours of he and I being the butt of the jokes from other neighborhood kids I learned I would have to be the one to defend us from the verbal attacks. I've always been creative and pretty decent at turning a phrase, and with a little practice on timing and delivery I could put up some resistance against the other kids, especially the older ones.

Please understand, attempting to be the bigger person and deciding not to participate was not a wise strategy; at the first sign of your unwillingness to defend yourself, you would receive the label of "scared", one of the worst titles you can assign a young black man. In fact, any name or title that questions a young black man's masculinity, like soft or scared was considered to be fighting words. I was talking to somebody the other day about how certain words still trigger emotional responses in me after hearing two young men play with words that were traditionally used as gay slurs - bitch and faggot. As much as I believe that I have evolved, internally my mind and my conditioning still process those words as a precursor to a fight. One of the biggest topics that fueled these joaning sessions was fashion. Fashion and style has always been a part of black culture. As a child, you learn the importance of being well dressed anytime you appear in public. It was always a shock to the black kids at my school that the white students had very little regard for how they dressed. Although our young white contemporaries may have had on clean clothes of decent quality, they lacked the style and swagger the black students felt was important. For us, being clean and wearing the latest styles was a necessity, and any violation of this norm was subject to punishment by joaning. Shoes, the most important style element, had to be clean and of a certain brand in order to be acceptable. This was during the start of the "tennis shoe revolution", when pop culture made tennis brands to be an integral part of fashion, and they began to cost around $100. Indeed, the black youth at my school were baffled by the white kids that felt so comfortable wearing old, dirty shoes to school. This cultural difference further shaped our perception of the racial divide. There were other factors that fueled these joaning sessions such as weight, height, shoe size, skin tone, hair texture, and so on. The basic premise was that any perceived difference or variation from what was considered to be cool could be used as fodder for a joaning session. These cultural expectations helped to form the basis of hatred, specifically in black children who were subject to these mindsets.

We learned to be cruel to each other with our words and actions, to exploit each other's weaknesses and to prey upon disadvantages that were often outside of a child's control. We learned to devalue each other, to insult and to injure. This was an expectation, a practice that had been handed down to us from those who came before us and we would pass along to those who came after us. I never understood why it was necessary to act this way towards each other; my experiences with my white friends were nothing like this. Among other black children, however, it was understood we were fighting a war with each other.

The war that black children learn to fight is not only verbal and mental in nature, but physical, as well. One key component of your status as a black male depended on your willingness and ability to fight. As a skinny, emotionally sensitive child, I always felt this put me somewhat of a vulnerable position. Again, I was not a child who enjoyed conflict and violence, so it was my nature to avoid them as much as I possibly could. My older brother and cousins would help to "toughen me up" by sparring with me, often. Slap-boxing and body punching were the tools we used with each other in order to hone our abilities. As I said before, choosing not to fight was not a healthy option for young men in my community. If at any time other young men got the sense you had no desire to fight, you would automatically become the community punching bag. There was always a reason to fight; a basketball game that got too physical, an intense joaning session that got out of control or something as slight as a wayward glance in passing. A young black man learns at an early age there is only one acceptable form of conflict resolution: violence. In studying this part of my upbringing, I wanted to know if my experience was common among black men. I wanted to know if men from different parts of the country that are slightly older or younger than me, or that had a different familial experience, had experienced a similar introduction and indoctrination to violence. I began to talk to men who were in prison with me - federal prisons house inmates from across the country, from across the world, in fact. I spoke with men from

California, Indiana, Texas, New York, Detroit, Florida, and other parts of the country. I didn't do a formal study per se, just held a few informal group discussions with other black men where we talked about our experiences.

As these discussions began to develop, I was surprised by how similar our stories sounded. Except for a few variations in the details, almost everyone said they were exposed to violence by the older men in their neighborhood. Everyone noted these men were the ones who gave them their earliest definitions of masculinity, and were the ones responsible for teaching them what it meant to be tough. One man shared with me that his heroin addicted uncle would make all the neighborhood children fight each other as a source of entertainment for him. He also shared with me how all the "street guys" began to participate in encouraging these gladiator matches, with promises of money and sugary treats for the participants. Some men would even go so far as to place bets on their favorite child street fighter. One theme that was common among nearly all the men I spoke with was the requirement of an appropriate response to violence that was instilled in them. Almost everyone shared that they were instructed by their mothers (as most were products of a single parent household) if they were attacked and did not respond with the appropriate level of violence, they would be subject to even worse violence at the hands of their mother. As the product of a loving, compassionate family, I could not relate to this. My mother and father certainly encouraged me to defend myself, but they also allowed me the discretion to forgive and forget. This principle of forgiveness put me in direct conflict with other men in my community, however, as reconciliation was only to be sought when first prefaced by violence or the attempt thereof, and attempting to circumvent that process was usually interpreted as an act of cowardice. I also discovered our combat training was similar in nature. As I said before, slap boxing and body punching was a regular activity for me and my brothers, and I learned this was true for most of the men I spoke with. Another common practice, I found, was backyard sparring matches with boxing gloves. My brothers and I had all participated in martial arts classes, and we all had these lightweight martial arts gloves with very little padding on the knuckles, similar to the gloves worn today in MMA fights. I'm almost certain these gloves weren't designed for the full contact sparring we were using them for. Needless to say, as the youngest and smallest of the group, I was often the recipient of a bloody nose or lip. At some point, we got some real boxing gloves, but it was still pretty much the same for me. Even though I was fairly decent with my hands, my brother and cousins were a lot bigger and stronger than me. This type of training was common among the men I spoke with as well; because there are no referees or weight classes in a street fight, a young man learns early on he must be fearless and able to hold his own against any opponent, regardless of his height or weight. In fact, some of the most vicious people I have ever come across are small in stature, and I firmly believe this cultural expectation exacerbates this "Napoleon complex" mentality. One of my Aunt Jacci's (who is small in stature but large in courage) famous quotes when I was growing up was "grab a rock, a stick, or a brick"; the lesson being to do whatever it takes to hurt your opponent because they are trying just as hard to hurt you. The sport of boxing has always been quite popular in black and pop cultures and, although I won't say it contributes to violence, I do believe it contributes to how we perceive violence. In today's culture the sport of boxing is a mere shadow of what it once was; not too long ago some of America's greatest cultural icons were boxers.

The martial arts were also a huge part of pop culture, as movies and cartoons featuring samurai, ninjas, and Kung-Fu masters filled the movie theatres and controlled television screens across America. I think a combination of parental concern for violent images, over-saturation, and readily available content provided by technology has made that part of American culture less relevant than it once was, but a lot of young boys aspired to gain the respect and attention the men in these images commanded through their combat prowess.

I remember as a child watching Sugar Ray Lewis, Marvin Hagler, Tommy "Hitman" Hearns, and other great boxers. "Iron" Mike Tyson, known for his aggressive style of boxing, would become a hero to many black men; who sought to emulate the sheer power he displayed in the ring by his multiple knockouts. In fact, the "knockout game", a surprise attack that young men would commit against unsuspecting people walking down the street with the goal of rendering them unconscious with one punch, came about at the height of Mike Tyson's fame. Although this vicious "game" became popular in the 1980's, it has recently resurfaced in communities around the country. I had heard stories from older guys who were supposedly participating in this savagery, but the game became infamous when a videotape of a young black man executing one of these vicious attacks aired on the nightly news in Washington, D.C. As these expressions of senseless violence became commonplace across America, young men began to become desensitized to the harm being inflicted on people, and the stage was set for the escalations of violence we now find to be all too common. One aspect of violent culture that varied among black men in different geographical regions of the country was the relationship between violence and gangs. Gangs as traditionally understood were not prevalent in the Washington, D.C. area. There were no groups (at least none that were well known) with a formal structure, comprised of a leader at the top and underlings who acted at their leader's behest. The groups in D.C. were based around a particular neighborhood and loosely formed, with each person being independent and able to act autonomously. This contrasts greatly, I learned, with the experiences of black men in the Midwest and on the West Coast, who had been raised in the tradition of organized crime and understood what it meant to have an allegiance to something outside of their own self-interest. The idea of following orders or of being subject to another man's will was completely different from what I saw and learned as a child; the mentality that was present in the minds of the people in and around my community was that it's about self above all else. I doubt these subtle differences made any significant difference in the amount of violence and hatred any of us were exposed to, however. As we discussed our collective childhood it was clear that although the cause or method may have varied slightly, violence was the commonly intended result. As for the whole concept of independent thinking, that, too, was a double-edged sword, especially for a child. On the surface, pop culture seemed to promote the ideas of being your own man, following your own star, living life on your own terms, doing your own thing, and all the other clichés that seemed to speak against emulating anyone else. This was a large part of the early hip-hop music, as well. For instance, it was considered to be a cardinal sin for early rap emcees to bite someone else's style. This concept of individuality would be fleeting and ultimately prove to be a facade, however. Most of the hatred we were inflicting on each other was rooted in some non-conformity to a cultural expectation of style and behavior. This fine line still exists for me as an adult, and though I have become more adept through the years at knowing when to walk the line and when to ignore the line altogether, as a child I suffered countless hours of mental anguish trying to make sense of it all. One of the biggest misconceptions about violence that is inflicted on poor, black communities involves the methods and mentalities by which young black men are exposed to firearms. I, like most young Americans, was fascinated with firearms. Most of my earliest toys were some version of a firearm and I kept a whole "arsenal" at my side that I could play with. Water guns, cap guns, dart guns, pellet guns, laser tag guns-you name it, I had it. The corner store around the corner from my grandmother's house always had some cheap plastic gun for sale, and I couldn't wait for my aunt Jacci to finish with one of her hair appointments, so that I could get a few dollars for a trip to the store.

I would pick up a pack of Kool cigarettes and a soda for her and the rest of the money would be mine. Often, I would be faced with the choice of purchasing a few snacks or a new toy gun and the snacks were often in second place. My first real experience with an actual firearm would come in an entirely different context, however. My family was heavily involved in the Boy Scouts - my dad was the scoutmaster of an all-black troop of young scouts - and every year we would go to Goshen, Virginia for a week on the camp compound surrounding a lake where the scout summer camp was held. They had a shooting range that was run by an older, white guy who was retired from the military and worked at the camp. You could train with a bolt action .22 rifle or you could purchase tickets to shoot clay targets with a shotgun. Not only did I learn the proper mechanics of shooting, like how to control my breathing and to squeeze rather than jerk the trigger, but also, I learned to have proper respect for the immense power of a firearm. This is an important point in the discussion of access to firearms for young black males. I think that most gun control advocates are naive to the culture associated with firearms in black communities. Most young black men have their first encounter with a firearm through someone that owned and/or used that firearm in an illicit manner. A lot of men I talked to told me stories of older men teaching them to shoot in residential areas like alleys, abandoned houses, and wooded areas behind a housing community. Shooting pistols in the air to celebrate the New Year is common in black neighborhoods, and I was always surprised by the amount of firepower I heard being unleashed. The report of so many weapons firing at the same time, many of them fully automatic, is a sound that drove home the reality of the danger of gun violence.

Most of us witnessed gun battles in the street as children, as rivals in our communities shot at each other with reckless disregard for the homes and people nearby. This, too, is a part of the apprenticeship, as I would come to understand.

The idea of malevolence and disregard for life is a necessary part of a young man's upbringing, if he is to participate in this system of violence and destruction. Exposure to these types of situations is completely opposite to the experiences most young white males have with firearms as children, I'm told. The stories I've heard from white men about their experiences with firearms in their childhood involved hunting trips with their dad or some other family member as a mentor and guide. Through the experience of taking the life of another living being, these white men were more intimately exposed to the power of life and death associated with firearms. I'm not suggesting these experiences alone are enough to foster respect for human life; values must be taught early and reinforced often. But, I do believe there is a sense of awareness that develops when the mystery of what it looks like to see bullets pierce flesh is removed.

These are some of the experiences that would begin to shape my foundation of hate, the hate I would begin to feel towards others and towards myself. My hatred would become a learned response, a response to the fear of being rejected by my peers, a response to the confusion I felt in trying to lead dual lives, each with their own set of rules and expectations.

I began to see this world view that was based on love and principles as unattainable, a fantasy of a by-gone era. My reality was based on opposition, and it demanded I conform to its precepts of violence and I believed if I was ever going to be accepted, I had to learn how to destroy the parts of me that wanted peace, that wanted to love and to be loved in return. I believed it to be my duty as a man to mask, conceal, and camouflage any emotion or indicator of empathy.

I had to learn to be hard, cold, and to represent the only emotion respected by my peers: hate.

SEX

For as long as I can remember, I have had a huge appetite for the opposite sex. I was definitely more of a lover than a fighter and it would be fair to say that I was what older folks would describe as a "nasty lil' boy". I've always been drawn to intelligence and beauty in females. Ever since kindergarten I've had a soft spot for bright wide eyes and a pretty smile, and when you add a brain to that mix, it definitely has an effect on me. I don't know if it was because of the strong, beautiful women in my extended family, the lack of estrogen in my own house (besides my mother), or just human nature, but I had a natural thirst to have, to know, and to explore the mystery of a female figure. My Uncle Terry would be the first man in my life to influence my interaction with women. Terry, my mother's brother, was definitely a ladies' man. He lived in California so we didn't get to see him very often, but the experiences I had with him sparked something in me. I remember traveling around with him to run errands on one occasion, and watching how he interacted with people. He had a smooth, easygoing style about him, and there was a "control" he seemed to have when he talked to women - any woman. If I had to try and define it now, I guess it would fall somewhere between polite conversation and flirting, but I remember that my young mind was amazed by how easily he shaped conversation. His bright smile and attentive manner would draw women in, and it appeared to me like he could have any woman eating out of the palm of his hand. As for me, I was articulate and outspoken but I lacked the self-confidence he readily displayed, and I wanted to understand his secret "tricks of the trade". I began to question my uncle more and more about these things, and so began what my uncle called "charming lessons". Thinking about it all now, I'm sure my uncle probably intended for my charming lessons to be

80% humor, but to a young, insecure man who wanted to be a "player", this meant the world to me. He told me about how to talk, to smell, to dress - nothing too deep, just a few words of wisdom to a young man from his uncle. For me though, it was the beginning. I began to incorporate my uncle's advice into my style, my elementary school swagger. Again, I was always fairly decent at turning a phrase, but armed with a bit of charm I was now on my way. I'm not exactly sure what I was on my way to because in my young world having a girlfriend didn't carry any real "privileges" other than conversation and companionship. Kissing was a huge deal back then, but women weren't my biggest priority in the third grade. It was more important to me to have a girlfriend as a status symbol, a rite of passage, or as most black people would commonly say, I was "trying to be grown". My mom still teases me about the first girl that called our house for me. I won't use her name here, but it makes me smile every time I think about my mother's fairly accurate rendition of the way my third-grade sweetheart would squeak into the phone as she asked to speak with me. We would talk every evening after school; of course, we didn't have a whole lot to talk about but we managed to stay on the phone with each other every day. As far as I was concerned, you couldn't tell me I didn't have one hell of a talk game. I thought I had this whole smooth thing figured out. That theory would soon be put to the test though.

I remember that there was this young white girl in our class who seemed to enjoy talking to me, apparently a little too much for my girlfriend. Keep in mind that at this time, interracial dating was not as common a thing as it is today, especially among naïve third graders. Our class regularly divided into groups according to reading and math abilities and, more often than not, I was one of a few black students in my group, and usually the only black male. This young white girl and I had been paired up on a few occasions on different assignments and over time we became more familiar with one another and actually began to enjoy each other's company. This was a no-no, not only because I had a girlfriend, but because I was being friendly with a white girl.

Of course, this was no problem for a young player like me, or so I thought. I was supposed to talk to more than one woman because players always had more than one woman. I tried to talk my way out of it at first, but there was no way that my girlfriend was going to allow "her man" to keep embarrassing her by talking to this white girl right in front of her face. This would also be one of my first experiences with the stereotypical attitude that black women are known for accentuated by hand gestures, eye rolls, and a back and forth of the head and neck unique to only them. I had seen it from my aunts and cousin but I had never had it directed at me, not in this way. After explaining to my young sweetheart that I was going to talk to whoever I wanted whenever I wanted, we broke up, as much as eight-year olds can break up anyway. We would eventually begin to talk again, but this was the first of many break-ups and arguments that I would face over the years. These early experiences would be some of the most formative in helping to shape my experiences in future relationships. I never really paid much attention to how my dad interacted with my mom. It's not that they didn't have a healthy affection for each other, but I don't think anyone likes the thought of their parents getting "freaky" – it's still very disturbing to think about now, in fact.

Much of my early exposure to sex came through what older kids told me. Sex, body parts, and their purpose are usually discussed by children in graphic detail long before parents ever decide that it's time to have "the talk" with them. I know how fast and curious that I was growing up, so I can only imagine what my children have seen and heard, especially with the internet being readily accessible on almost every electronic device in existence today. My mom was very good at explaining about a penis and a vagina, but "wee-wee", "coochie", and a few terms a whole lot worse than that are what we used to talk about our body parts when talking to other young people. I think that the biggest impact on my sexual education, as far as the early stages of the apprenticeship were concerned, came through cable television. The 1980's were a pivotal time in American history; the technological advances that were made in the entertainment industry gave Americans greater exposure to film, video, and media from around the world, all from within the confines of their homes. For me and my brothers, that meant two things: rap videos and soft-porn movies. In the 1980's, rap/hip-hop music was in its infancy and had yet to become the commercial juggernaut that it is today. In my community however, it was a part of who we were, signifying the way we talked, dressed, danced, and related to each other. There were different viewpoints and styles represented by hip-hop music at that time, but the videos that showcased scantily clad women were irresistible to my young eyes. This is natural, as I'm pretty sure that any young, heterosexual man would gravitate to images of beautiful women with little to no clothes on. As I have said before, there is a natural curiosity that all young people have about sex and sexuality as they begin to mature, but some of that is also influenced by what they see and hear. There was also somewhat of a cultural revolution in the black community during the eighties, in terms of how men spoke of and depicted women in black music.

Sex has always been a theme in music, especially in black music. The eighties would be what I consider to be the beginning of black music becoming increasingly direct and overt in its suggestive nature. Like most black children, I grew up listening to groups like the O'Jays, Earth, Wind & Fire, Stevie Wonder, and other singers who were popular at the time. This music that I heard, although sometimes sexually suggestive, had a romantic quality to it. Even Marvin Gaye's "Sexual Healing" was considered a love song. Rap music would soon change all of that.

The rap song that I remember exposing me to this new, hypersexual depiction of women was 2 Live Crew's "Me So Horny". Now, by today's standards, this song's video would hardly be considered worth mentioning, considering some of the content now available on the internet. But at that time, this video was life changing, especially for young men in the black community. Images of women wearing barely visible bathing suits and skin-tight outfits, gyrating and moving provocatively to this new sound of music were captivating to say the least. This "celebration" of a black woman's' physique, especially of the large buttocks and wide hips common to a lot of black women, would be one of my earliest validations of black standards of sexuality. At that time, there was a station called "The Jukebox Network" that allowed you to call and request a video to be played on TV, for a small fee, of course. "Me So Horny", "Baby Got Back", and other videos featuring attractive black women with little to no clothing were in constant rotation. Music videos and the cable network shows that featured them were cultural staples. Rap City, Yo! MTV Raps, and similar programs were the dominant subjects of our schoolyard chatter, and of our very lives. I feel the need to point out here that in no way am I suggesting that black music is responsible for any of the decisions that I made, as a child or as an adult. I will explain my thoughts on personal responsibility in greater detail later in this book, but for now let me emphatically state that in no way am I "hating" on any of the images that were presented in these videos. In fact, I am quite appreciative of the courage it took to display the reality of what a lot of black men, in particular, found attractive. Before rap music, black sexuality had never been displayed in such a raw, base manner; this music was not about love or passion - it was about sex, pure and simple. Although some argue that these images were derogatory towards women, we have to be honest about the contribution that this music made to pop culture by allowing a more direct expression of human sexuality. I, for one, was thankful to be able to see our women, our bodies, and our culture on display as attractive. Although I didn't understand it in those terms at the time, this music provided one of the few outlets for black men to express their admiration of black women. No matter how much progress was made by the generations of black people who came before the hip-hop era, I know in its own twisted, exploitative way "booty-shaking" videos helped a whole generation of black men to celebrate what we are physically attracted to in a woman, specifically black women. No, I'm not suggesting that these videos are the totality of black sexuality or of a black woman's worth, but during a time when white women were the only standard of what beauty was considered to be, I believe that black men needed to see some depiction of a black woman outside of Claire Huxtable. In many ways, this music was a natural progression of some of the films and themes expressed by black artists in the seventies. Also, I don't believe that these videos influenced young women to act like "hoes". In my opinion, as long as the divide remains between what people profess as acceptable and what we actually enjoy, we will continue to stumble along in this awkward hypocrisy of American sexuality. This crisis of identity affects all Americans, is magnified in the black community, and is personified in the curiosity of children as they struggle to find a sexual identity in this broken framework that the apprenticeship creates.

My exposure to porn would also shape my early views of sexuality. I remember seeing "adult" magazines as a child. The 7-Eleven by my house sold them, and just like anything else in my neighborhood they weren't hard to get. Older kids would bring them to school, my cousins would have them, and eventually I started getting them for myself. In fact, by the time I entered sixth grade I'm willing to bet I had "read" porn magazines featuring women of every shape, size, and color. Still, none of that excited me like the soft porn that used to be shown on late night cable. When I was around nine or ten, my older brother and I would sneak into our living room late at night to watch; knowing that it was past our bedtime, we would keep the volume turned down very low so that my mom and dad didn't hear us. We would watch these low budget "love stories" featuring women from all around the world. We were always anxious for them to get to the love scenes, and we were super-excited to get a glance of a woman's nipples or a bare bottom during one of the many love scenes that these movies had. The sex and nudity weren't the only thing that excited me though; I enjoyed living vicariously through the different roles that these actors were portraying. The exotic cities, the parties, the scandal, the passion-I was thrilled by all of it. I would study the swagger and authority that the male actors would project, that smooth sense of control and awareness that would incite women to passionate love-making. I was impressed by their ability to combine charm, class, and machismo into sex on a table, beach or hood of a car. In a lot of ways, it appealed to my creativity, to my love of reading and the progression of a good plot. Even as I got older and began to appreciate porn for its intended purpose, there is still a part of me that enjoys erotic literature. In fact, I was recently the butt of one of my homie's jokes for taking too long with a porn magazine that we had floating around, all because I was taking the time to read the stories. Surprisingly, this was how I learned that a lot of other men enjoy reading the stories in porn magazines, as well. These stories also provided me an insight into what I thought women were attracted to. In my own way, I began to piece together parts of my game and the aspirations of what I hoped to one day personify for women. Again, I don't blame any of my actions past or present on the existence of porn; I'm simply stating my personal experiences with the information that was available to me, and how I used that information to form who I wanted to become. One of the other issues that these soft porn movies helped me to explore is my attraction to women of all ethnicities. I never believed that interracial dating was an issue, or that it should have been an issue. In my early years of elementary school, my classes contained a fairly diverse mix of children. I remember playing with kids who were Caucasian, Mexican, Chinese, Vietnamese, African, Polish, and other ethnicities. I noticed how most of the students who were born into a foreign culture had the same affinity for learning that I did. Not only did they have the desire to participate in class, they had the desire to compete and excel. This common interest would be the foundation around which our relationships would be built, especially during some of the group activities that the teacher put together. But with all that we had in common, it seemed impossible to ever feel close to people from other races. The girls of other races were especially hard to deal with; no matter how much we interacted it always felt like there was some invisible wall between them and me, besides the one that exists already for children of different sexes. I found beauty in all of the different skin tones and hair textures, but none of that mattered in the context of the rules that the apprenticeship of sin had already established. The charm and easygoing manner that I used to hold conversation during those group activities didn't seem to transition into social conversation, and although I was determined to know more and experience more from other cultures, the divide began to feel too big to cross. Porn helped to satisfy some of the curiosities I had, at least.

As I said before, I already had a basic understanding of how things worked from my access to porn magazines. I also had seen pretty much every ethnicity of woman fully nude, so I understood some of the basic variations of body size, shape, nipple color, and build. For me, porn was the only tool available to learn these things, and these soft porn movies allowed me to see human bodies and stories of human sexuality in action. I'm sure to some that it may seem as if I'm trying to defend the use of porn by minors, but that's not it. We expose children to animals and their habits at a very young age. We teach babies and toddlers animal sounds, and take our children on countless trips to the zoo in order to view animals in action.

Most children are more familiar in fact, with the sexual habits of animals than they are with the sexuality of humans. For children in America, sex and sexuality was and is a taboo subject. Sex is some secret activity that only adults are mature enough to understand, and the concept of a child using the parts of his or her body for the purpose for which they were intended is unacceptable, criminal even. We teach children everything else related to their bodies through visual demonstration-fractions, cooking, knot tying, and more. Sex is the only subject in which our society makes children, as well as a lot of adults, feel ashamed to be human. Again, I'm not suggesting that we plop little Johnnie and Susie down in front of the TV and turn on the Playboy channel so that they can get a little "education". I do believe, however, that parents should be able to expose their children to "appropriate" images of human sexuality without fear of shame or even criminal charges. On so many levels, this system of shame and secrets is what creates a niche market for sexual predators. The predator has an advantage in that they are willing to satisfy a basic human curiosity for the children that the adults they trust the most are unwilling or unable to. Add that to the fact that it's a child's nature to test boundaries and break rules, and it's no wonder that the sexual abuse and child pornography epidemic is so problematic. A child's curiosity, combined with the allure of social rule-breaking, is one of the best recipes for victimization and exploitation.

One of my earliest opportunities to physically satisfy my curiosities would come at the beginning of my fourth-grade school year. At nine years old, my parents felt I was still too young to stay at home alone after school, and so me and my five-year old brother began to go to a babysitter. We were cared for by a woman who lived down the street from my elementary school and ran a day care out of the basement of her home. She had a daughter who was a year younger than me, and she also cared for three or four other girls around our age. My brother and I were the only boys there, which annoyed him greatly at the time but provided a great opportunity for me. All the girls were black, so there was an ease of conversation and communication that came along with being around people of the same culture, and in a lot of ways I found that to be a welcome relief from the frustration I felt in navigating the complexities of juvenile interracial relationships. All the young women were attractive, at least in my nine-year old mind, and I knew that eventually we would find a way to practice "being grown". Our afternoons were uneventful at first, filled with innocent childhood games and play. But at some point, someone suggested that we play "truth or dare". Now for those who don't know, the concept of the game is that all participants take a turn in which they either A) have to answer a true/false question, or B) do something that someone else dares you to do. We added our own local twist, which allowed another option called consequences, in which you had to suffer some penalty for not answering a question or completing a challenge. Our game started off innocently enough, with most of the participants choosing to answer a "truth", and with the challenges being light-hearted and in good fun. As we became more familiar with each other, however, our group dynamic began to shift. There was a certain attraction that I felt on some level with each of the girls, and as we began to form relationships with each other, human nature and natural curiosity would begin to take over. All three of them had just begun to sprout breasts, and this further prodded my young hormones into a frenzy. It started off with touching, hidden inside dares of provocative "dirty dancing" or "grinding" like we had seen on TV, and quickly progressed to grabbing and touching each other's genitals. Eventually, our truth or dare games began to involve more sex acts; kissing, petting, rubbing, touching, and even licking became common. We would all go into the backyard where we were supposed to be playing, and sneak into the tool shed for privacy.

We exposed ourselves to each other and found creative ways to explore each other's bodies. I never actually achieved penetration; in fact, I don't think I even had hair on my genitals at that point. But I can say that I put my hands, tongue, and penis about 70% of all the places that a sexually curious fourth grader could ever imagine. I'm sure many assume that I must have been the ringleader of this whole operation, but surprisingly these young women were just as eager to explore my body as I was theirs. One day, the babysitter's daughter and I were alone in the wooded area behind the school. We had tongue kissed several times before; at first, while playing truth or dare, and later on by ourselves in order to "perfect" our techniques. Out of all the girls in the group, she was more of a free spirit than the others, and she possessed that sharp confrontational attitude common to a lot of black women that men find both attractive and impossible to deal with. At some point, she suggested she would like to attempt oral sex on me. I obliged, of course, as this was the fulfillment of many a young man's sexual fantasies. I remember that she didn't do it that long; I definitely didn't ejaculate and I think she bit me once or twice, but none of that mattered. I only remembered the pride I felt in telling my older brother that a girl had "sucked my dick". This was a dirty term we used all the time in jest; to actually achieve placing your penis in a girl's mouth, especially at my age, was a legendary accomplishment in my eyes. Of course, my brother and my cousins all thought I was lying, so my excitement was short lived because I couldn't bask in the glory of my success.

As the father of a daughter and two sons, I will publicly admit that I still harbor a huge double standard when it comes to sex and sexuality. I can instantly feel anger surge through my body by imagining my daughter and some young man participating in any of the acts described in some of my previous stories. As progressive as I consider myself to be, the fact remains that most men hate to think of their daughters as sexual beings.

My sons on the other hand are a completely different matter. If I am completely honest, I would probably feel a little pride in discovering that my son was attempting to become sexually active. I can also admit that I probably wouldn't feel that same sense of pride if I found out that he was engaged in homosexual activity. As for my daughter, I would feel as if she had been violated; I would be even angrier to discover that she was a willing participant in anything sexual. In my admission, I hope I can help someone consider what the process of sexual identity and exploration should look like for our children, and that we as a country can begin a conversation founded in reality. In an age where we are attempting to figure out how to help children who identify as LGBTQ, I think we need to acknowledge the fact that we are still stumbling in the dark with the heterosexual maturity process. Our current model is obviously not working, and is tainted with an expectation of shame, fear, and apprehensiveness about the rule of law. As a father, I understand the necessity of allowing my children to escape this dated concept of shameful sexuality, despite the cultural bias that I, and most of America, was and still is apprenticed into.

This paradigm was the foundation of my apprenticeship of sexual sin, upon which all of my future sexual experiences were built.

HYPOCRISY

My earliest experiences with religion came through my upbringing in the Roman Catholic Church. Everything I thought and believed about God, man, and the universe was taught to me by the church and by my mother, who had been raised Catholic, as well. My dad's side of the family is Baptist, and as a child I remember he rarely came to mass with us on Sundays, except for Easter, Christmas, or a special event that involved our family. The parish where we attended mass was about five minutes away from our house by car. At the time, St. Joseph's in Landover, Maryland was extremely diverse in terms of its racial make-up due to large numbers of older, white families who had been longtime members. However, white flight would eventually make its way inside the pews, as well. As more black families like ours began to arrive, we saw less white families on Sunday morning. Our church day usually began with Sunday school which is known as C.C.D. classes in the Catholic Church, followed by mass. These C.C.D. classes were where I received my earliest introduction to Christianity, as practiced by Catholics. I think it is important for me to point out I have only recently come to understand the doctrine of the Roman Catholic Church with enough confidence to actually comprehend at least a part of what they profess as truth. I was baptized as an infant in accordance with Catholic tradition and doctrine, and the C.C.D. classes that I took were designed to prepare me to receive the sacraments. As a child, I had no idea what purpose or significance any of these rituals held; in fact, most of my early religious "education" was centered on the rote repetition of pre-formed prayers. In my attempts to explain my religious origins, I began to independently research Catholicism.

I did so because I wanted to compare and contrast my childhood beliefs with what I understand to be true today. I don't profess to have all the answers, nor am I attempting to disparage anyone else's beliefs or faith tradition. My family members are still very much practicing Catholics; my mother is a C.C.D. teacher, my father is a deacon, and my son and daughter are altar servers. My goal is simply to explain the progression of my religious and spiritual journey and the challenges I have faced along the way. I think that is necessary in order to demonstrate the gap between my naive allegiance to what I was told to believe and my conscious awareness of who and what I now profess God to be. Interestingly, I never thought of God as a loving, compassionate spirit as a child. God was always more of an obligation, a name to insert as the "person" responsible for the rituals I performed before I ate and went to bed each night.

In a practical sense, my parents were my true god. I believed them to be in control of every aspect of my life and, as far as I was concerned, there was nothing that was outside of their control, nothing of importance anyway. The idea of talking to God or of having a relationship with Him seemed kind of silly to me, and I put Him and the whole religious experience in the same box as Santa Claus, the Tooth Fairy, and the Easter Bunny. The only difference was I knew it was "wrong" for me to feel that way about God. I had heard and understood enough about the term "blasphemy" to know even the thought of God being less or different than what I was taught was an absolute no-no. Part of that expectation of conformity was implied through our religious education, but a large part of it was cultural. In the black community, at that time, children didn't often question authority, but were expected, instead, to stay in a "child's place." As a curious black child, this expectation would be the source of countless punishments for me and as much as I would like to believe that I have granted my children a greater amount of discretion to explore their thoughts and feelings, I know that old habits die hard. I think being a father has been one of the most informative tools in understanding my early religious journey, in fact. My youngest son is curious, inquisitive by nature and very aware of subtle nuances. I can tell that like most children, he really sees no need for God in his life right now. His immediate needs are being met quite adequately, as well as some of his less immediate needs like snacks and video games. Religion, especially as it was taught to me, became another assignment to complete, another set of facts to be memorized like the state capitals and the multiplication table. Of course, I had issues with the story of creation, and even though I could recite the facts, I can't say I whole-heartedly accepted the entire story. The "let there be light" statement, the creation of the world and all living things, and the story of Adam and Eve's creation didn't bother me too much.

It seemed a little far-fetched, but I figured this creation story was much more plausible than all the other explanations I had heard. I was really into cartoons at the time, so this story was no more a stretch than the cartoons I loved. Plus, it's a good story with an entertaining plot, and as I said before I have always had an affinity for a good plot. I think my earliest questions about the foundation of my religious beliefs began with the story of Adam and Eve in the Garden of Eden. As I understood the story, Adam and Eve were frolicking around in this huge garden, naked and happy, with all the animals in the zoo as their pets, and all the trees full of their favorite fruits. God gives them permission to do whatever they want, except for eating from this one tree. So, along comes a slick-talking snake, who convinces Eve that God is lying to them and doesn't want them to eat from this tree because he's a hater. So, the serpent tricks Eve, who then goes and tricks her husband, Adam, because he is incapable of resisting the temptations of this beautiful woman and thinking for himself. In the end, God is angry with all of mankind for the rest of eternity, all over one piece of fruit.

Let me first say, before I get into the millions of questions I had about this story, I sincerely made an earnest attempt to accept this story as truth. For those of us who come from a Christian tradition, you understand the intense expectation placed on people today to accept the bible as absolute. I struggled with this even as an adult. As a child, I felt absolutely alone, ashamed to be critical of the lessons being fed to me. I couldn't understand how I profess that God created everything, and then explain the existence of Satan. If God knows all and created all, then He had to have created "the devil". In fact, God had to have created lies and evil as well, and since He is all-knowing, He must have known Eve would listen to the serpent instead of following His command to her. Speaking of those instructions, why would God create one tree He didn't want Adam and Eve to touch? Why wouldn't He just keep the tree and the knowledge that came with it to Himself? Did God make a mistake? Can God make mistakes? Even if Adam and Eve did make a mistake, how can God be mad at everybody, forever? Isn't that a little harsh, petty even, especially when you consider it's over one piece of fruit? Again, I tried to just believe it all, I really did. As I began to ask more questions though, I received less answers. I think one thing most religious scholars, preachers, teachers, and historians are hesitant to admit is they don't know all the answers to that which they teach and claim to believe. After all, if you admit you don't know how it all works, then you have to admit you're taking a guess at it, just like everyone else. I always felt like people just accepted the answers that had been told to them because that's much easier than admitting not to know, so they try to do what I did for many years. They pretend. They learn the answers through what their family, their culture, and their communities say God is and how He works. They learn it until they can recite it, or at least enough of it to recall the appropriate responses at the right time.

The Roman Catholic Church defines this process as catechesis, an "education in the faith of children, young people, and adults which includes especially the teaching of Christian doctrine imparted, generally speaking, in an organic and systemic way, with a view to initiating the hearers into the fullness of Christian life." (Catechism 5) This catechesis was the platform on which all of my early understanding of God would be founded. I never did arrive at a full understanding, but I definitely learned to pretend well enough to make it look like I did. According to the catechism, there are four pillars of catechesis - the baptismal profession of faith, the sacraments of faith, the life of faith, and the prayer of the believer. (Catechism 13) The first pillar, the baptismal profession of faith, is said to be for "those who belong to Christ through faith and baptism" and requires that they "confess their baptismal faith before men."

I was an infant when I was baptized, so I certainly couldn't have professed or confessed anything. I had no faith to profess; I didn't even have teeth yet. I understand the concept is the parents and godparents take on this responsibility for the child, but my point is that this ritual is designed for someone who can't consent to the words being stated. The Catholic Church says this about infant baptism: "born with a fallen human nature and tainted by original sin, children also have need of the new birth of Baptism to be freed from the power of darkness and brought into the realm of the freedom of the children of God, to which all men are called. The sheer gratuitousness of the grace of salvation is particularly manifest in infant Baptism. The church and the parents would deny a child the priceless grace of becoming a child of God were they not to confer Baptism shortly after birth." (Catechism 1250) As I matured, I witnessed countless families bring their children to the altar to receive baptismal rites, but I had no idea that this ritual was designed to free anyone from "the power of darkness". Although I certainly did my fair share of wrong in my youth, I never thought of myself as an evil person, and that made the whole concept of original sin much harder for me to grasp. I remember on several occasions, I or one of my brothers would do something wrong or break something at home, typical mischievous childhood behavior. When one of us failed to claim responsibility for whatever we had done, we were all punished. Except for the instances I was actually the one responsible, I remember how unfair it felt. Some might argue the punishment "evens out" when you consider all the things one may have gotten away with, but to me that isn't the point of it or at least it shouldn't be. Even more so, I struggled to understand what sin an infant needed to be freed from. The Catholic Church admits "original sin is a mystery we cannot fully understand." (Catechism 404) The church also teaches "original sin does not have the character of a personal fault in and of Adam's descendants" and "Baptism, by imparting the life of Christ's grace, erases original sin and turns a man back toward God, but the consequences for nature, weakened and inclined to evil, persist in man and summon him to spiritual battle." (Catechism 404) As I said before, this whole concept is exactly what the church says it is: a mystery. All I knew as a child is I was born a bad person because of Adam and Eve and Jesus came to make it all better. That didn't help me to understand why people did bad things to each other, especially in the face of all the violence that was happening around me. It didn't help me to understand why God made me, what he made me to do, or how I was supposed to do it. My job was not to question, but to believe.

Another one of my big issues had to do with the identity and the role of Jesus. I had a hard time accepting the story of Jesus, and I still do to this day. My current understanding is founded on the studies I have done of religion, history, and culture, but my arguments as a juvenile were based on the limited set of facts I had available to me at that time in my life. I began trying to understand Jesus at the same time that I really began to consider the plot behind movies like "Superman" and "Star Wars." Although there are plenty of similarities in the underlying themes, and supposedly the characters in these stories are loosely influenced by the bible, the story that was told to me of Jesus was the one I was supposed to accept as truth, a reality that actually happened. Not to mention the fact that I had been told by an older relative that Jesus was, in fact, a black man. The only representation of Jesus that the Catholic church has ever supported is that famous painting of the blonde, blue-eyed white guy. Despite of the inaccuracy of this depiction of Jesus being well-known, the Catholic church continues to deify and promote this representation of Jesus. On one hand, something about the whole story felt quite wrong; on the other hand, it was a nice story overall. Plus, as a kid I really liked having Christmas, no matter what the reason behind it was. The miracles with the wine and the fish, the blind man, and the walking on water were definitely straight from fairy tale land in my book, but if it made everyone else happy and I got to have Christmas, then I figured, "Why not?" I was still lost on how His betrayal and brutal murder were supposed to be the gateway to reconciliation with God, though. How could we profess that God was so angry with the world that he had to allow the only son he had to be born, betrayed by his friends, and hung on a cross just so that mankind could be in His good graces again? That is how a "loving" God was taught to me. I wanted so badly to understand, to be able to just believe and go with it. I remember days that I sat in church during mass, looking around at people and wondering what they really thought about what they were listening to, wondering what they really believed. My place as a child was not to question, however. My place was to listen, to believe, to do what I was taught and what I was told. Not that I considered Jesus to be a "bad" thing or I didn't find value in the story, I just couldn't relate to the circumstances and conditions of how it all supposedly came about, especially in the face of all that I saw and was experiencing. The Catholic Church states that "revealed truths can seem obscure to human reason and experience, but the certainty that the divine light gives is greater than that which the light of natural reason gives. Ten thousand difficulties do not make one doubt." (Catechism 157) They profess that "a believer desires to know better the One in whom he has put his faith and to understand better what He has revealed", but they also state that "though faith is above reason, there can never be any real discrepancy between faith and reason." (Catechism 159) These statements reinforce what my understanding of religion was: Feel free to question all you like, just make sure at the end of it all you arrive at the same conclusion we've been teaching to you. The Catholic Church states the second pillar, the sacraments of faith, is "made present in the sacred actions of the Church's liturgy, especially in the seven sacraments." (Catechism 15)

The sacrament of penance and reconciliation, also known as confession, would prove to be transformative in my early views of God and religion. The Catholic Church states the purpose of this sacrament is to "obtain pardon from God's mercy for the offense committed against him," as well as to be "reconciled with the Church which they have wounded by their sins." (Catechism 1422) Of course, my understanding of how that process works was a lot simpler in my youth. To me, it seemed as if the priest was supposed to act as God's "middleman," an intermediary between God and man charged with the task of brokering an acceptable form of restitution for my numerous character flaws. The process of learning about confession was more of the same, a routine and a ritual to be performed along with a set of pre-formed prayers to be memorized.

There were discussions and explanations of the concepts, but I never walked away feeling connected to the words I was expected to profess. I remember my experiences in making confession as awkward and uncomfortable. But, I didn't have any problems with learning the process, so I would enter the confessional and begin with the appropriate statement, a request for a blessing from the priest and the amount of time since my last confession. My parish priest also happened to be my baseball coach, so it was always a bit uncomfortable going through this routine with someone I was so familiar with. Nevertheless, I said the appropriate words at the right time, and when it came time to confess I would admit to some trivial wrong I had done, usually involving some argument I had with my brother or a household item that I had broken. I would then receive my penance; usually that meant repeating one of the numerous, pre-formed "church-sanctioned" prayers a few times. As a child, I thought the concept of apologizing to God was one of the craziest parts of the whole religious experience; I had no problem apologizing to my parents, my siblings, or even a schoolmate, but apologizing to God just seemed to be unnecessary, especially if I was to believe in his omniscience.

As for the role of the priest, the church teaches that the priest has been given authority to forgive sins. In the Contra Novatus, Athanasius states "As the man whom the priest baptizes is enlightened by the grace of the Holy Ghost, so does he who in penance confesses his sins, receive through the priest forgiveness in virtue of the grace of Christ." The Catholic Church cites John 20:22-23 as the basis of this authority given to priests: and when he had said this, he breathed on them, and saith unto them, Receive ye the Holy Ghost: Whose soever sins ye remit, they are remitted unto them; and whose soever sins ye retain, they are retained. (KJV) As an adult, I have an entirely separate set of reasons why I object to this entire practice, but as a child I just remember how phony and ceremonial it all felt.

The sacrament of the Eucharist was the most important part of my religious experience in my youth. Because communion (as it is commonly referred to) is given or "celebrated" during each mass, there was an urgency on my part to reach the age that allowed me to participate. By this time, my family and I began to attend the Church of the Incarnation in Washington, D.C. This parish is where my mother and father were married, where I was baptized, and where my mother's side of the family had attended mass for years. As far as diversity was concerned, Incarnation was and is overwhelmingly African-American; in fact, the only white faces we ever really saw were members of the clergy. I began preparations for my first communion right around the time I began to be an altar server, now commonly known as an altar boy. The Catholic Church teaches that "the holy Eucharist completes Christian initiation" and that Catholics "participate with the whole community in the Lord's own sacrifice by means of the Eucharist." (Catechism 1322) The church also declares "that by the consecration of the bread and wine there takes place a change of the whole substance of the bread into the substance of the body of Christ our Lord and of the whole substance of the wine into the substance of his blood. This change the holy Catholic church has fittingly and properly called transubstantiation." (Catechism 1376) This teaching, that the communion bread and wine become the actual body and blood of Jesus during the communion ritual, was and is the hardest thing for me to understand and accept. I tried as hard as I could to accept the other parts of the Christian story as taught by the Catholic Church, but this was the limit. I refused to accept this teaching, this obvious lie. It felt like being asked to trust the entirety of your spiritual existence to a magic trick, minus the trick, minus the disappearing bird or flowers out of thin air. How could the church and my parents ask me to accept any part of this as truth?

I became increasingly frustrated at my inability to question, to demand proof, to demand that somebody tell the obvious truth. I continued to participate in the rituals; I was an eager altar server, and I had no problem serving as a lector on youth Sundays. But deep down on the inside, I began to disconnect. I disconnected from God, from Catholicism, from religion altogether. I began to hide in plain sight, camouflaged by my ability to look the part of a faithful child. I had no one who could help me, no one who understood. These feelings only reinforced my closely-held views of God as an obligation, as a duty to my parents in the same manner that school was. I believed the expectations for my life at that time to be good grades and going to church, and that everything else would work itself out. But it didn't work itself out, it couldn't work itself out. My parents gave me what they believed to be right, but it wasn't enough for me. I needed to know more, to know about the world and what this power of darkness felt like. I understood darkness, because it surrounded me. It walked past my house every day, on its way to and from the liquor store. It lived in the stories I heard at N.A. meetings with my aunt.

Its influence could be seen in the kids at my school, the ones who were considered trouble. This darkness, this sin we spoke about every Sunday, was readily available, so I decided I needed to understand it. I needed to speak its language, to wield its power, in order to earn the respect of its students who were already enrolled in the apprenticeship of darkness and sin. I had to move transubstantiation and miracles and confession out of my way, in order to have something more useful, something real. I needed to learn about the dark side. I had to find a way to take my place in the call of sin, of the destruction and chaos that was a part of my everyday reality. I didn't quite know who would teach me or I how would learn, but I knew I would find a way to figure it all out.

DISFUNCTION

I don't remember exactly when I became aware of my racial identity, but if I had to guess I would say it was when I started kindergarten. Naturally, I recognized the differences in skin color before I started school, but kindergarten definitely helped to shape my understanding of racial identity. I had previously been exposed to people of other nationalities, white people in particular, but I think that because my everyday experience was limited to black people, my early perceptions of how the world looked were defined by what I saw. There have been numerous studies done on racial identity as perceived by children, and I will defer to the "experts" on how that whole process takes place. But in exploring the issues of race, culture, and their influence on the disfunctional attitudes and relationships I became a part of, the awareness of how limited my worldview was from an early age becomes important for several reasons. Some of these reasons I will explain in later chapters; for now, I will start by saying that this understanding of the world was the lens through which I saw my reality. Kindergarten was my first exposure to peers of a different ethnicity.

New Carrollton Elementary in New Carrollton, MD is much different now than it was in 1983 when I enrolled. I transferred from Kenilworth Elementary school, an all-black school in my grandmother's Northeast D.C. neighborhood, to this integrated school located in the suburbs. Again, at this time the neighborhood surrounding the school had yet to fully begin the "white flight" that I discussed earlier. I'd like to think my transition went fairly smoothly, however. As I've said before, I'm a pretty easy guy to get along with, and playing with kids of a different race was no big deal for me. My awareness of the obvious differences between cultures was rooted in fascination and curiosity, not in a desire to segregate or stay separated. I still feel a huge sense of awe at the innocence of children, and yet sadness in knowing that part of their process to maturity will be to learn the mandates of race as defined by this apprenticeship of disfunction. As I said before, it started off for me by internalizing the physical differences between ethnicities like eye color and hair texture, but somewhere along the way I began to think of those qualities in terms of better and worse. I can't point to one specific influence on my interpretation of physical qualities, but there were a number of cultural influences that helped to shape these views. As a brown-skinned child with very coarse, "nappy" hair, I understood how undesirable these traits were to mainstream society, even in kindergarten. I received those messages from the black community, as well, as many of the discriminatory practices created by slavery became a part of how African-Americans related to each other. There was a white family that used to live in the house directly behind ours. Our backyards were separated only by a fence, so we saw and interacted with this family quite often. There was a grandmother who lived there along with her drug addicted daughter and her two children. The grandmother would babysit my brother and I sometimes, and although I rarely saw or interacted with her daughter I would come to know her later on in life in a much different way. The drug addicted woman's daughter went to school with my brother and me. Our neighborhood was all black except for this one white family; despite this, they never seemed out of place. Maybe I was just too young to recognize the differences, or maybe they had been around black people long enough to "blend in." Either way, they seemed to get along quite normally with everyone else, at least from my young perspective. I do remember how pretty a lot of the boys thought that the girl was. She was about six or seven years older than me, and so naturally I looked up to her with that childish attraction most younger boys have for older girls. But I was also captivated by her long flowing hair, her pale skin, and her light blue eyes. Remember that this was the early eighties, a time when straight and processed hair was the "in" thing, and beauty was defined by the fairness of your skin.

With this understanding in mind, a white girl that was, for all intents and purposes, a part of our community was considered a precious commodity. Light-skin women were already prized possessions, but a white girl that was "just as black" as the rest of us was something that most of the young boys were fascinated by. As time went on, I began to understand the structure of this cultural dynamic more and more. Regardless of my intellect or personality, there was an unwritten hierarchy of attractiveness and favor for those with lighter skin. White children were seen as off-limits; they had no place in our relationships because we believed them to exist in a world totally separate from ours. Even though we all went to the same school, we were expected to segregate ourselves as much as possible. There were exceptions to that rule, however, and the more that we interacted with each other and became familiar with each other, the more those expectations became difficult to maintain. As I got older and experienced more activities attended by a larger demographic than the members of my immediate community, I became less comfortable with the social norms of the status quo. One of my best friends from school was a young white kid. We enjoyed many of the same activities, and he and I were two of the most intelligent, articulate young men in our class. We played soccer at recess together and got along quite effortlessly, and it seemed as if the friendship that we shared existed outside of the realities of our environment. But it always became difficult when other kids outside of our immediate circle were around. When other white kids were around us, the conversation always felt a little more strained between us. My friend fell into a pattern of speech and behavior that made him seem much more "white" than he did when we were by ourselves. I was guilty of the same thing, though. When the black kids would play with us, especially the ones from my neighborhood, I felt the need to change, too. My speech, the way I walked and behaved, and all of my mannerisms reflected the social norms of the black community.

At home my parents spoke clearly and intelligently, and they demanded the same of me and my brothers. Outside of our house was a totally different matter though. Slang was and is a part of how people communicate; although pop culture today has become increasingly comfortable using slang that originated "in the hood," there is still a huge double standard about the rules of when and how it is appropriate. As a child, slang and the standard of proper speech was one of the tools used in the practice of discrimination the concept being that blacks who used slang in their speech lacked the intelligence or education to speak "proper" English. This was a part of my apprenticeship into disfunction, as well, because I was being taught how to exist in the duality that is American society. As an adult, I understand now that most minorities are burdened with the necessity of having an identity influenced by white society, an identity apart from the one they present in their communities. This separate identity is a uniform of sorts, a mask that is intended to hide the parts of their culture that offend white people's sensibilities. This identity was born of necessity and has evolved since its creation in slavery into a routine of sorts. It has become a ritual, a rite of passage that marks a black child's introduction into white society at-large. You are taught not to talk or act black in the presence of white people capable of withholding the resources necessary for your survival, lest your blackness offend them. You learn to smile, to say "yes" instead of "yeah", to be pliant and malleable and willing to conform. You learn to put this identity on every morning. As a child, I carried my other identity to school like a lunchbox or backpack. I could be black at the bus stop and on the way to school, but in class I knew that I was expected to be fully dressed as my alter ego. This presented problems for me for several reasons. The main problem I had with this other identity is that I performed well with it on, and that did not go unnoticed by my black peers. As the product of two parents who valued education, along with my exposure to white culture through the Boy Scouts and the Catholic church, my other identity was much harder to take off. I liked reading, science and social studies, and I enjoyed learning about what the world had to offer. Books and education had the power to transport my mind to places I never dreamed existed. My mind began to crave this knowledge that was being fed to me, this exposure to belief systems outside of the hatred and destruction that was a part of my everyday life. This attitude would prove to be troublesome, however, because this was not normal behavior for children in my community. It was uncommon for a young black child to take interest it school, especially a black male. It was culturally acceptable for black females to do well in school, but for young black males the only acceptable areas of achievement were sports and entertainment. Those were the only legally acceptable areas of achievement; the other areas of culturally acceptable achievement were crime and violence.

In my early years, I was in group activities with mostly white children, besides the few black girls who were also good students. As the school became less and less integrated, all the activities for "gifted" students were filled with mostly black girls. The desire to do well in school and being recognized for academic excellence put me at odds with other black boys because we were so often seen as problem students, it was quite noticeable when one of us excelled. I began to feel torn between what my peers considered normal and my aspirations for success. I was teased, bullied, and even assaulted because of my love for education. I had to fight often, and I found it difficult to make any real friends in my community. Of course, this affected my self-esteem and, although I received lots of love and support from my family, I hated the feeling of being alienated from my peers. I didn't know how to reconcile the values of my peers with the expectations of my family. The effort required to maintain these dual identities became emotionally draining, especially for a child who was just beginning life.

I know that to some, the idea of social identity as a problem may seem trivial when compared to some of the other social ills that plague the black community and, in a broader sense, American culture. It is my belief, however, that this struggle for identity in our children and young adults is the battleground in the fight against the mentality that breeds self-hate and sin. We have been losing this battle for years because of our reluctance to acknowledge its relevance. The reality is that no matter how much our children are exposed to positive influences outside of their immediate surroundings, it is nearly impossible for a child to totally resist the influence of culture and community. In no way am I suggesting that people are unable to overcome the circumstances of their youth; there have been many of people who started off much worse than I did and went on to achieve some of the greatest accomplishments known to man. I just think it would be naive not to consider the impact of culture and community in the discussion of the apprenticeship of disfunction. Race and class would prove to be a factor in other areas of my childhood life, as well. One of the most important activities at the time was a sports league made up of young men from various Catholic churches in the D.C. area. As I said before, our church was almost entirely black and located in an economically poor section of D.C. Our uniforms were old, and had been donated to the church by some wealthy school that bought new uniforms for their kids every year. Our baseball team even had old softball uniforms from an all-girls' high school softball team. I bet that those uniforms are probably still in the basement of my parents' church right now. In contrast, most of the teams that came from the churches that were majority white had the best equipment and gear, in addition to their sparkling new uniforms. The stands were usually full of their supporters and family members. We participated in two sports, basketball and baseball, but the experiences I had were a shining example of the apprenticeship of disfunction.

Baseball was not a very popular sport in the black community when I was growing up, and most of us would have never played the game at all had it not been for this league. Our teams always played considerably worse than all the other teams. They seemed to be quite organized, and you could tell that they put a lot of time and energy into baseball. Although our team practiced fundamental baseball skills, we lacked the discipline and enthusiasm to do well at the sport. Basketball was a different matter, though. Most of the guys on our basketball team had been playing since they were old enough to walk. We had practice weekly, but even at our worst we easily dominated the teams from the majority white churches. Culture was the biggest factor in the difference of our team's performance in these two sports; most of the white children had practiced and studied baseball more than basketball, and the opposite was true for black children. Even though this was supposed to be a church league, racism and discrimination began to surface in our games. The problems began when the referees began to blatantly discriminate against the teams with the black youth on them especially in playoff and championship games. Although I felt like our churches' teams got it the worst, it was not restricted to only us; in fact, I heard later that there had been some of the same complaints made by other churches with black players. I remember one year the team that my older brother and cousin played on made it to the championship game. This game was held in the gymnasium at Catholic University in Washington, D.C., and so for us it was a pretty big deal. Although the game was competitive, the team from my church had the better athletes. The referee made sure that would not be a problem for the other team, however. Fouls were called against our church's team almost exclusively, and they were usually against the tallest or most athletic team members. By the beginning of the second half, two of our team's best players were in foul trouble, and toward the end of the game I believe three players had fouled out. Not only did these tactics allow the other team to "stack the deck" by keeping their tallest players on the floor against smaller players, it also affected the morale of the game. It was obvious to everyone that our team was being cheated, and despite protests by the coaches and the parents the referees continued to call a one-sided game. Our team lost, and I remember the sense of helplessness that we all felt, mixed with the anger we had at the obvious display of racism. I couldn't believe that this was actually happening to us. I had heard about this type of racism in school from the limited information that was provided during Black History Month, but I had never experienced blatant discrimination this up close and personal. In my naiveté, I believed that if a person worked hard and tried to treat people fairly then the world would respond in kind. I went to school with white kids and did all types of activities with them, and although

I always understood that there was an invisible line of separation, I truly believed overt expressions of racism to be a thing of the past. This experience opened my eyes to a whole new reality. I could no longer ignore that invisible line or the causes of that line. I could no longer assume that the white people I knew who seemed to care did not secretly harbor the same racist mentality as those referees. Everyone who was not black was now suspect and I began to question the true intentions and strength of those relationships.

Teachers also played a part in my introduction to disfunctional beliefs and racism. For as long as I can remember, the black children in my classes were more likely to be subject to disciplinary actions. I'll admit some of this was warranted at times; a lot of the black students, especially the young men like me, were not focused and participating in class at an appropriate level. Black children were also less likely to read and write at an appropriate pace for the grade level in which they were enrolled, and this disconnect from what was being taught exacerbated the classroom discipline issues.

Although I personally didn't have issues with the classroom material, the mentality of diminished expectations was being reinforced by the constant failure and subsequent expectation of defeat experienced by other young black men. I remember one year during black history month, one of our substitute teachers gave a short "presentation" on her interpretation of diversity. She pointed out how good diversity was, because each race had some talent to contribute to the world. Hispanic people or "Mexicans" were known to be hard workers, Asians were really good at math, and white people were known for their intelligence. Black people, she explained, were good at sports, and they made really good music. I couldn't make that up if I tried! Looking back on it now, it seems almost incomprehensible that someone felt that comfortable saying that to a group of children. At the time, my young mind didn't quite comprehend what she said as blatantly racist. A few students asked her some questions, but I don't remember too much of what was said. There was an uneasy silence in class, in part because she was a substitute teacher, but also because I think everyone was trying to process what she had just said. I never told my parents about that until years later in a passing conversation, and I'm sure they probably wish I would have said something about it at the time. I think that I honestly accepted part of that statement to be true, as I tried to internalize what I had heard with everything that I saw in my young life. It is true, after all, that black people take exceptional pride in our athletic prowess and our music, and at that time if I had been asked to define what black culture was about, those two traits would've definitely been at the top of the list. The complexities of racial identity as defined by black comedians, TV personalities, and elders in my community gave these statements a measure of value; I had no real sense of what it meant to be black, so I accepted whatever definition that was given to me at face value. I couldn't reconcile the inherent limitations of my race with the expectation of success instilled in me. I had been a participant in the Boy Scouts for as long as I could remember, and I had learned the values of self-reliance and working together with others in order to achieve a common goal. I participated in camping, fishing, hiking, and other activities that were designed to help young men grow and develop. My scout troop consisted of young black males from all black, low-income neighborhoods. My dad was the scoutmaster, and he would have up to twenty young black men out in the woods doing various outdoor activities. We attended the different events sponsored by our local district, and as I said before we were usually the only black faces present. At first, I think everyone had an initial culture shock - both the kids in my scout troop and the white kids in the other troops. As time went on we all got used to it, though. We enjoyed participating in all the activities, and in a lot of ways we were just like all the other boys. Of course, there were still some people who treated us differently or looked at us funny, but for the most part we were all just scouts.

As I said earlier, every year we would go to Goshen, Virginia to the big campgrounds on an old Indian reservation, where we could enjoy the miles of open land and the big lake that sat in the middle. I enjoyed canoeing, rowing, swimming, sailing, and other outdoor activities. I earned several merit badges, and I learned a lot along the way. The most important lesson that I learned was that I could function in the world that existed outside of my neighborhood. I found that I could compete with my white contemporaries, and that I could do so quite successfully, in fact. The young black men in our scout troop enjoyed proving how capable we were, to ourselves as well as to all the other white scout troops. There was another way of life that existed outside of the insanity of my community, and contrary to what the world had been showing me, that way of life was fully accessible to me. What I didn't understand was how I could still be a proud black young man and choose to participate in this alternate reality, without conforming to what I now know to be the mentality of white supremacy? Being a part of this larger society meant assimilating, conforming to a white expectation of culture and standards. I had yet to develop the maturity to understand certain tenets of human decency and civilized societies were universal, and not limited to definition by the expectations of whites.

One day while I was attending mass, I noticed for the first time that in the very back of the church there was this crucifix with a depiction of Jesus as African-American; for those who don't know, Catholics use a crucifix with an image of the body of Jesus still attached to the cross. I don't know how long it had been there, or why it stood out to me in such great clarity on this particular day. I began to think about that more and more, especially when I considered that there was a huge image of "white Jesus" hanging at the front of this all black congregation. I questioned a few adults at the church, who either didn't know, explained that that was how it had always been, and rationalized the fact by explaining that "there were a lot of people who worked hard and spent good money to purchase that statue." Nobody could explain to me where and how black people were depicted in the teachings and history of this "one Holy Catholic and Apostolic church" that I professed to believe in every Sunday as I recited the Nicene creed. This struggle to find myself in a world that placed so much emphasis on my race was only beginning, though. On one hand, I loved being black; I loved black people, black accomplishments, and most parts of our cultural identity. On the other hand, I hated the ignorance that was expected of me, and the limitations that I felt my peers and, to a larger extent, my community placed on me. I didn't think it possible to take some things and leave the rest; It was a zero-sum game to me, all or nothing.

I wanted to experience that other world, where values meant something and education is celebrated. I longed to feel good about the person I was raised to be, but instead I learned to kill a part of that person every day. I learned when to be "blacker", and how to turn my neighborhood mannerisms on and off like a light switch.

I learned when I needed to conform to the expectations of white society, and when I needed to conform to the norms of my peers in order to escape the wrath of other young black men who had learned to despise that which is different.

This was the beginning of my disfunction, born out of a need to conform and forged in the fire of low self-esteem. This part of my apprenticeship would transform me into someone I never wanted to become.

Chapter II
THE APPRENTICESHIP

{POVERTY, HATE, SEX, HYPOCRISY, DISFUNCTION}

POVERTY

My formal introduction to the streets began in 1991. I was in the eighth grade at the time, thirteen years old and still very naive. My older brother was three years older and in the eleventh grade, and because he and I both had very few friends we experienced most things together. My brother did have one guy from our neighborhood that had begun to come around; I wouldn't necessarily say that he and my brother were friends, but they were definitely associates. I didn't really know too much about him at first, but right away I could tell that he was much more worldly and in tune with the streets than my brother and I were. He had a sharp tongue and a slick, sly way of doing almost everything. He was the type of person that you never really trusted, not in the way that you would trust a true friend. I'm not saying that he was a "bad" person per se, but he always gave me the feeling that he might try something sideways at any given time. I had been exposed to people like him all of my life, but it was always from a comfortable distance.

I had definitely never hung around someone who was so involved in the streets - that's not to say that he was a huge "street guy", and to me that didn't really matter. He and my brother would discuss girls, school, and all of the latest happenings, and I would always be around joking back and forth with them. As I said before, the house where we grew up was directly across the street from a liquor store, so even though the owners knew very well that we were underage, we never had a problem getting anything that we wanted. We began trying our hand at buying forty ounce beers for us to pass around, even though I've never been much of a beer drinker. To this day, I doubt seriously if I could or would drink a whole forty. One day, my brother's friend came by with some weed that he got from somebody. This was during the time that hip-hop music was beginning to openly celebrate the use of marijuana in a lot of the popular songs. I knew a few guys from my school that had tried weed before, but I never hung out with guys who were into that. He pulled out a cigar and began rolling a blunt, and I was fascinated by the whole process involved in splitting the cigar, removing the contents, and re-rolling it with the marijuana inside. I had tried a cigarette before once or twice, but the sweet, pungent marijuana smoke was a lot stronger. My throat and lungs burned as my body struggled to handle the heavy, resinous smoke, and I coughed and choked as I inhaled as deeply as I could. In my younger years I had heard all of the anti-drug campaign speeches, from "Just Say No" to "D.A.R.E." classes taught in school, to the "brain on drugs" commercials that were shown on TV. None of that mattered to me at the time, and I was well past the point of worrying about any of that. I can't say that I ever felt pressured to try weed or alcohol; I think that there is a certain curiosity inside of all men to taste the "forbidden fruit" and, when coupled with a culture that encourages anti-social behavior, the perfect conditions are in place for the rampant drug use that has become prevalent in so many communities today.

For me, trying marijuana was as much of an act of defiance from my parents' standards as it was about the desire to feel something new, something different.

Looking back on it all, I find new meaning in the story of Adam and Eve in the bible. As I discussed before, I have significant issues with how the bible details the story of creation, but I do think that there is a lot that can be extracted from the story if you are willing to go beyond the literal interpretation. The significant part of this story to me is found at Genesis 3, when the serpent approaches Eve and questions God's intentions in his command that they not eat from the tree of knowledge of good and evil. According to Gen 3:4-5, and the serpent said unto the woman, ye shall not surely die, for God doth know that in the day ye eat thereof, then your eyes shall be opened, and ye shall be as gods, knowing good and evil. (KJV) I can relate to the position Adam and Eve were in at that moment. I know what it feels like to have what you need and most of what you want, but to still desire more. There was something in me that longed to feel more, to know more and to understand this counter-culture that existed all around me. I could feel the lure of it tickling the tips of my fingers, calling out to me to extend my hand into its grasp. This struggle was the crux of the battle being fought every day right in front of me, a war between hard working people like my parents, people who played by the rules, and people like the ones who hang in and around my community, people who made their own rules. I never understood why God would want to deliberately withhold knowledge of anything from his beloved creation. In spite of my own personal pain and struggles, I couldn't seem to put this concept into focus. It took becoming the parent of a teenager to really get a good sense of that line of reasoning, not that I would ever claim to understand the reasoning of God, but I understood the desire to shape how much of life your children will come to know. I have known evil; some of the deepest, ugliest acts one human being is capable of committing.

I have seen and experienced this evil in a way that can't be learned by reading about it in a book or hearing about it in a story; rather, I have gained the knowledge that came from the fruit of that tree, the knowledge of good and evil, in the most intimate of settings and circumstances. As much as I understand the need for children to be informed and aware, I sincerely pray that my children will never come into this knowledge of evil, not as I have come to know it. Maybe that is foolish on my part. Maybe in my desire to shelter my children from the reality of all that I have experienced I am, in fact, sending them into the world unprepared. Even so, it seems to be a better option than the alternative that this apprenticeship of sin offers. Oddly enough, I didn't get high the first time that I tried smoking weed. I kept at it though, and needless to say I eventually got the hang of it. This new habit that I was developing also coincided with another problem that I was beginning to have - paying for all of the activities that I wanted to do. In my younger years, I received an allowance from my parents weekly and I supplemented that income by cutting the small patch of grass in the lot behind the liquor store across the street from my house. Eventually though, this would not be enough money for me to live on. In the summer, I got a job through the D.C. summer jobs program that then Mayor Marion Barry started. I was assigned to an African dance studio, where I learned to play drums for a dance troupe comprised of people around my age. It was a great experience for me. As a musician, it was my first real opportunity to play a percussion instrument and to play rhythms that weren't mainstream or Eurocentric. There were stilt walkers, costumes, dancers, and drummers, and I was proud to be a part of such a massive production. Besides, there were lots of very, pretty young ladies there and the outfits they wore were minimal and left little to the imagination. On more than one occasion I was able to see several girls almost naked as they rushed to change in and out of various costumes.

Even though I enjoyed this job and all of its perks, my small paycheck was still not enough to finance this new lifestyle I was beginning to lead. I had become friends with the older brother of a girl I went to school with. He was a few years older than me and had a car, and I would ride around with him and some of the guys he went to school with, smoking weed and talking to girls. We would travel all around town going to parties, shopping, and enjoying our teenage years. I also began playing the keyboard in a go-go band that some older guys from my neighborhood had started. Music was something that had always been a part of my life in one form or another. I started playing the clarinet in the fourth grade, and I actually got to be fairly decent at it. I began singing in my church choir simply because I loved music. I discovered that I had a fairly decent "ear", that is, the ability to hear a pitch and play it on an instrument. At thirteen, I received a small keyboard for Christmas, and I would spend hours picking out melodies of popular songs. The first song that I ever learned the chords to was Mary J. Blige's "Real Love". I was super-excited by my ability to figure out this song by just listening to it, and I spent hours teaching myself to make my fingers play the progression of notes. By the time I reached ninth grade, I was able to play a lot of the popular songs that were out at that time. One day, I was hanging out with a few of the guys around my neighborhood, and when they learned that I could play the keyboard they were surprisingly excited. All of the guys were older than me by a few years, and so up until that point I was just the "youngin'" tagging along behind the big dogs. There was one guy who had an assortment of equipment in his basement that he used for informal band practices. He played congas, but there were drums, microphones, percussion instruments, and a keyboard. I had known this guy for years, but I had never been invited to hang out at his house until now. We all went over to his house and began to play, and everyone was surprised by my ability on the keyboard.

That day led to the start of us forming a band, but I had no idea what I was really getting myself into. Our band played at different venues all over D.C. and MD, and although we weren't that good, we felt like we were on top of the world.

I finally had an identity outside of the sheltered kid from a good family, and it felt good to feel like I finally fit in. I'm not saying that I didn't have any friends growing up or in school, but I was finally "in with the in crowd". If there is one thing that transcends all racial and cultural boundaries, it is the desire a person has to feel accepted and to belong. Not only was I hanging out with the popular kids, I was the youngest in a group of guys three to five years older than me, and so I thought that I was "grown". Again, trying to live like a grown-up meant I had to find a way to finance my lifestyle. At first it was okay going out to eat and smoking weed all the time, but the few dollars that I was getting from my parents weren't enough to last, especially when you're with people who had already begun to sell drugs. This was around 1992, and the crack cocaine epidemic was well established in my neighborhood. I remember that when I was about nine or ten years old, our local neighborhood civic association attended a hearing at the city council to address the use of drugs and violence that was occurring at the liquor store. The civic association asked me to give a speech on the concern I had about all that was going on across the street from my house, and so I read a paper that I wrote that expressed all of the issues I had as the upright ten-year old member of society that I believed myself to be. A few years later at fourteen, I became one of the same people that I claimed to be afraid of. I don't exactly remember who I bought my first package of crack to sell from, but I do remember that some of my earliest clientele were split between people who frequented the liquor store, transvestite prostitutes and their customers, and patrons of the crack house a few houses up the street from mine. I wouldn't say that I made a lot of money starting out, but I kept enough to eat out every day, smoke lots of weed, have pocket money to spend, and buy more drugs to sell. I remember the feeling of pride I had when I was able to buy my first pair of shoes from drug money.

It wasn't the point that the shoes were all that expensive; in reality, I could've worked at a fast food restaurant or somewhere similar in order to afford some shoes, although I would've had to work much longer and harder for a lot less money. It was more about the thrill of having this alternative lifestyle, combined with the pride of being my own boss and becoming my own man. This time period would also be my earliest attempts at living in two separate worlds, with two separate identities. I was involved in the marching band at school, and we also had a "top 40" band that played cover songs off of the radio. I enjoyed playing different instruments, so I tried to learn to play every instrument that I could get my hands on. I had a phenomenal music teacher - this old, white lady who let you know right away that she was in charge, and I learned a lot about music and about life from her. Nevertheless, the allure of the streets was calling my name. I began hanging out in an apartment complex up the street from my school with a couple of guys who were in the band with me. They were also into smoking weed and selling drugs, so they understood my whole struggle with attempting to exist in both lifestyles. We decided to form a go-go band, and because the guys in my other band had other things going on and weren't as dedicated as I felt they should be, I agreed. That was pretty much the extent of my first two years of high school - smoking weed, making music, selling drugs and chasing girls. My brother began selling drugs with me at some point, and although we never became super rich like the guys you hear about in all of the movies and stories that are told, it felt good to have money in our pockets and to be able to do what we wanted. We sold crack at night, and although we had a few customers here and there it really wasn't all that lucrative. Everybody had crack for sale; in fact, between the two locations that I was selling drugs I was lucky to make $1000 a week, simply because there was so much competition. Selling weed proved to be much more lucrative early on.

I don't remember who we started buying weed from originally; there were always random guys I ran into who had quarter pounds and half pounds for sale. Eventually we got turned on to some Jamaicans who had moved into an old Wonder Bread distribution warehouse off of Georgia Avenue, and began buying pounds of weed from them. In those days, $800 for a pound of the compressed, greenish-brown commercial weed was considered fair; nobody would even consider smoking that type of weed nowadays, but in the early nineties it was all over D.C. Besides, the only thing most guys cared about back then was how "phat" the bags of weed were. Most people wanted to be able to roll two blunts out of a dime bag, or three small ones if they were trying to stretch their weed because money was tight. My brother and I would make up these huge twenty dollar bags (or dubs), and sell them all over the neighborhood. I went a step further and made up some five dollar bags (or nicks) to take to school with me; these were better suited for kids who were pooling the one or two dollars they had for their lunch money together, and for everyone else who was trying to stretch a dollar. We had steady clientele, and eventually people started knocking on our front door looking for us. With all of the increased foot traffic I'm sure my dad had to know something was going on. He knew we were smoking weed, but I doubt he knew we were running a fairly decent retail marijuana operation right out of the front of our house. Between the money I made selling weed and crack, I was content in my stupidity. I had enough money to enjoy my teenage activities, and even buy myself a few clothes and shoes every now and then. Most of my extra money went into smoking weed, so I didn't worry about my profit margin as long as I had money to spend and weed to smoke when I wanted to.

Of course, I was still trying to juggle dual identities, and between school, band, selling drugs, and my social life, things stayed pretty busy all of the time. I would go and live with my grandmother off and on when I wasn't getting along with my parents, and since she didn't live too far from my school and the neighborhood I hung out in, it was easy for me to go over there whenever I wanted. One day, I was over my cousin Courtney's house when another one of our cousins stopped by to visit. He asked me if I knew anything about music production and making beats, and I told him that I did. He had recently opened up a studio on Georgia Avenue and he said that he was looking for some producers. At that time, I had messed around with music equipment before, and I had even hooked my keyboard up to my computer at home using some basic software, but in no way was I prepared for all of the equipment that my cousin had purchased. I tried to "fake it until I make it", but it became obvious after a while that I had no idea what I was doing. Nevertheless, I persisted in trying to be a part of what he had going on, not only because I looked up to him for his reputation as a successful "street dude", but also because I felt like I finally had an opportunity to be somebody. This period of the mid nineties was a very significant time in black culture because, along with the explosion of crack cocaine and the money that came with it, "gangsta rap" or rap based on elements of street life and criminal behavior, had begun to gain mainstream notoriety. Rappers and their affiliates were portraying a lifestyle that showcased all of the supposed spoils that came from living a life of crime: cars, money, houses, women, jewelry, clothes, power, and respect. These images were the definition of the American dream for me and most of the young black males that I knew, and combining my musical abilities with my adolescent experiences in the criminal underworld seemed like a natural progression. This initial venture would not be the success I had hoped it would be, however. More often than not, the studio sat empty as my cousin pursued other ventures that were more lucrative, and I continued to lead my multi-faceted life. The relationship I began to develop with my cousin and his associates had other benefits, however. For one thing, I now had access to the best weed in D.C.

Up until this point, I had been satisfied with smoking the brown, dry, compressed, "commercial" weed that was being sold and smoked all around D.C. My cousin and his friends introduced me to a new name for this type of weed - bush. The new weed that they were smoking was much lighter, greener, and fluffier. It had a fresh pine smell and a much milder taste. I knew from that point on, I would never smoke bush again. I also began to hang out in the neighborhood with my cousin. The atmosphere was totally different from what I was used to; I had never seen so many drug sales take place that fast, and it went on like that all day long. Everybody seemed to be making money, if they had drugs and were willing to stand outside and sell them. It was also the first time I had ever met any older hustlers, men who had been around and were well known in the streets. The most memorable of all of the people I met was an older hustler named John Lee. John Lee was well-known all over D.C., both from his time in the street and the time he had spent in prison. His commanding style and his deep knowledge of the street matched well with his nickname - the General. I would sit outside with my cousins and the other guys from around there, and he always had some game to give me about getting money and how things go in the street. Now at this time, I hadn't begun to sell drugs with the other men who were selling drugs in that neighborhood. I would still sell the small packages of crack I had bought from various places in MD. I was cool with two guys that played in my old go-go band, and I would hang out in their grandmother's apartment with them and hustle. She moved around a few times, but we could always go to any of the places that she had lived and sell our crack. I still sold weed with my brother too.

It was bush, but it was cheaper than the "lime green" weed, and most of our clientele wanted quantity over quality. Between spending time uptown with my cousin, hustling and hanging out in MD, my social life, and my extra-curricular activities at school, my life was all over the place.

Something had to eventually suffer, and that thing was the marching band, first, and later on school. I couldn't meet the demands that my band teacher placed on me and run the streets, so I chose the streets. One day, I decided I was going to try my hand at hustling uptown with my cousins. I bought a quarter of crack from my connection, or seven grams, cut it up and put it in bags, and took it uptown with me. I had stood outside with my cousins for months, learning faces, making trips back and forth to the store, getting to know how things worked, and now I felt like it was time to throw my hat into the ring. They definitely did not share my enthusiasm, however. For one, I was young and inexperienced, and two, my family was not going to be happy to find out that I was uptown selling drugs with them. None of that mattered to me, though. At first, my cousin wouldn't let me sell my crack; he took it, gave it to my other cousin to sell, and gave me my money. We had a talk about why I couldn't sell drugs around there, but at that time I didn't care - I knew I would be back tomorrow with another package of crack to sell, especially after I got a taste of how fast the first package sold. I was persistent, and I made it clear that I wasn't going away, and that this is what I wanted to do. My family, my teachers, my former dreams and hopes - none of that was as important as learning to master the streets. I needed to become worldlier, more in touch with the experiences of the black men all around me. I needed what our culture told me was important. I needed to gain respect in the street, to be admired by men and women for the money I made and the lifestyle I lived. I needed to become an apprentice of the game of the streets and all of its ways. There were clear lines between wealth and poverty in the hood, and poverty was a weakness as far as boys and men were concerned. You are expected to get money, to get outside and make something happen for yourself, to "get down how you live". I had no idea what lied in store for me behind the door I was walking through, but I would find out soon enough.

HATE

Violence began to take on a whole new meaning as I got older. As I said before, I'm not naturally inclined to violence, which is a huge liability for a young black man in an urban community. The expectation of violent behavior that black people place on one another as the only acceptable form of conflict resolution is implanted in our psyche at an early age. A child learns early on that you are either a wolf or a sheep, and no one naturally wants to be a sheep. I was not raised to respond with violence as a first option, and so in a lot of ways that made me a sheep by default. I know that that's not a popular thing to be and I'll be the first to admit that I was hesitant about admitting that here in this book for the world to see, but in my heart I know that being honest about my hatred of violence is necessary in order to combat the apprenticeship of hate. I know that there are plenty of other young black males who are peaceful by nature, and that wish that somehow they could call a "cease fire" to the war that they were born into. Many feel drawn to the darkness of violence by the world in which they live, and so it seems unfair at times to many that they are held accountable for following the rules of their culture and their community, rules that they didn't create.

The turning point for me was high school, and my ninth grade year was one of particular significance. As I said before, I was in the marching band, but I had just begun to dip my toe into the dark waters of the streets. There was a guy who was a few years older than me who was in the band as well. Initially we got along, but at some point we had a disagreement that led to us falling out. I think there were several things involved: I was in a relationship

with a girl he had previously dealt with, I played in the drum
section and earned my respect as a musician, and I was young
and inexperienced. One day, the school had an event for all of the
students that participated in extracurricular activities, a pool party
at one of the local pools.

I hadn't really had any interactions with the guy outside of what
we were doing at band practice, but for some reason the tension
was thick between us on this particular day. I felt like he was
being extra antagonistic, in an attempt to show off for the guys he
was hanging with. I shrugged it off and did my best to avoid him.
It wasn't that I was afraid of the guy, but I really didn't have a
problem with him and I felt like I was being the bigger person by
avoiding any conflict. Towards the end of the party as everyone
was preparing to leave, I was leaning up against my brother's car
talking to my girlfriend with my arms around her. That's when
the guy approached and spoke briefly to my girlfriend. I turned
away for a second to let them talk, and the next thing I knew the
guy sucker punched me in the eye. Now the thing about getting
hit in the eye is that you really can't see that good after getting
hit. I had been in fights before and been hit in the eye, but this
guy hit me in the right spot. This guy was older, taller, and
stronger than me, so I had a challenging fight on my hands
already; it only made matters worse that I was now fighting with
only one functional eye. As I started to fight back, I guess this
guy figured out that I only had one functional eye, because he
would move to that side and hit me as I tried to adjust my vision.
Someone broke up the fight, eventually, but it would be fair to
say that I lost that fight by a landslide. Of course, I was
embarrassed, especially since this all happened in front of my
classmates and my girlfriend, but I also felt angry at myself for
trying to "play nice" and avoid a violent confrontation altogether.
I don't think anyone enjoys losing, but I felt like I lost all the way
around the board, because maybe I should've met the conflict
head on when the situation first developed.

I felt like my cooperative spirit and mild manner was a weakness, and weakness is a cardinal sin in the eyes of black culture. I hated myself for not being more aggressive, more inclined to "go hard" and be violent at the slightest sign of disrespect.

I felt like I was cheated out of some sociopathic genetic disposition that was supposedly standard issue with black skin. To add insult to injury, I felt like now the whole world knew it, and had just seen my weakness. I'd lost a fight, and now the world was waiting for my response. According to the code of the streets, the only acceptable thing left for me to do was respond with violence of equal or greater measure, in order to prove to everyone that I wasn't weak or soft. At the very least, I was supposed to attempt to fight him again, and if I really wanted to make a statement I was supposed to jump him, stab him, or shoot him. Whatever the violent response I chose, it had to leave the message that I was not one to be played with. I didn't do any of those things, however. My band teacher sat us both down to talk about the incident, and we actually got along quite fine afterwards. I'd like to think that I didn't choose violence because of my gentle nature, but I don't think that is the case. I know the violence that I'm capable of- I won't go into detail about what I have or haven't done, but I think that it is safe for me to say that I have the capacity for violence in a manner that is commonly seen as a part of the urban African-American experience. I think that at that point in my life, I had not learned to hate myself enough, yet. I have always, among other things, been very sentimental and idealistic, and so up until that point I believed my duty to be attempting to live peaceably among all men. I had witnessed the violence of the late eighties, as countless numbers of my cousin's drug-dealing boyfriends were laid to rest. I believed it to be honorable, noble even, to avoid violence whenever possible. This fight opened my eyes to reality, however, and I understand what a fool I had been.

I could no longer afford to give place to civility in the face of men who defined their status by their ability to display savage behavior. In order to survive, I needed a new skill set. I needed to disregard all that I had been taught, all that I had been brought up to be, and become someone else.

I had to learn to replace compassion with intolerance, fear with egotism, respect with wanton disregard, and love with hate. I had to surrender myself to the cultural influences I inherited by virtue of being born black in Washington, D.C. I had tried to outrun it, but its pull could no longer be denied. My options were clear: learn to become a wolf or accept the fate of a sheep. The bible makes a lot of references to the roles of wolves and sheep. During the sermon on the mountain, Jesus tells his followers to beware of false prophets who come disguised as harmless sheep but are really vicious wolves (Matt. 7:15 NLT) In this example, Jesus was talking about people who manipulate the truth in order to exalt themselves and fleece the people. They disguise themselves as authentic, but in their heart they only desire that which is self-serving. What intrigued me about this lesson, after sitting down and meditating on it for a while, is that this type of mindset is totally acceptable in today's culture. In fact, not only is it acceptable, it is often encouraged, especially in the black community. Nobody likes a bully. Sure, you can try and intimidate people with brute force and scare tactics for a while, but eventually someone is going to figure out how to stop you. It may come by the use of greater force, calling the police, or some other method, but eventually someone will put an end to the reign of a tyrant. This is true for rulers of countries and members of a community alike. Yes, there are some who continue the tough guy routine, and there are even a few who are successful at it for a while. But in my observations of history and life, the person who appears openly as the big, bad wolf usually goes down hard. That, however, does not mean you should desire to be a sheep.

Sheep were considered sustenance, used for food, valued for their soft coats and the nourishment of flesh they provided. But when you think about it, sheep only look like food to a predator, to a creature that has the appetite and intent to devour. One definition of predatory is "inclined or intended to injure or exploit others for personal gain and profit" (*Webster's, 11th Ed.*) In my community, that is really the person almost everyone wanted to be respected as. No one respects sheep, except for the shepherd who the sheep belong to. Certainly no one fears a sheep, which is why this analogy of being a wolf in sheep's clothing is so relevant. In order to be readily accessible to the sheep, a wolf must first learn to appear like a sheep. He needs to walk humbly and meek, present himself as non-violent, non-threatening. I felt comfortable in that place; I never gravitated towards loud, obnoxious types, but I needed to gain that quiet, cool confidence that I saw displayed by older men that I respected. I wanted to be cool, naturally charming but with an edge that made violence a real possibility. Some might say that attitude or "swag" is a natural thing, but I believe that as adolescents we are all trying on different people and personalities in an attempt to figure out what works for us. And so, I set out to learn the ways of the wolf: the way he moves, the way he thinks, and most importantly, how he does the things that make him dangerous. As I got older, the level of violence that was displayed by my peers increased. Jumping someone - two or more people fighting one person - had always been a part of the violence of my youth, but it became more common as I got older. I never got jumped myself, but I have participated in jumping other people. One thing about wolves is that they travel and hunt in packs. No one wants to be a lone wolf. No matter how strong a person may think themselves to be, you can't beat a pack of wolves by yourself. As I said before, I didn't hang with guys from my neighborhood, and so my integration into a wolf pack was awkward to say the least. For the most part, I hung out with my brother and my cousins, but in high school I started associating with the other guys from my neighborhood who went to school with me. Most of them played in our neighborhood go-go band, so that gave me some common ground. I began to associate with more and more people from around my neighborhood through the band, and that also became a valuable source of networking for my efforts as an aspiring drug dealer. But belonging to a neighborhood was important for other reasons as well. We didn't have "gangs" per se in D.C., at least not when I was growing up. I mentioned earlier that most of my contemporaries from the mid-west and the west coast grew up in a formal, organized gang with a hierarchy, rules, dues, and so forth. But in D.C. it was all about your neighborhood, or the crew that you ran with. There were never any official chiefs or leaders. Sure, you had guys in your neighborhood that everyone respected for their ability to sell drugs, be violent, or whatever personality trait that you may have gravitated towards, but there was never anyone who was a definite "shot caller". That independent spirit is one of the most unique things about being from D.C. Most men learn from an early age to be your own boss, and that being a follower or "flunkie" is for weak minded people. The ability to stand on your own two feet is what men respect, and although I have come to understand these traits through a somewhat psychotic, twisted process, I am thankful for the life lesson. That doesn't mean that there were no similarities to gang life, especially when it came to violence. It's one thing to be surrounded by a bunch of young men who have been indoctrinated into a lifestyle of violence, but when these same men begin to form alliances, bad things often happen. There was no respect for a fair fight; maybe for a friend with whom you'd had a misunderstanding, but it was perfectly acceptable to grab two, three or more guys and collectively beat and stomp someone, especially if he wasn't from your neighborhood. A lot of these types of incidents played out in local clubs where go-go bands played. Part of the go-go culture is the call and response between the band and the crowd, where people are asked to put up their hands and represent their neighborhood. In that atmosphere it becomes competitive, especially when you are dealing with testosterone-filled young men. The combination of loud, aggressive music, drugs, alcohol, and men full of adrenaline led to a lot of the violence.

It didn't take a whole lot for a brawl to break out; everyone knew that at any moment a go-go could go from being an enjoyable party to a violent free for all. Most neighborhoods tried to be as "deep" as possible, or to have as many people from their neighborhood present, in order to overwhelm any potential rivals with their numbers. In fact, it wasn't uncommon for different groups of guys to show up to a go-go with the sole intention of starting a fight. There were plenty of times that I ended up in a fight with someone I didn't know and had never met, simply because they were from a different neighborhood. I remember playing at one particular club called Barnett's, which was basically a little "hole in the wall" club in northeast D.C., right in the heart of some of the most well-known housing projects on that side of town. Our band was having a fairly decent set; there was a nice sized crowd, and they seemed to be enjoying our music. There were different groups of girls in attendance, which is always a good sign for any band. All of a sudden, a commotion broke out in the back of the club, and before I knew it there was a full-on brawl between these different groups of girls. Two or three girls drug another girl in the bathroom and began stomping her. Another group of girls began fighting by the stage, and they ended up tussling onto the stage, nearly knocking my keyboard over. The fight spilled over outside, and one girl got hit over the head with a bottle. Eventually the police came and cleared out the street, but I never forgot that day because it was a prime example of how the violence that is ingrained into the black community and our culture affects both males and females. Eventually, as I got older, the violence I was involved in and surrounded by became a matter of life and death. The reality of violence struck home my ninth grade year, when a guy who played in the marching band with me was murdered. He wasn't the type of guy that you would consider as being involved in the streets, but I guess the same could have been said about me, so you never really know.

In some ways, all of the black men my age that I knew had access or involvement in the street life, because the lifestyle had become so linked to black culture. I can't say that death was something new; I had seen plenty of deaths before, but it was different this time. This wasn't some older hustler who I had heard about through my cousins or through the streets. This was someone I ate with, someone I talked to and someone I could relate to. This death made the consequences of the streets real to me in a way that no other experience could. Of course, he was not the last person around me that would be murdered in the streets. Death and murder were a part of this lifestyle that I chose, and regardless of how I felt about it I needed to come up with a plan of how to navigate through it all. One night, I was leaving out of a go-go and was standing on the wall waiting for a friend of mine. I was slightly distracted, because I was talking to a girl I had met earlier, but out of the corner of my eye I remember seeing a car turn the corner and cut off its headlights. Something about that didn't feel right, and I began to move further down the street. There were a few cars in front of that car, but the driver swerved around them and someone in the car began shooting at everyone that was standing in the area I had just left. I initially froze, out of fear and also because I doubted that I was the intended target. I snapped back to reality, however, after a bullet whizzed past my head and ricocheted off the wall behind me with a loud pop. I took off running as fast as I could down the street, as I contemplated how close I had come to being shot. I think that I remember hearing that four people got shot and one person died. That was the first time I had ever been so close to deadly gunfire, but it would not be my last.

Another incident that helped shape my perception happened one night after playing a show with my neighborhood band. We had just finished performing, loaded up our equipment and began the drive back to our neighborhood.

We were riding in a van that was owned by the drug-addicted daughter of the grandmother who lived behind my house; she had passed away by this time, and the daughter had turned the house into her personal crack den. She would allow us to "rent" her van whenever we needed to use it, in exchange for crack. Anyway, as we were riding we noticed two men in a car following us. I didn't know if someone in the band had "beef" with somebody, or if they were trying to rob us for our band equipment. All of a sudden, the car sped up and the guy in the passenger seat let off a shot, and we began to weave in and out of traffic trying to lose them. At some point the guy must have gotten stuck behind another car as we returned to our neighborhood. My brother's friend, who was in the band with me, ran in the house and returned with a .38 revolver that he passed to me. It wasn't the first time that I had held a gun, but it was the first time that I felt like I needed one. He had another gun on him, and we stood outside for a while waiting to see if the car would ride through our neighborhood. We didn't want to have to worry about whoever this was creeping up on us later, so we were prepared to deal with whatever they wanted that night. That car never came through that night, but I went home with the pistol anyway. My band mate let me hold onto it for a while, and told me he would sell it to me if I decided later that I wanted to buy it. Having a pistol on me at fourteen made me feel more powerful, in a way that I never had before. I had the confidence that I always wanted, because I knew that no matter how big or strong a guy was, I could win with my pistol. I'm not saying that having a pistol turned me into a tough guy all of a sudden, but I certainly didn't have the same apprehension that I used to about being a sheep.

I carried my pistol to school with me every day, like it was part of a school uniform. I was still in the band, still trying to be a "good guy", but my alter ego was beginning to develop the edge I needed.

I continued to attend go-go's, both as a keyboard player in a band and as a fan of some of the more well-known bands. I became more and more comfortable with all of the violence, too; I guess just like anything else, the more exposure you have to something the less sensitive you become to it. Fights, brawls, shootouts, injury, and death were all commonplace in the black community at this time, and I was slowly becoming another product of my environment. By the time I reached the 11th grade, everybody was bringing their pistol to school. This was before the days of metal detectors at school entrances, and so coming to school with weapons was a common thing. Miraculously, no one got shot inside of my school during my time there, but I do know a guy that I grew up with who shot someone at school. As I write this, I can't help but to reflect on how insane all of it was, but the reality is that this culture of violence and hatred is the theme by which black men have learned to relate to each other.

Jesus uses the analogy about wolves and sheep again in a similar fashion, by telling his disciples look, I am sending you out as sheep among wolves. So be as shrewd as snakes and as harmless as doves. (Matt 10:16 NLT) Jesus was telling his followers that the Pharisees were like wolves, because of the cultural and social influence they held over the people of their time. But even in the face of all the opposition that the disciples would face, Jesus commanded them to be cunning but passive. Imagine what a frightening concept that must have been, especially in the face of such open hostility. I think few people today see the similarities between the challenges that Jesus faced with his disciples and the plight of a black man growing up in America. The truth is that if you don't teach your children how to navigate inside of this culture of violence and hatred, you are sending them out as a sheep amongst wolves. There are no other options: either you choose to stand up for yourself and defend your life and well-being, or you accept the fact that at any moment a predator could choose to make easy prey of you.

I think one of the biggest hypocrisies we see in our society today involves our understanding of how violent culture influences human behavior. We readily acknowledge the psychological damage that occurs from exposure to extended periods of violence when it comes to the care of our soldiers, but society has been less willing to give the same deference to the thousands of black men born into this cycle. For those who have never experienced this culture of ignorance firsthand, it is easy to assume that a young black child has the support system and resources in place to opt out at any time. One only need to look at the violence that continues to plague inner cities year after year to understand that it's not that simple. I continue to acknowledge the power of individual choice and personal responsibility, because without them a man is nothing more than a slave. But in a lot of ways some men never had a choice, because you can't choose an option that you never knew existed. The lack of options due to ignorance makes some a slave by default. Their only choice becomes what they have learned and seen: sin, death, and hatred. I wish at times I could've walked away from it all, but that wasn't my reality. I knew if I was going to survive in my community, I had to learn the ways of the wolf, the ways of sin, the ways of hate. I became a slave to that sin, bound by the expectations of it and trapped inside of the hopelessness that it brings. This apprenticeship of hate would continue to call me deeper into its darkness and I made up my mind to answer its call.

SEX

Out of all the problems I may have had over my lifetime, I can honestly say that dealing with the opposite sex has not been one of them.

I'm not saying I didn't have a learning curve or an awkward stage like all kids do, but my natural charm helped me out a lot when it came to dealing with women. As I progressed through my early years, I continued to talk to girls on the phone, practicing my adolescent game.

My first time having actual sex would be at the age of twelve. Up until that point I had rubbed, touched, and even had oral sex, but I had yet to actually "get it in". The girl I had sex with went to elementary school with me, but had transferred to another school years earlier. I think we ran into each other at the store one day and exchanged phone numbers. She wasn't the most attractive girl I had ever seen, but my hormonal twelve year old mind wasn't concerned with looks. This was another opportunity to practice my "rap", and I thought maybe if I found the right words to say I could talk her into coming over to my house when my parents weren't home. As I said before, I had been watching and reading porn for years, so not only did I feel like I knew everything there was to know about sex, I was eager to try out some of the moves I had pictured in my head. I had a road map of how I planned to start, what move I would do next, and so forth. The only element that was missing was a girl who was willing to try all of this stuff with me. At that time, I didn't view sex as something women enjoyed or participated in because they desired it as much as men. I thought of it as more of an obligation that a woman had to fulfill for the man with whom they were in a relationship with. For the female participants of "casual" sex, I believed that their participation hinged on the man's ability to deceive the woman, to present them with the opportunity to have or be whatever they desired - to "sell a dream". This idea of selling a dream is what I was attempting to practice, at least that was my game plan going in. Surprisingly though, I didn't have to do any of that. When I called this young lady on the phone, we really didn't talk about much at all. We made small talk for a minute, and then I suggested that she come over to my house.

I was surprised that she agreed so easily. I began making all the necessary preparations - I "cleaned" my room (more like threw all my stuff in the closet), I changed my sheets, sprayed a little air freshener, took a quick shower, and splashed on a healthy amount of my best cologne.

Minutes later, the doorbell rang and there she stood wearing a nice summer dress and some open toed sandals. As I said before she wasn't all that attractive as far as her face was concerned, but she had begun to develop the body of a woman, with the firm breasts and shapely behind that came with it. Many men before me had been willing to overlook a woman's looks in the name of easy sex, and in my horny twelve year old mind, looks didn't matter one bit, especially not when I was this close. I invited her in and we went straight to my room, and that was the first time I ever had a woman in my personal space in that way. She kicked off her shoes and laid on my bed while I fumbled for something to watch on TV. Of course the TV was just a distraction, and I remember being shocked at how easy it had been to get her to actually lay in my bed. She had the cool confidence of someone who had been through this all before. I, on the other hand, was struggling to maintain my composure. I tried to appear calm, even though I was eagerly excited in anticipation of what I hoped was about to happen. I laid back on the bed next to her and she immediately snuggled up next to me, rubbing her soft, curvaceous backside against my throbbing erection in the process. It was then that I remembered a conversation I had overheard on the bus one day between two older guys. One guy was explaining to the other the importance of always masturbating before sex, so that you wouldn't ejaculate too quickly. I didn't know if what he was saying was true or not, but I did feel like I was ready to explode every time her body brushed against mine, in spite of the fact that we were both still fully clothed. I excused myself, went to the bathroom, and relieved myself of the aforementioned pressure. I returned to my room a little calmer, but still very excited. I laid back on the bed and again the girl snuggled up to me. My erection returned with lightning speed, as we began to kiss, fondle, and touch each other. I was surprised when the girl climbed on top of me and began to remove her dress and bra.

It was then I knew I wasn't dealing with an amateur. This helped me to relax, as I removed my clothes and began to put on a condom. I'll spare you all of the graphic details, but I will say that I experienced every sexual position and curiosity that I had in my mind. I think when you experience that type of "no holds barred" sex at such a young age, especially for your first time, it sets the bar pretty high for all of your subsequent experiences. I'm not saying that sex got boring or uninteresting after that, but once I had truly experienced every body part and position a woman had to offer sexually, the childish curiosity and behaviors associated with the unknown were gone. I matured that day, if not by a shift in my mentality then by sheer virtue of an adult experience. No longer did I have to sit silent or pretend as my older brother and his friends described their sexual conquests. I could now throw my hat in the ring along with the rest of the young men. I continued to mature in my relationship skills as the years progressed. I had normal teenage relationships throughout my middle school years, and because I associated with older guys who were always chasing sex, I also tried to have casual sex with young women every opportunity I could get. My arrival in high school would be the turning point for me, however. I became involved with a young lady early on in my ninth grade year who also had her own experiences with sex and the whole process involved in coming of age. She had aunts who were only a few years older, and I think that her personal experiences combined with all that she had seen gave her a maturity that I had not yet experienced in a woman my age. We were compatible on so many levels, and it didn't take long for us to become intimate. This relationship was different than the casual sex that I had been having; this was my first real relationship, a relationship based on love and passion. I had real feelings invested into this relationship, and so the sex that we had meant a lot more to me than curious exploration of female flesh.

I know some may think it is impossible to really experience those types of relationships at fourteen years old, but I know it to be true. I would submit I certainly didn't have the wisdom or maturity to handle such a relationship, but every feeling and emotion seemed real to me. Besides, "puppy love" is always easy, because it doesn't cost anything. Our relationship didn't have the pressures of bills, kids, and other responsibilities that come with real adult relationships, and so I was free to focus on all of the other parts of this "grown-up" relationship that seemed so important at that point. For me, that meant lots and lots of sex. As for my newfound love interest, she lived right next door to my high school, and so that made for easy access to her. We would wait until her family left for work and then have sex before school. Some days, if we just didn't feel like being bothered with school or if we were having an intense round of lovemaking, we would just stay in her house all day until it was time for band practice. I was always over her house during the week, and she usually was over my house on the weekends. My parents didn't allow me to have girls spend the night at the house, but they did allow me to have girls in my room with the door closed. At first, my room was on the first floor of our tiny house, so that meant I had to be extremely quiet if I was trying to have sex. As I got older, we converted the attic into another bedroom, which worked out perfectly for me. My brother had been the first to live up there, but after he left for college it became mine. It really didn't matter where I stayed, or where I was for that matter, because I was going to find a way to have sex regardless. My room being upstairs and away from the rest of the family just made things easier. As far as safe sex went, that was a complicated thing. We started off using condoms the first few times that we had sex.

The condoms in the store fit best, but with no job and sporadic income from my early attempts at selling drugs, buying condoms wasn't a priority.

The clinic provided free condoms, but those often fit poorly, smelled bad, and broke easily. Besides, after you become so familiar with someone, and you do all of the things my girlfriend and I were doing to each other so frequently, condoms were not important to us. Of course, the inevitable happened - my girlfriend got pregnant. I remember the first time that my girlfriend told me she was pregnant. I was filled with a mix of pride in my ability to procreate, and fear of the real-world consequences of having a child. I had no idea what I was going to do, and neither did my girlfriend. Neither of us told our parents, and we found comfort in each other the only way we knew how: more sex. One day, my girlfriend began bleeding uncontrollably, and I had heard enough about a miscarriage to know that she was having one. The girl who lived across the street from my girlfriend helped out and showed her what to do because I certainly didn't have a clue. I remember feeling somewhat saddened, yet relieved at the same time. I talked to my older brother about it, but he had never experienced anything like that either, so he couldn't relate to how I felt. I dealt with my emotions with drugs and alcohol, the only way I had learned to deal with things. Again, I'm not suggesting I didn't have any other options besides drinking and smoking weed, or this issue "forced" me to get drunk and high. I used drugs and alcohol anyway, but especially during stressful times in order to help me deal with the symptoms of stress. If some chose to view that as drug abuse, then, so be it. I always feel the need to mention that point whenever I reference my drug and alcohol use, because I hate some of the preconceived notions that continue to exist. But more on that, elsewhere. Long story short, I smoked weed and thought about how the miscarriage affected me and my girlfriend's lives.

I think we both knew that we weren't ready, and I remember contemplating if this was somehow God's way of saving us from a situation we couldn't handle. I never discussed any of that with my girlfriend though.

I wasn't sure what to say to her really, and I provided her comfort in the only way I felt comfortable expressing my emotions: with more sex. We both got past the miscarriage, but because of all of the unprotected sex we were having, this would not be our last experience in that situation. Over the course of our relationship, during my ninth and tenth grade years, my girlfriend would end up having three more miscarriages. We were both pretty numb to it all after the first one, and in a way we were emboldened in our disregard for prophylactics, because we felt confident that she couldn't yet carry a child to term. We ended our love affair at some point during my 10th grade year, but we remained friends and occasionally still had sex. We were comfortable with each other, being so close together made sex convenient, and at fifteen years old, I didn't turn down sex. I began to deal with a girl I went to church with. She was a senior in high school, so I took pride in the fact that I was dealing with an "older woman". She had her own car, so that made sex a lot easier. We enjoyed each other for a while, I went to prom with her and we went out often, but I was still too immature to be any good to her. I wanted to have high school fun, run the streets, and she was getting ready to begin her adult life. Throughout my high school years, I would have a few more girlfriends, some of whom were temporary and some who I am very much still connected to today. But I think it's important to note that despite the fact that I may have been in a relationship at any given point, I was never faithful to one woman. Monogamy wasn't something I considered important, at least not when it came to abstaining from other women for the sake of maintaining a relationship. Several factors influenced this way of thinking. The first and most obvious is that I was a horny, hyper-sexual teenager - most young men are in their teenage years.

In spite of our current culture, God created our bodies to be that way for a reason. We now make young men and women feel ashamed of being sexual beings at that age, but if you examine history and culture outside of the current Eurocentric paradigm this country subscribes to, you will see that teenage sex and sexuality is quite normal. More on that point later. As for me, I was young, horny, and I wasn't going to change for anybody. Part of it was my self-esteem issues; I never felt like I was "cool", and so finding a female who found me attractive enough to share the most intimate parts of herself with me felt like a validation of my worth. Another part of it was that rebellious, independent attitude teenagers develop as they begin to come of age. Sex was an adult activity, and because I was having sex (along with drinking and using drugs) I was therefore an adult. The third part was cultural. Remember we are talking about the nineties, what some consider the golden age of rap music, and when machismo and misogyny were the foundation of all the most recognized artists' tunes. Jerry Springer and Maury Povich were emerging as daytime TV celebrities by giving people, mainly African-Americans, a place to showcase their ignorance by making a mockery of our broken relationships and disfunctional families. I wouldn't say that I was simply a blind follower of all that surrounded me, but when in Rome it's definitely much easier to do what the Romans are doing. I'm still not a big believer in monogamy, but I think that my reasoning on the issue has matured. Back then, my only goal was to have as much sex as possible with as many different women that I could, and at that age I didn't have a whole lot of discretion about how that happened. By the time I made it to the eleventh grade I was skipping school frequently, smoking weed, selling drugs and having sex. There was always a girl at school willing to leave with me, especially if she liked to drink and smoke. Fat, skinny, ugly, cute, it didn't matter. I'd usually end up over someone's house for the day, and pretty soon it became normal.

Some days it would be with a random female I met somewhere. Girls usually liked to travel in groups, so if I had a girl it was usually pretty easy to get another girl to come for my friend, or vice-versa. Some days that didn't work though, and we'd have to resort to other measures.

I remember on a few occasions, there were girls who everyone in the neighborhood talked to, or at least tried to talk to, just to have sex with her. We would have the one guy that she would agree to come and see arrange for her to come over, while another two, three or four of us were over there. Sometimes the girl would know we were there and other times we would hide in the next room or even the closet. We would wait until the girl started having sex with the guy she agreed to come and see, and then come in the room with them, sometimes one at a time, and sometimes altogether. Sometimes the girl would get upset and leave, but there was more than one occasion where the girl would allow all of us to have sex with her, sometimes all at the same time. We called it "running a train", and we considered it to be something normal that guys did together whenever they found a girl who would allow them to. Maybe it was the peer pressure that made the girls do it, or the combination of drugs and alcohol, or maybe the girl liked sex as much as we did. There were a few girls who we didn't need to play any tricks on in order to convince them to let us run a train. Those girls were usually overweight or unattractive, and so we preyed upon their low self-esteem in order to get what we wanted. In talking to other young men from around the country I found out running a train is a common practice, and many men had stories about taking part in it. Some guys I know used to have handheld camcorders, and would secretly videotape girls having sex with them by placing the camcorder under a towel or a blanket. This was before camera phones and the internet were household items, and so being able to be the "star" of your own personal sex tape was a much bigger deal back then than it is nowadays.

Looking back on it all, I wonder how some of the women turned out after going though those type of experiences. I've seen a few who have transitioned into adulthood successfully, but I'm sure some of these experiences have affected their ability to have a healthy relationship.

Everyone has regrets, and although I'm sure there were some who may have enjoyed that carefree period of their life, I know there are a few who wish they had it to do all over again. Relationships are hard enough, but the climate and conditions we create for each other is largely due to the unhealthy behaviors we were apprenticed into from the beginning. When you have two broken people trying to work together in a relationship but that have never stopped to consider the effects of their past, things will eventually fall apart. The main idea of it all was women were only valuable for sexual gratification, and that a woman was to be used for enjoyment by a man in any way possible. Somehow, I viewed the women in my family as exempt from this apprenticeship; the idea was that, like all things in the street, if you were dumb enough to fall for it, then you deserved whatever you got. These are the stories and lessons I tell to my daughter and my nieces, early and often. They think all men don't think the same. Sure. One of the easiest sources of sex was tied to the drug trade. I think the first time I ever "tricked" with a crackhead was when I was fourteen. I hadn't been selling drugs long, and so I didn't really understand all of the games people play that well. One night, I was outside waiting on customers to come through, when one of my regular female customers approached me. She explained that she was a little short on money, but she would be willing to give me oral sex in exchange for crack. Now I wouldn't say that I found her attractive in any sense of the word - she was probably in her late thirties or early forties, with a rough complexion and short, nappy hair. I could tell in her former years she could have been somewhat attractive, but the drugs and alcohol had long since claimed any looks she once had.

None of that was important to me, though. I had already heard stories of her exceptional talents at oral sex from some of the older guys around the neighborhood, but I didn't have the desire or the opportunity to experience it for myself until now.

I was a bit bothered by the thought of paying for sex, but the thought of easy sex won out pretty quickly. Besides it was only one rock, and it wasn't like I really needed the money anyway. After my first experience with tricking, it became a lot easier. I never had a problem trading crack for the quick, convenient sex acts that were readily available. I could do sexually any and everything I wanted, without fear of rejection or judgment. I didn't even consider it as cheating on my girlfriend; I viewed it more like a business transaction. The fact that most of these women were old enough to be my mother never crossed my mind. As for the women, the sex seemed to just be another part of the lifestyle that they chose, and I know that quite a few of them enjoyed some of their sexual experiences with virile, young men. I'm sure that prostitution in order to support a crack habit was probably not their first choice as far as life goals, but the women I came across seemed to be long past any reservations about that. Some guys gravitated to the control that drugs gave them over addicted women, and combined with a culture that endorses taking advantage of others, many guys became abusive and exploitative. I've seen guys make drug addicts put all types of foreign objects in their body, and on, more than one occasion I've seen men tell women who were desperate for crack to perform oral sex on a dog in exchange for crack. As most psychologists would tell you, these demeaning types of sex acts are not about sexual gratification; rather, they are expressions of dominance and control. The mentality is similar to that of a rapist, in that the man finds satisfaction in the act of exerting control over the woman. Although the threat of violence is traded for the symptoms of withdrawal as the means to bring about compliance, the desire to humiliate and exert one's will on another person is the same. I never got into the abuse; that wasn't something I was into, and I wouldn't want someone to have someone in my family out there like that. Besides, I was excited by all of the sex I got to have with these older women, even if they were "crackheads". Although my experiences with these drug-addicted prostitutes were some of my earliest experiences with older women, that was not the last of them. My older brother was in college by the time I was fifteen, and had begun to explore the world of nightclubs. I, of course, wanted to experience this too, and so I obtained a duplicate copy of my older cousin's I.D. to use. The bouncers at most clubs weren't paying that much attention and I rarely had a problem getting in. It was at these clubs that I would begin to further develop my game. At fifteen years old, I really had nothing of value to offer a grown woman; I had no house, no car, and very little money from my sporadic drug sales. What little money I did have usually went to food and smoking weed. I had to learn to rely on my charm and intellect in order to not only meet women, but to keep them interested. My brother and his friend were into reggae music, and they would go spend a lot of time on the dance floor showcasing their moves as a part of their game. That wasn't my thing, so I was usually on my own while they held court on the dance floor. It's not that I can't dance, but I didn't enjoy it in the same way they did. I began to mingle among the crowd, searching for women that I thought I could get. I really didn't discriminate as far as looks were concerned, because my only objective was to meet as many women as I could. I got rejected a lot, but I also got a lot of phone numbers. Besides, I was only interested in having fun. I enjoyed the feeling of maturity that came from dealing with older women, especially women I had met in the club with nothing more than my "rap" as bait. I had sex with plenty of women who were much older than me, some who even had children my age. Although I wasn't at the point where I was taking care of myself like a real adult, I believed my limited drug revenue and, perceived sexual prowess to be enough for any woman. As for the women, at some point most of them found out I was underage. Some had their suspicions right away, and while a few refused to continue to deal with me, most of them simply accepted it because we were already dealing with each other. My brother and his friend met a lot of women, too, and so I usually ended up "taking one for the team" by dealing with a girl who was the friend of one of the girls my brother and his friend had. The girl was usually the least attractive or most overweight out of the women in the group, but I didn't care. I went on like this throughout my high school years, chasing casual sex and the women that came along with it. I'd like to believe that I was at least a bit more romantic to the women that I actually had relationships with, but any relationship that I had was founded on a false promise of fidelity and monogamy. It was during this time that I began to compartmentalize the relationships with women I cared about into a different space than my casual sex partners. In my mind, the two had separate, distinct places in my life, and that was how I intended to keep it. Over time I got better and better at playing the game. I would lie and deceive women at will, as long as I obtained the results that I wanted. For those I had no attachment to that meant meaningless sex. For the women I did actually have feelings for, I learned how to use lies so that I could keep things how I felt they should be. This would be the beginning of my destructive sexual relationships, it wouldn't be the end.

HYPOCRISY

By the time I was really old enough to understand religion and God for myself, I had already begun to rebel. In a lot of ways, I associated God and church with parental and social authority, and so anything associated with that had no place in my life. This was not an immediate decision, however, like everything else, I was learning and experiencing, this too was a gradual process.

I continued to be active in my parents' church throughout part of my high school years. As I said before, I sang in the choir at the church that I originally joined out of a sense of duty to my mom, but I enjoyed all of the things I was discovering about music, as well.

The church had hired some very talented choir directors, and they helped to open my mind to a lot of different musical possibilities. The early nineties was a period of transformation in the world of gospel music, as well, as more and more artists and musicians began to incorporate the stylings of hip-hop, R&B, and funk into gospel arrangements. This piqued my curiosity, especially as a black Catholic who had always found the music that was a part of the mass to be uninspiring. I was just beginning to develop an ear for music, so I tried to absorb as much as I could. Of course, being a drug dealing, weed-smoking choir member didn't exactly work too well together and so eventually I gave that up. I was also a part of the Catholic Youth Organization, or CYO. CYO organized events for the teenagers at the church, and a few times a year we participated in events with parishes throughout the region. We did a lot of the routine events young people enjoy - bowling, movies, amusement parks, etc. One year, we attended a conference for all of the Catholic youth in America, called youth day. The conference was a three day weekend event in Philadelphia, with events at the conference center and lodging at the surrounding hotels. I enjoyed the sights and sounds of the city, and although this wasn't my first time outside of D.C., this was my first time experiencing another city without my family. As for the youth conference, that was another matter. Almost immediately the members of our youth group noticed that we were some of the only faces of color present. That wasn't an unusual thing for us, the majority of the events sponsored by the larger Catholic church were majority white except for a few events held at the parishes in the inner city.

We all knew going in that we would not likely find an experience that felt inclusive to us, and so almost immediately we began to disconnect from all that was going on around us. The youth from the large white churches looked at us like we were aliens, and so we never got to form those bonds of commonality from a shared experience, in the same way the white children did.

In hindsight our group probably could have done more to involve ourselves in the events that were being offered but we felt so out of place that we refused to even try. In our minds, the only people we had were each other, and that was okay by me. I knew that this so-called religious experience that we were supposed to be having didn't include people who looked, thought, and talked like me. I spoke previously about how I had begun to understand the stronghold of white supremacy embedded in the teachings and images of the Catholic Church, and that a lot of these practices were present at my parents' church although it was and is overwhelmingly African-American. When I began to truly desire to know who God was to me, I knew that this version of religion would no longer have a place in my life. Our youth group continued to go through the motions that were required of us, but we never felt any real connection to the conference activities. We were more interested in exploring the city and all it had to offer. One day, the group of guys from our church decided to visit the girls' hotel room. We knew it was against the rules, but at that point we really didn't care. Yes, there were some teenage hormones and physical attraction involved, but it was also about sharing our experience with the only people we felt comfortable with. Plus, I had bought a S-curl kit for my hair, and I wanted the girls to put it in for me. I experimented heavily with my look and style back then, and the S-curl kit was all part of the process. Anyway, off to the girls' hotel room we went. I can't really say that we sneaked into their room, but we did attempt to avoid the prying eyes of other church members and their chaperones.

I thought that we had done that by taking the stairs, but I knew some of the conference attendees had seen us. At that point we really didn't care, though. The girls opened the door for us and let us in, and we began to enjoy ourselves as always. We laughed and joked as the girls applied the relaxer to my hair, and for a while we forgot about the rest of the conference.

At some point, we heard a knock at the door and, of course, it was a chaperone from one of the other youth groups asking if there were guys in the girls' room. We knew that we were caught, but it didn't matter to us. We were escorted out of the room and reprimanded, but like most things with rebellious teens, it all went in one ear and out of the other. The rest of the conference went by without much participation from us and we returned to D.C. shortly thereafter. That was one of the last youth events that I attended at my mother's church, or any church for that matter. I had pretty much decided that this whole church business had no place in where I was going in life and, at some point, I stopped going to mass altogether. My cousin, Courtney, had begun to attend church around this time. She had been shaken by the passing of another member of our extended family in a homicide and had decided to seek a relationship with God. After attending the funeral for our cousin and being moved by the service, she decided to begin attending the church of the pastor who presided over the service. At that time, I was constantly getting into disagreements with my parents over one thing or another, and so I would go and live with my grandmother whenever things got to be too much between us. Like most black families, my grandmother told me that she was praying for me and believed that going to church would help me to change from the direction that I was headed in. I was not feeling any of that, especially not at that time. I had no place in my life for any more religion, and besides, I wasn't trying to change my life for the better. I wanted to run the streets, and that was the only thing that I was focused on. But I also wanted to keep my grandmother happy.

She didn't ask for much, and in the grand scheme of things I figured that if showing up for a few Sunday services was all it took to keep her from nagging me about my lifestyle, I could certainly make that concession. And so off to church I went with my grandmother, aunts, and my cousin. What I found when I got there was much different than expected.

The service was being held in an old banquet hall around the corner from my grandmother's house. There were black, padded chairs set up, instead of pews, mirrors on the wall, and old party decorations tucked into the corner. The pulpit was set up in the middle of the dance floor, and the musicians were set up behind the pulpit in the corner. The congregation was made up of a large number of young adults and the atmosphere looked and felt more like a club than it did a church. The dress code was casual, at best, and this further added to the club atmosphere. I remember that on one particular Sunday, a young woman came to church wearing a camouflage-patterned, skin-tight body suit. This was unreal to me, not only because we were supposed to be in church, but also because she was so shapely. I saw plenty of disapproving looks from many of the women in attendance, but no one said anything. She wasn't the only woman who dressed provocatively, and that made it hard for me to focus on anything that was being said. This was a totally different experience than I was used to at my parents' Catholic church. Although both churches were filled with black people, the religious experiences were worlds apart. The most meaningful difference to me was the use of music in worship. As I said before, the nineties were a defining moment in the tone and structure of black music, and gospel music was no exception. The music incorporated into the parts of mass at my parents' church had begun to reflect some of this change, but not to the extent that it did at this Baptist church. The accompaniment at the Catholic Church consisted of one musician playing an upright piano; in contrast, the Baptist church featured a seven-piece band, complete with multiple percussion instruments, synthesizers, processors, and electronics of all sorts. The service usually began with traditional praise and worship songs, or old familiar hymns. There would be two or three people who led that part of the service, and although the stated purpose is to usher in the spirit, praise and worship service at most black churches serves the dual purpose of allowing habitually late church members both inside and outside of the ministry to arrive and get into position. Once the service was underway, the choir usually sang three or four songs at different parts of the service. The band also accompanied various ministers during different parts of the worship service by playing soft music as someone prayed or spoke. The music set the tone of the worship service in a way that I had never experienced before. I believe that because the music had the feel and flavor of what was being played in the club and on the radio, the congregation was able to connect to the service with more ease. The black church has an inseparable connection to its music, and some of the most well-known artists in all genres of music got their start in the church. Most of the popular styles of music throughout American history were influenced by what was happening in the church as well, which is one of the reasons why most "successful" black churches try to retain talented musicians and singers that are able to bring popular music to life inside of the church. The central figure, around which the church revolves, however, is the pastor. Pastors, or preachers as they are commonly called, have a much different disposition in black churches when compared to the pastors of Eurocentric congregations. The priests of the Catholic Church had a humble, pious manner about them, and every word they spoke during mass felt pre-formed. The various recitals and responses had the weight and tone of a judge handing down a sentence in the courtroom. When the priest spoke, the church sat in reverent silence as though his words were flowing out of the mouth of Jesus Christ himself.

Usually the priests at my church were white men, but even when guest priests of color would visit - usually an African priest visiting the U.S. - they did their best to mimic the stylings and vocal inflections of their white contemporaries, despite their African accent. The pastors of black protestant churches that I've attended were completely opposite, however. The pastor at my cousin's church was a far cry from the older, white men I had listened to most Sundays.

Whatever his true age was, he had a youthful spirit. He had a worldly sense about him; his mannerisms and style were of someone who knew what was really happening, and even without knowing anything about his background you could tell he had been around. I had never heard a preacher like that, someone who took the bible and made it relevant to what was happening in the streets and in the world I lived in. He spoke like me, moved like me, and had walked the same streets I walked. This preacher used humor and told stories in order to make his message feel more like a conversation than a sermon. He seemed to hold the congregation captive, with a mixture of the style and finesse of a motivational speaker, stand-up comic, and car salesman all in one. As the sermon went on, the volume and intensity of his words grew, and the congregation began to respond in kind. The preacher started "whooping", a rhythmic, melodic, call and response style of preaching that is usually emphasized with percussive musical runs by the church musicians. Amongst all of the fanfare and reverie, someone in the congregation usually "catches" the Holy Ghost, a state of deep spiritual connection that is almost trancelike and causes a person to dance, jump, shout, weep, faint, and praise almost uncontrollably. Sometimes several people would catch the Holy Ghost in one service. As the service would begin to wind to a close, the pastor would make an altar call. The musicians would begin to play softly, as the pastor invited everyone to the altar who wanted to become Christian, rededicate their life to Christ, or who simply needed prayer. People would walk forward out of the congregation, some with their hands raised, some crying, as they opened their hearts to the words and prayers of the preacher. The preacher would pray for them and lay hands on them, and some would faint as they felt overwhelmed with the Spirit. Finally, the service would end with the preacher saying a closing prayer, and after service people would fellowship with one another.

The church has a long, complex history in the African-American community. Due to what I have studied over the years, I believe all world religions can find their origin in African history, but a lot of the traditions and practices we now see in the church have their roots in slavery. While I won't go into all I believe on the correlation between Christianity and the mentality that slave owners imposed on the African diaspora, it is certainly true that slave owners used the bible and their version of Christianity to their benefit. While some may have considered themselves to be following the true teachings of Jesus Christ, the reality is that Christianity was one of the methods used to pacify black people. Blacks accepted the doctrine taught to them by their slave masters, combined it with elements of our culture, and by doing so this cultural-friendly version of Christianity had the ability to connect to the black psyche in ways that the white preacher could not do by himself. Even to this day Sunday mornings are referred to as "the most segregated hour in America", mainly because of the cultural differences in the way people worship.

In his book, *Christian Doctrine*, Shirley C. Guthrie, Jr. states "for churches in the Presbyterian-Reformed tradition (in distinction from churches in some other traditions), the church is not a 'voluntary association of believers' who get together and decide to form a church. It is God who creates the church and calls people into it. The church therefore is not like a club or group of like-minded people who enjoy each others' company, form an organization for their mutual benefit and enjoyment, and set up a constitution, rules of membership, and policies and goals to suit themselves. It is not 'our' church but God's church". While this concept of what the church should be is noble, the sad reality of what the church actually looks like is far from this. In my experience churches are segregated and separated on so many levels, and for people who are seeking to find God in the midst of all that life has to offer, it can be disheartening to discover that reality.

The idea of the church being Catholic, or universal, was one that was introduced to me at an early age as a Roman Catholic. I used the term to identify how I related to God, and I affirmed this principle every Sunday as I recited the Nicene Creed. I never really felt like a part of this global, universal movement I professed to be a part of though. Guthrie goes on to say "the church is catholic in that it unites in faith and life Christians in all times and places; of all races, classes, languages, cultures, nationalities; in all kinds of political, economic, and social situations. There is one Lord, one Spirit, one Baptism, one shared bread and cup - and therefore one body, the one holy catholic church."

I had yet to experience that type of church, especially as a young black man seeking to understand my place in a culture that was anti-social and a society that made me feel devalued. I didn't expect much from religion or from God for that matter. I know now that a large part of that was based on the sheltered, spoiled perspective with which I viewed life. At that point in life, I had never been in a position to really need God, not in the way I understand needing God as an adult. I "kinda sorta" believed He existed, and I felt that as long as I acknowledged that much I was good. Even the prayers that I said before I ate my food were more about habit and tradition than it was about relationship with Him. I certainly didn't think there was any "unity of believers". The feeling of being marginalized as a Catholic had made me bitter, so I didn't expect much going into a new church. The divide at this church looked different, though.

There was a lot more gossip and petty arguments between church members, who were mostly women. They all smiled in each others' faces, but they rolled their eyes at each other and talked behind each others' backs without shame. Everyone seemed to be jockeying for attention from the pastor, being seen and recognized seemed to take priority over what was being taught. Most of the people who came to the church had spent some time running the streets, and even though they were now at church they still related to people and situations in the same way that they did before. Part of that is habitual, and some of it is cultural; when you have a group of people who are used to dealing with others through a broken set of communication skills, it takes a lot of time and awareness to change those behaviors. That is why, in my opinion, the culture of a lot of black churches looks like the controversy that we see on all of the popular reality shows today. The pastors do little to curb these behaviors, at least not the ones that I've seen. When you examine the church as a business, most people who attend a black church want to see a show. For a long time, the black church was the only option black people had for entertainment, social comradery, and instruction. That tradition has been handed down over the years, and it would be safe to say that any successful black church has a dynamic, entertaining pastor, along with a lively music ministry. Sermons about hope and future blessings tend to be the most popular, while lessons about being accountable for one's current behavior tend to be a source of contention. A lot of the formalities of dress and behavior have faded away, and people seem to want affirmation that God finds whatever they choose to do acceptable. Therein lies the heart of my spiritual struggle: Did God understand and accept this destructive path I had chosen, or did he require me to follow this exacting standard that some interpret the bible to

outline? In his book, *My Utmost for His Highest*, Oswald
Chambers states "we shall all feel very much ashamed if we do
not yield to Jesus on the point He has asked us to yield to Him.
To get there is a question of will, an absolute and irrevocable
surrender on that point". He goes on to explain "God's order
has to work up to a crisis in our lives because we will not heed
the gentler way. He brings us to the place where He asks us to be
our utmost for Him, and we begin to debate; then He produces a
providential crisis where we have to decide - for or against, and
from that point the 'Great Divide' begins".

This idea of yielding and surrendering was next to impossible for
me at that point in my life. I had just begun to achieve some of
the freedom and individuality that I thought would bring me
happiness, and I refused to willingly cede that power over my life
to anyone. There were a few times after a particularly moving
Sunday service that I really considered giving the whole church
and following God thing a try. I thought that I could will myself
into the power of the Holy Spirit, and that if I truly prayed a few
times really sincerely that I would feel something change inside
me, something new that I never felt before. I even decided to get
baptized, with the hopes that this ritual would be the catalyst for
the mystical, magical transformation that others professed to
experience. But in reality I felt nothing. I continued to look at life
with the same misguided viewpoint that I had before, and I
continued on the path that I had been on. I was confused,
confused about who I was and what I was supposed to become. I
wanted desperately to be happy with who I was, and I hoped that
I could find it in church like all the people that I saw crying and
rejoicing. I was not willing to work for it though. Work meant
changing my behaviors, and I had already decided that if I was
going to be who God wanted me to be then He would have to
change me Himself. He would have to perform a miracle on my
heart, my mind, and my life if He wanted anything different from
me. The only thing I had to offer at that point was sin, and

anything else would have to move aside. That's what I thought at the time anyway; God had other plans for my life, however.

DISFUNCTION

My apprenticeship of disfunction progressed rather rapidly during my teenage years, and there were several events that would prove to be pivotal in that process. I began working as a lifeguard for the summer when I was fifteen. I was still playing in the go-go band and selling drugs, but I decided to try and get a steady paycheck to support myself with as well.

I went to work at a pool in an apartment complex not too far from my house. There wasn't much to do most days, but I did get to meet a few girls that came by the pool, and what fifteen year old doesn't like girls in bathing suits? One day, a man came by the pool and approached my co-worker with an offer to be a lifeguard at a private party. She said she was unavailable, but she would set it up for me if I wanted to do it. I figured that it was easy money, so I accepted. The party started off without incident, but toward the end of the evening things took a turn for the worst. I was on a break getting something to eat, when one of the partygoers called my attention to a man at the bottom of the pool. I could tell right away something was wrong with him, and I jumped in to pull him up. He was unconscious and had stopped breathing, so I began to perform CPR. The man began to cough and vomit, but he never fully regained consciousness. I was told that he was alive for the trip to the hospital but later died on the operating table. Surprisingly, I was sort of numb to the whole thing. I felt sorry for the man and that he died, but I was selfishly more concerned I would get in trouble. This was far from my first experience with death being that close to me, and besides, after I was told about the amount of drugs and alcohol that were in the man's system, I honestly felt like he brought death on himself. Jumping into a pool with your system full of cocaine and alcohol was stupidity, or at least it was in my mind at the time. The fact that the man hit his head on the bottom of the pool, probably from diving off of the diving board into water that was too shallow was lost on me.

I had yet to really live and experience enough of life to see the value in that man's life, especially once drugs and alcohol were put into the equation. I think subconsciously I tried to devalue him so I wouldn't fault myself or feel any guilt about this incident happening on my watch. This was supposed to be easy money, and now I had police asking me questions and people looking at me as if I didn't do my job.

Plus, I had seen the recklessness that comes along with using intoxicants for most of my life, and I guess that helped me to become contemptuous towards anyone who suffered misfortune due to their choice to become intoxicated. My own drug use was guided by this paradigm in a sense; I was not very fond of alcohol at time, and on the occasions I did drink, I was careful not to allow myself to become drunk to the point of being out of control. That would not hold true later on in life, however. As for smoking weed, I held that in a class by itself. I felt like weed didn't cause a person to become out of control; in fact, I felt like it helped me to focus. Cocaine use was absolutely off-limits. Again, at that time the black community was in the midst of the crack cocaine epidemic, so all of my understanding of cocaine was filtered through my experiences with crack users. If there ever was a caste system or hierarchy in the black community, crackhead would definitely be at the bottom.

My parents would probably tell you the drowning incident affected me much more at that time than I am able to perceive. Whether that is true or not I don't know; they claimed at the time that my behavior and attitude changed significantly after this incident, but I think they may have just started paying more attention to behaviors that were already there. As a parent now myself, I'd like to believe I'm perceptive enough to recognize changes in my children, but through my own experiences I also understand how clueless a parent can be to what is really going on in their child's life. Right after this incident happened, I got caught smoking weed in the bathroom in the house.

To them this was "acting out", but I just wanted to finish the last piece of a blunt I had rolled earlier. I thought I was home alone and opening the window would help, but I guess I was wrong. Between this incident and my troubles in school, my parents decided it was time for me to see a mental health professional. For most black people the idea of going to see someone about their problems was and is taboo.

For a long time, there weren't many mental health professionals of color, and that made it difficult to find someone capable of understanding the cultural dynamics of the black experience. Not to mention the fact that no one was going to pay good money to sit and talk to someone about how we felt; that was a luxury reserved for white people. Black people didn't do that; we found a family member to talk to, an older aunt or uncle, or our grandparents. If it wasn't something we could keep as "family business", we would talk to a pastor at the church. Whatever we did, we certainly weren't going to go see a white man about what was wrong with our family. Our culture teaches us to suck it up; our history demanded we function at our best in spite of our circumstances, and for most black people it is common for them to be constantly moving from one state of chaos and crisis to another. As far as children were concerned, our culture taught us that there wasn't a problem that a belt couldn't fix. There have been numerous comedy sketches made by black comedians about the black parenting style, and although the parenting styles of younger generations has somewhat moved away from the traditions of the past, there is a large part of that history that still influences black families. Changes began to happen as the field of child psychology began to gain acceptance, and even I could notice some of the differences that were beginning to come into effect. As I said before, my mother's mom was a strict disciplinarian. As the mother of eleven, I can only imagine how hard it must have been for her to maintain order, especially with eight boys and three girls. Growing up, I remember seeing a long wooden paddle lying around my grandmother's house. I was told my grandfather had made it before he passed away. The paddle had all the names of their grandkids written on it. On the back side of the paddle, my first and last name was at the top, in big capital letters. I'll be the first to admit I was a handful; what we called "hardheaded" in those days would be classified as curious by today's standards.

However you describe it, I got my fair share of spankings growing up. I also remember children being spanked at school by the teacher. This was not uncommon at that time; parents understood young children needed to be disciplined from time to time, and besides, no one was going to keep leaving work and running back and forth up to a school simply because their child couldn't sit still in class. Kids act out, that's what they do. The solution was simple - beat their behind, tell them to sit down somewhere, send a note home with them, and the child would get disciplined again at home. Around my first or second grade year, that way of doing things all but went away, however. I don't know if it was due to this new paradigm of child psychology, fear of abuse charges and lawsuits, or a combination of both, but teachers would no longer physically discipline a child. Instead, children who had behavior problems were now given a "time out", and told to sit by themselves in the corner of the room. Teachers would also take a child's recess away. As an adult, I can see how counterproductive that idea is. Why would you take away the only opportunity a hyper, growing child has to exercise? Around the fourth or fifth grade year, I got to experience this new way of thinking firsthand. My younger brother began going to school with me around this time, and it would be fair to say that his transition into the social setting of elementary school was not the easiest. The most memorable incident I can recall happened one morning towards the beginning of the school year. I was called out of my classroom to go and speak with my brother, because allegedly he had decided to cut some young white girls hair with a pair of the arts and crafts scissors. The fact he had cut someone's hair was significant by itself; the fact this happened to be a young, white child, especially in the early eighties, made this situation that much worse. I don't know what the teachers expected me to say. I couldn't have been older than ten years old and besides, there was only one punishment I thought to be appropriate for a transgression like this: a good spanking. Nevertheless, I went and spoke with my brother to find out what happened. He explained that the girl had done or said something he didn't like, and after their disagreement incited him to rage; he thought cutting her hair was appropriate. I didn't know how to respond to that; I mean, he obviously knew his actions were wrong, but he did it anyway. I told him the only thing I thought to be right: sit down, leave the little girl alone, do what the teacher tells you to do, and when you get home Mom and Dad were going to deal with you. Sadly, this would not be the last incident of this kind. My brother continued to act out in class, and after a few disturbing incidents, the most severe being my brother throwing a chair at the teacher, my brother was no longer allowed to attend school with me. Throughout this whole ordeal, my parents had received the recommendation that our family begin attending group counseling. My father's health insurance plan covered our sessions, so despite any reluctance I'm sure he must have felt, at least it wasn't another cost out-of-pocket. In spite of that, family counseling had little effect on any of us. As I said before, sitting around talking to some random white man about how we felt was not normal, and after a while even the counselor acknowledged how pointless these sessions were. One thing did come out of all this psycho-analysis that my brothers and I went through: a diagnosis of ADHD for my younger brother. Several studies have been done on the effects of ADD and all of its variations on African-American children, and again I will defer to the experts on the finer points of the issue.

What I will say is that at the time my brother received his diagnosis, the concept of misbehavior as a symptom of a psychological and/or physiological condition was new, at least in the black community. I believe that to be due not only to the cultural beliefs I expressed earlier, but also to the severe lack of access to mental healthcare providers in the African-American community. My brother began receiving medication for his condition, and after a few more incidents at school my parents put him in a program at Psychiatric Institute of Washington. I didn't know how to process all of this; in my mind they were basically saying that my brother was crazy. My parents had to have been at their wits' end by this time. Although all of this was new to them as well, I can appreciate now their willingness to do all that "the experts" told them they should do, and to put their money and resources into those solutions. As I got older I began to see more and more kids around me get diagnosed with ADD. Lots of kids with behavior issues ended up in special education classes, and by the time I got to high school almost every kid who had ever been in any type of trouble received some type of mental health diagnosis of impairment. Even I would end up with a diagnosis of ADD, but the circumstances that brought it about were quite different from my brother's. As I said before, my parents took me to see a counselor after the drowning incident and several other incidents I had been involved in. Between my earlier negative interactions with mental health professionals and my rebellious teenage attitude, I had absolutely no desire to talk to anyone about how I felt, and I made that clear every time I went. Eventually I stopped going altogether, and I continued to live my life as I had been. I continued to drink, smoke weed, sell drugs, and hang out in the street. My lifestyle would not go on without any challenges to my behavior, however. Like most black men across America, I began to have interactions with the police. Growing up I didn't have a natural distrust of law enforcement.

In fact, at one point in time I wanted to be a police officer. My parents weren't involved in a criminal lifestyle, and so I believed the police were there to protect me, to keep us safe from all of the "bad" people. That way of thinking held no merit in my new lifestyle, however, and I learned quickly if this was to be my path then I must learn how to navigate interactions with law enforcement in a manner consistent with the rest of the black men in my community. That meant an open contempt for law enforcement and anything associated with it. I learned you were supposed to answer any and all questions from law enforcement with as much disrespect and virulence one could muster, otherwise your peers might view you as scared. Most importantly, I learned that if there was ever a chance that you might go to jail, you should run. I ran from police early and often, sometimes because I had drugs in my pocket, but other times just to see if I could get away. One day, I was hanging out with a group of guys in an apartment complex near my high school. This day was like most days; we drank, smoked weed and sold drugs. All of a sudden, two police cars pulled up in the cul-de-sac we were standing in. We had just finished smoking weed, and although the smoke was still heavy in the air I knew I wasn't "dirty", so I decided not to run. Two of the other guys with us did run, and I was curious to see if the police would chase them or not. The police opted to search us, and they jumped out of their cars, weapons drawn, demanding to see our hands. They ordered us all to our knees and began to search us one at a time. They didn't find anything, and they told us one of the neighbors called and reported that one of us had a gun. This happened to be true - one of the guys had stashed an old .357 revolver underneath a car not too long before the police arrived. Of course no one admitted that to the police, and we complained about harassment in the most belligerent way possible. The police told us all to leave, and as three of the guys and I were crossing the street up the hill from the apartment complex, one of the officers was driving up the street. When the officer saw us in the street, he stepped on the gas as if he were trying to hit us. We ran across to get out of his way, and as he passed one of the guys with me gave him the finger. He hit his brakes as if he were slowing down to come back, and when we saw his reverse lights come on my associate picked up a bottle and hit his rear windshield. We all took off running after that. That incident made it a lot easier to feel contempt for law enforcement, but that would not be the only incident I witnessed or experienced that heightened this sentiment. I remember a police officer who was moonlighting as a security guard at the liquor store across the street from my house was shot dead while he sat in his patrol car. This happened during my younger years, when I still had respect for law enforcement. As I became a young adult, I began to look at that incident with a twisted sense of justice, a gratitude that someone had done to a police officer what I believe police did to black men every day. I remember a female police officer getting knocked out in the neighborhood where I hung out uptown, by that time I was firmly entrenched in my negative perception of law enforcement. After witnessing the brutality that was done to Rodney King, my hatred for police was firmly cemented. When I began to examine all that was happening, along with the anti-establishment culture expressed in rap music, my negative feelings towards law enforcement were a cultural norm and necessity. Nothing highlighted this dynamic more than the O.J. Simpson trial. I was too young to remember O.J. as a football player; although I had heard from older guys in the community that he was a dynamic athlete. I simply knew him as the guy in the rental car commercials. None of that mattered though, what was important was that a black man stood accused of murdering a white woman. What's interesting in examining that case is how little regard people had for the facts, even when juxtaposed with the issues that were supposedly important at the time. For instance, most black women did and do have contempt for black men who date and/or marry white women, especially wealthy, successful black men. The idea is that black men get an education and/or become successful, and no longer have an interest in dating black women. In spite of the fact that this progression pretty much defines O.J. Simpson, most black women still wanted to see him go free.

None of the domestic violence that he was accused of or other cultural sins mattered. I heard a few mumblings from a few women that he should have known better than to deal with a white woman, but the main focus was about seeing a black man get a fair trial. Race relations have come a lot further today than they were in the nineties; in spite of all of the real challenges that exist today, the cultural divide is not as pronounced as it was back then, especially in the area of interracial dating. In fact, the O.J. Simpson trial could arguably be considered one of the most polarizing events along racial lines in American history. This incident happened only two years after the Rodney King trial, in which four white officers were acquitted of charges stemming from the vicious beating of a black man that was caught on videotape. The O.J. trial took over the country, as everyone waited for a verdict. TV's were set up in most of my school's classrooms during the trial, as teachers and students alike followed the events of the case. I remember cheering along with my schoolmates as the not guilty verdict was announced. I also remember the images of tears and anger on the faces of the white people shown on TV. It all seems crazy, in a sense that black people would be so excited to see another black man not go to jail and that whites would be so angered by it. This trial put the thinly veiled racism of this country and its criminal justice system on display once again, for all the world to see.

Of course, I would soon understand that fact on a much deeper level. One day, the car I was riding in was pulled over by

Montgomery County police. My friends and I were ordered out of the car, searched, and made to lie face down on the side of the road.

Police officers searched the car and found nothing, but they continued to demand we tell them where the guns and drugs were. I felt confident enough to ask them what this was about, and my response was given via a police boot to the back of my neck. Another officer stepped on my hand, as another officer proceeded to kick me in the ribs, with the first officer maintaining pressure on the back of my neck with his foot. I felt myself losing consciousness as I gasped for air, and right before I blacked out I heard one of the officers say, "let him get some air". The officers returned to their cars, as we picked ourselves up off the side of the road. My ribs were bruised and tender for the next week or so, but I've never forgotten that incident. I never did get an answer as to why we were stopped and searched. This was one of the most memorable experiences I had with police, but it would not be my last. Over the years I have been stopped, frisked, questioned, and harassed so much that I've almost become numb to the whole process. Police have taken money from me and my associates on several occasions, without providing us a seizure receipt. Again, police interaction and encounters like these are a normal part of everyday life for a lot of black men. Almost every black man I know has a story of some kind about the abuse and mistreatment inflicted on them by law enforcement officers. There are a lot of incidents that go unreported, because at the time of the incident, many men may have been involved in criminal activity, and so the fear of future reprisal outweighs any desire to hold these officers accountable. Men learn to just "charge it to the game", and accept abuse by law enforcement at one of the hazards of the lifestyle. This mindset has become so prevalent even men not involved in criminal activity fail to report police abuse, due to the belief things won't change, or somehow police abuse is normal and therefore must be acceptable. The increased incidents of law enforcement being captured on video in recent years has helped to expose this issue to mainstream America, but in reality much of what goes on continues to go unreported. My interactions with law enforcement would not always end with me walking away from it unscathed, however. After skipping so many days of school during my eleventh grade year, I was told I would need to take English in summer school in order to graduate. I had no intention of staying at summer school all day, especially on the first day.

I assumed that the first day was only for registration, so I planned to go and register for my class and then head uptown to sell the package of crack I had recently purchased to sell. After I learned I was expected to stay all day, I was pissed. I ran into a guy I knew from school, and we stepped outside to smoke cigarettes and talk. While we were outside, a school police officer snuck up on us from a side entrance of the school. He asked us what we were smoking, and requested to pat search us. He pat searched me first, but didn't find the stash of drugs I had on me. When he searched the other guy, he felt the stash of drugs he had tucked in his underwear. Before I knew it, the guy took off running, with the officer chasing him. I had considered running when the officer first appeared, but we were standing at the top of a staircase landing, so the only exit was down a flight of steps. I figured I had passed the pat search so I was good; I didn't even try to run, and I casually strolled down the steps to go about my business. What I didn't know was during the chase of the other guy, the police officer had tripped and broken his ankle, and he had called an "officer down" distress call over his radio. When I walked down the stairs and around the corner, I was met by a football tackle from one of the officers responding to the distress call. Another officer joined him, as I was subjected to a knee on the back of my neck. The officers proceeded to search me again, this time quite thoroughly, by checking inside of my boxers and removing my shoes. This time one of the officers felt my stash, and I was arrested and charged with possession with the intent to distribute cocaine base within one thousand feet of a school.

I had no idea how much trouble I was potentially facing at the time; now I've been in prison and studied the law, I've seen people with fifteen to twenty years for the same type of offense. Amazingly, the lab tests on the drugs didn't register any cocaine, and the courts gave me probation on the charge in exchange for pleading guilty.

To this day I don't know how to explain how those drugs came back negative for cocaine; I had personally watched someone smoke some of it, and from what I was told it was pretty strong. One of the conditions of my probation was I attend counseling, because like most people arrested for a drug offense I told them I smoked crack. I had never so much as snorted a line of coke, much less smoke crack, but this is one of the things I was taught to say early on in order to obtain mercy from the court. I went to counseling, but this time I had to stop smoking weed because I was being drug tested. I was also diagnosed with ADD and depression. Somehow, the doctors concluded that my behaviors were the result of my condition, and instead of smoking weed I should be given a prescription. I began taking Wellbutrin, and I guess the idea was that the drug would help me feel "better" somehow. In reality all it did was make me feel like I had drunk a cup of coffee, and I couldn't keep my mind from racing all day long. I gave up on the pills, and went back to the only medicine that I believed worked - weed. I had found a way to get around the drug tests, and so I was back to my old routine once again. It was different now though, because I was no longer untouched by the reality of my lifestyle. I was beginning to suffer the consequences of criminal behavior; to most it would be considered a step in the wrong direction, but at the time arrests and encounters with the police were considered a rite of passage of sorts among black men. Being on probation or parole is a normal thing, especially at that time in my community. I had taken another step in my apprenticeship, and I began to feel like I was somehow authentic now.

As for the mental health component, I'd like to believe that this diagnosis was given to me out of a desire to understand and explain my behavior, but the sad reality is that for a lot of young black men the mental health system has become a tool used to medicate a social and moral issue. For some it is a win-win; drug companies make a profit, and teachers get compliant, controlled classrooms.

This method has proven to be a dismal failure, however, because as drug companies' profits soared, our children were being turned into a group of medicated zombies. Using medication as a cover-up is a lot easier than dealing with the disfunction caused by broken lives, broken communities, and the apprenticeship of sin. One thing was certain; I was getting ready to transition into the next phase of my apprenticeship. All of the lessons I had learned up until this point were practice, and now I was ready to officially get in the game. Little did I know it was a game I stood no chance at winning.

Chapter III

THE MASTERY

{POVERTY, HATE, SEX, HYPOCRISY, DISFUNCTION}

POVERTY

I graduated from high school in the spring of 1996. There were a few teachers who tried to help me get a scholarship to Hampton University if I had been willing to do the work in school, but I wasn't. I was surprised I graduated at all, really. If there was any question as to what I was going to do before, there was absolutely no question now that I was going to be in the streets. I had already committed myself to this lifestyle while I was still in school, and despite all my family's pleas and protests I was determined to keep at it. I would leave school and catch the metro uptown, so I could stand outside and sell my drugs. Now that school was all finished, I felt like I would have more time to run the streets. I didn't completely abandon "square" life at first, though. As I said before, my family has always been very supportive and because I didn't want to completely distance myself from them and their expectations, I made a half-hearted attempt to do something positive. I got a job at UPS part time, and I enrolled in community college.

Neither of those lasted very long, though. There was no way I was going to keep working inside of hot, dusty trailers unloading boxes every day, especially when they were only paying me for one hour what I made for selling one rock. I tried to tough it out to keep my family happy, but I think the breaking point was when I was asked to unload by hand a trailer full of garden lawnmowers by myself. The boxes were compact and heavy, and by the time I had finished the first trailer full I was sore and soaked with sweat.

I'm definitely not the most muscular person, so I knew my body wasn't going to enjoy being pushed that hard.

I've gained a few pounds since then - a bit of muscle from my prison exercise regimens, and a bit of fat due to getting older and moving slower - but for the majority of my life I've been kind of scrawny. I found out there were two more trailers just like the other one waiting for me, and I quit right then and there. It wasn't that I was scared of physically demanding work - between the boy scouts, odd jobs, and chores around the house, I had been exposed to my fair share of physical labor. I just didn't believe this was what I was meant to be doing with my time. I definitely had some pride issues and a sense of entitlement that made me feel like I was above moving boxes. But there was a spark inside of me I couldn't understand, a spark that made me want more out of life. As for school, it was hard for me to focus and take my classes seriously. I tested out of some of my basic credits, but even the classes I should've taken seriously I didn't. Even though I didn't have a full-time schedule, the truth is I wasn't focused and disciplined enough for college. I started socializing with people at the school, and before long I was selling weed to some of the guys I'd met, and I tried to meet all of the women I could. I couldn't see life past that moment in time, and before long I dropped out. Things were going fairly well for me as an ambitious, young drug dealer, at least by my definition of fairly well at that time.

I didn't want to take over the city or be Tony Montana; as a matter of fact, I had no idea what I was hustling to achieve. In a lot of ways I was hustling just to hustle, and because I had no end game in sight that made me satisfied with little to nothing. My cousins had a house they used on a very popular drug strip in northwest D.C. I had been coming uptown to sell drugs with them for a while now; at first, they were absolutely against it though. I didn't grow up around there and didn't really know anybody, and for the most part I was very naive or "green" as far as street life was concerned. The fact that I thought I wasn't green made it that much worse, but like most young people you couldn't tell me anything at that time. I was determined to get on with them, and I kept coming around to make that point known. I started out going to the store for them, running errands to the carry-out or going to buy empty crack bags. I felt like a flunkie at the time, but it was all a part of getting to know people around there, and them getting to know me. My cousin was always sharp in that way; besides the respect he had as a hustler, I always admired his style and the way he looked at life. We smoked a lot of weed, but I rarely saw him drink and I never saw him on the block drunk and out of control. He always seemed to have a plan, plans that were much bigger than standing outside selling crack all day. I learned a lot from him, not only about the streets but about being a man as well. He had come up under the old hustlers; his parents were both in the streets at one point, so he had been involved with the game for most of his life. He always conducted himself with respect though. He wasn't the loud, rowdy type, and he didn't hang around a bunch of people that were. I remember when I first started coming uptown we would sit outside on the front steps of a house in the neighborhood. Every so often we would clean all the trash and bottles off the sidewalk where we stood. It kept the neighbors fairly happy, and although it wouldn't keep police away from our hangout spot, it did make it a little less obvious.

At some point my cousins began hanging out inside of this house in the neighborhood. I still don't know all of the details of how everything happened, but the woman who used to live there moved and we ended up setting up shop inside. There was electricity but no running water/and we kept a jug of water next to the toilet just to flush it. We had a garbage disposal installed in the living room so that we could easily dispose of our drugs if the police ever raided us.

Although we sold a good deal of crack, we had customers come from all over to buy weed. Back in the nineties hydroponic marijuana, or "dro" was not easy to find in D.C. Because of its high costs and limited availability, it made for somewhat of a niche market for us.

We would buy little glass vials from the wholesale shop to put the weed in, and would give customers a bobby pin as an accessory to get the weed out of the vial. In a twisted way, that was how I learned the value of marketing techniques like packaging and brand differentiation. These techniques definitely worked and we had more clientele than we could manage. It was hard to keep enough weed, and even though I would get as much of it as I could, I always sold out. It got to be almost scary how many people were coming to buy weed.

I remember one day in particular, I walked outside of the house and looked up the street and there was literally a line of cars all the way up the street and around the corner of people coming to buy weed. I had seen lines like that for drive-thru restaurants and basketball games, but imagine a line of cars waiting to buy drugs on a residential street. I was making more money than I had ever seen in my life, and I enjoyed the care-free lifestyle that came with it. I usually spent most of my money almost as fast as I made it. I bought lots of clothes and shoes, ate at the finest establishments, and partied as much as I wanted.

I had no interest in saving any money; I was young and spoiled, both by my grandmother who refused to take any money as rent, and by the seemingly endless access to money. I really didn't have any bills other than car insurance for the various "buckets" that I would buy and drive as hard as I could. I would sometimes sneak to the electric company with my grandmother's electric bill to pay it, but other than that I had no responsibilities. My older cousins told me I needed to save some money, but like everything else I was too hard-headed to listen.

The only thing that I did take pride in was my music. I had started a rap group with two guys I knew from the neighborhood, and together we would write and record songs about the lifestyle that we were living. We were proud of what we were doing and what we represented, and other than selling drugs music was the only ambition that I had in my life at that time. We even got to go on the radio, introduce one of our songs, and do an interview with the radio deejay. In reality, though, I had no sense of direction, even though I thought that I did.

If you would have asked me back then, I would have explained to you how dedicated I was to my music, how much I wanted to "get on", or sign a record deal. But looking back on it now, I realize that the only thing I was really dedicated to was the streets, to hanging out and selling drugs. If I had truly been dedicated to my music, I would've spent more time networking to get my music heard and developing my craft. Instead, I spent my time living the actual lifestyle that so many artists now portray in their music. That was much more important back then than it is now, and I thought that because my lifestyle reflected the things I was rapping about, that would count for something. It didn't.

One of the things that drive me crazy is the number of rappers portraying the apprenticeship of sin and of the streets in their music, without the background and the consequences that come with it. I can accept that it's art, but when you begin to portray this facade as an authentic experience, I have a problem. Every day I witness a new way in which a life is damaged or ruined because of this lifestyle, and to watch people-who haven't had to suffer any of the consequences that comes with it-market the apprenticeship of sin to the masses as if there are no consequences is sickening. It's bad enough to have those of us who actually have suffered the consequences to promote it, but to allow a "square" to pretend is to add insult to injury.

Society is complicit in this deception though, because even those of us who know better sing along to the lies along with everyone else.

More on that subject later though. Back then, I also would have told you that my priority was getting some money, but that's not exactly true either. I didn't have a problem getting it, even if I had to stand outside all day and night. The issue was what to do with it after I got it. I could've afforded a really, nice house, my own business, expensive cars, or just about anything I wanted with the type of money I was making. The truth is none of that would've made me happy. I was satisfied with nothing back then. As long as I had money in my pocket, weed to smoke, fresh clothes, a "bucket" to ride around in, women to have sex with, and somewhere to party and have fun I was good. I felt like I had finally found somewhere I belonged, something that asked very little of me but gave me what I wanted, and at that time that meant more to me than anything else.

I remember one time when I first started going uptown, I spent all of my re-up money, or the money I was supposed to use to buy more drugs. I had gone out partying the night before, and now I was almost dead broke. I asked my "big homie" to front me some "work", which he did.

A few weeks later, I did the same thing again. This time however, the big homie refused to front me any work. I had to take my last $40, buy a wholesale, flip that, buy an "eightball", flip that, and so on until I got my money back up. I stood outside all night, but I learned a valuable lesson that day.

I never spent my re-up money again after that, and although I still wasn't ready to start saving my money like I was supposed to, I started watching what I spent more closely. Eventually, we got concerned that the house we had been hustling out of was getting too hot, so we found a house across the street that we could rent under someone else's name. We set up shop across the street, but we only sold crack. By this time, everybody who hustled outside had weed for sale, and business was booming for anybody willing to stand there long enough to make money.

It was not uncommon for six to ten guys to sell two pounds or more apiece every day, not including whatever money they may have made selling crack.

There were open air drug markets all across D.C. back then, and although it would be unthinkable for anybody to try and hustle like that today due to the huge influx of white people into once predominately black/poor neighborhoods, that was the reality of the time.

As for me, I continued to sell my crack out of the house, and I would stand outside and sell my weed. We installed another garbage disposal, this time in the bathroom sink. Like most homes there was already one in the kitchen sink, but the bathroom was right across the hall from the room where we cut up our crack.

We would store ounces and half ounces of crack inside of the garbage disposal, so that if we had to get rid of the drugs quickly all we had to do was turn it on. None of that would end up being beneficial though. One afternoon, my little cousin was at the door of the house letting a customer out of the door. All of a sudden, a fleet of police cars pulled up in front of the house to raid it. There was an iron security gate attached to the door frame; the lock extended all the way into the frame of the house so it would not be easy to pry open.

Back then, police didn't carry the right equipment to break locks on security gates as quickly; these days they carry a pneumatic jack that they can wedge between the gate and the frame, and some police carry a cutting torch as well. Back then they would attach a hook and chain to a vehicle in order to snatch the gate open.

Anyway, as the officers approached the house in full raid gear my cousin retreated into the house. He attempted to pull the gate closed and lock it, but he was moving too fast and didn't get the lock inside of the door jamb. My cousin ran upstairs to inform us that the police were coming, but before we were able to get rid of all of the drugs the police broke the door down.

We attempted to turn on the garbage disposal and get rid of all of the drugs, but we didn't have enough time. The police threw a flashbang through the door as they entered, and ordered everyone to lie down. They found the drugs, and I was on my way to jail for the first time as an adult. I was denied bail, and I stayed in D.C. jail for about a week before the judge agreed to allow me to go to a halfway house. I stayed in the halfway house for about three months while my case worked its way through the process. I got a job with the U.S. Department of Transportation during this time, and I actually lived like a normal citizen outside of the federal case hanging over my head. My girlfriend became pregnant, as well, and on top of everything else I was expecting my first child. In spite of all of that, I was sentenced to five years in federal prison in October of 1998. My daughter Zhane was born the following year. After serving three years of my sentence, I was released to a halfway house in November of 2001. I had more trouble finding a job while I was in the halfway house than I ever have at any other point in my life. Even though I was willing to do anything to get my feet on the ground, it was hard getting adjusted because of the difficulties I'd had. I ended up getting a job through a guy that I met in the halfway house, working at FedEx Field cleaning the stadium after the Redskins games.

It was a dirty job in the freezing cold somedays, and between the crew that worked there and the crazy fans that we ran into, there was always something going on. The only thing I liked about the job was I got to see the games for free. Football season ended and my job ended with it, but the guy I met at the halfway house hooked me up with another job. This job was with one of the largest concrete construction companies in D.C. If you ever want to know what real work feels like, get a job in concrete construction. The work was physically demanding to say the least, and to make matters worse I had the flu on my very first day. The weather outside was bitter cold, and there was ice and snow stuck to all of the materials I was handling.

I had never felt so physically miserable in my life, between my flu symptoms and the numbing cold biting at my face, fingers, and toes, I never thought I would make it through the day. Working was a condition of increased freedom though, and I wanted to begin to move around and live. I ended up working that job until I got out of the halfway house, but to this day I have never worked so hard for so little money. I worked a few different jobs after that but nothing significant. I managed to finish my supervised release period, which is kind of like a mix between probation and parole, and now I was a free man. I had managed to stay away from selling drugs. I still hung around guys who smoked weed and sold drugs, but I promised myself I wasn't going to return to that lifestyle.

I had been in and around the criminal lifestyle for so long, but now I found myself struggling to run away from it instead of towards it. That worked for a little while at least. I began working as an independent contractor installing satellite TV. I had learned how to do communications wiring in prison, but it was hard finding a company to hire me.

I couldn't work as an independent contractor while I was on supervised release, but once I finished with that I had my own transportation and tools, so I was ready to go.

I was excited by the amount of work that was out there at first, and I was excited to be self-employed again. I know self-employment has always been one of the biggest incentives that street life offers, for me and for a lot of people I know.

Most of the benefits of owning your own business, coupled with the low cost of entry, make illicit businesses very attractive to a lot of people. I still had that entrepreneurial spirit, but I was determined to do it the legal way, at least at first.

I made fairly decent money installing satellite TV, but I had no experience with managing the expenses and the maintenance on a vehicle and between that and paying to support my daughter, my money started looking funny.

One day, I ran into my brother's old club buddy from college.

He had a few girls with him at the time, and even though I didn't know what he was into then, I would soon learn. We exchanged numbers, and he contacted me a few days later inquiring if I knew where to get some good weed. By this time I had returned to smoking weed again, and even though I wasn't selling it I kept enough that I could sell him some out of my stash.

Eventually he began calling to buy weed more frequently, and between his phone calls and the other people I knew who were looking for weed, I began buying weight to sell.

I didn't get a whole lot of weed, just a pound at the most for me to break down, sell some, and smoke some too. One day, this guy invited me over his house to talk business. I tried to sell him ounces in the past, but he said that he preferred the weed in bags. He also suggested that rather than continuing to drive back and forth to deliver weed, I could just leave some bags at his house. It was then that he revealed to me that he was a pimp.

I had been wondering what was up ever since I heard the girls with him call him "daddy", and after being told that I should call him Diamond around them instead of his real name. He also told me his girls liked to smoke weed, but they also liked to have some in case their tricks wanted to smoke. A few girls had regulars who really liked my weed, and they didn't need to be bothered with trying to weigh and separate an ounce of weed into smaller quantities. He told me not to worry about the extra cost, because the tricks would pay for it. He also offered me a job.

He told me he needed someone to help drive the girls to and from their "dates". He was only one man, he explained, and when business got to be busy he could schedule twice as many dates. He said he felt like he could trust me, and he offered to pay me fifty dollars per date. I accepted immediately, and in my mind I couldn't lose. I got to sell my weed, and I could make fifty dollars just for driving a girl to a house or a hotel. Business was decent, and I could make a few extra hundred dollars a night driving somedays, in addition to the weed sales.

I still had a day job driving a delivery truck, and while I wasn't getting rich I kept up with my bills and took care of my daughter comfortably.

Diamond also started teaching me the game-how he arranged dates for his girls, what web sites he used, how he advertised, and how he communicated with potential clients.

He had been trying to convince me for a while that I should consider getting my own girls and starting my own "escort agency", but I kept refusing. I saw how much of a headache that his girls were causing him and besides, I was already running myself crazy. Between my jobs, my side hustles, family, and my social life I was constantly on the go. Two or three hours of sleep was normal for me. I actually tried to live a dual life for a while, but as always one lifestyle would eventually take priority over the other.

I had my son, Pili Jr., in February of 2004, and even though my personal life was unstable the added pressures of having a newborn made things much worse.

I got a job working as an electrician's helper, and I learned to test, troubleshoot, and repair fire alarm systems and components. As I got better I began making fairly decent money, but as always my problem wasn't how much I had coming in, but what I had going out.

Trying to keep up with my social life, maintain two separate households with children, and keep up with all of my other expenses was exhausting.

The tipping point came about because of traffic tickets. I racked up a few parking and speeding tickets; normally that wouldn't be a big deal, but because my budget was a lot tighter with two kids I didn't pay them right away. I had some unexpected car repairs come up, and because I had to be able to drive to make money that came first. Some of my tickets were speed camera tickets, and although I doubt they were accurate there was little I could do. The state of MD also charged me a fine for driving a car without insurance, in spite of the fact I had turned in the tags to the car a year prior. The timing of these steep fines came at a horrible time, and eventually my driver's license was suspended. I had no choice but to keep driving though. One day I was pulled over and subsequently arrested for driving on a suspended license.

The next day when I was released, I met a woman outside of the courtroom. She was also in the streets, and was looking for a partner in crime so to speak. She began selling weed for me at first, but as her customer base grew she began asking me to supply her with PCP and crack. Up until that point I had never even considered becoming a pimp, but one day we had a conversation about me driving Diamond's girls around.

She confessed to me that she had prostituted herself before, but she had never chose a pimp because she hadn't found one she trusted. She made it clear she wanted to choose me, and after some consideration I decided to enter "the game".

I took pictures of her with an old digital camera and posted the pictures on Craigslist, and although she got a few dates she made more money selling drugs and catching dates on the street.

I began finding other women to work for me too; some were women I knew through friends and family, and others were women I met on the internet or in the street.

Most of the time I had between four and seven women working for me; some lived with me full-time and some came out only on weekends or on certain nights.

I was all the way in the game now, and there was no turning back. We would stay at hotels all over the DMV area for two to three days at a time, and post ads on the Internet advertising where we were. I began to build websites for my girls later on, in order to give the business a more professional look. I stayed away from putting the girls on "the track", or a street where prostitutes ply their trade.

I never learned the rules of the track, and besides, I learned really fast if the tricks happened to see your girls on the track, the word would spread and no one would want to pay Internet prices for a "track ho". I ran into a girl who used to work for Diamond, and she decided to come and work for me as well.

She had a section eight apartment in a high-rise building out in suburban Maryland where she stayed with her daughter, and me and my "stable" ended up using that apartment as well.

She had a coke habit and rarely cleaned up her house, but I didn't have a problem getting the girls to do it so we could conduct business there. It beat paying for hotels, and I liked the place because I could watch the customer pull up and investigate whether it was the police or not. We didn't stay there every day, but I got a few good days out of that apartment.

Her daughter was never home when we did anything of course, but in reality I know I did help in exposing her daughter to a lot more things than I would have wanted my own child to be around. That is definitely one of the many things on my list of regrets. Eventually, the police began closing in on my operation. One day, the police ran a sting operation and arrested a young woman who was working for me that was underage out in front of the apartment building.

The girls would always go downstairs and meet clientele just in case it was an undercover officer, but the police returned later on, raided the apartment, and arrested the woman who lived there. I went back to the hotels with my team, but I began to feel like the walls were closing in.

I was running back and forth all day trying to keep up with all that managing women entails, plus I was trying to continue to have a family. My daughter's mother and I still dealt with each other, and at this time I still had a job. Eventually I would get fired from my job and break up yet again with my daughter's mother, as I devoted more and more of my time to pimping. Around this time, I met a woman from Germany on the Internet. She had a house she was renting where she lived with her daughter, and she told me she used to work as a stripper. She had a job as a waitress at a German restaurant downtown, but once I moved in I slowly convinced her to come and work for me. We turned the basement into a dominatrix studio for her to work out of, and slowly but surely she began to prostitute herself as well. My daughter's mother was pregnant with my youngest son, and Zhalil was born in February of 2007. I now had three mouths to feed, along with all of the women on my team who relied on me every day.

Eventually the young woman who was underage was released, or so I was told, and after telling me a bunch of lies and convincing me that she was in fact of legal age, I agreed to go and pick her up. My cousin had begun working for me as a driver, and I was attempting to teach him the game as it was taught to me. I immediately set up a webpage and Internet ads for the girl, and she went right to work. She received a call to go to northern VA for a date, and I arranged for my cousin to drive her there. It turned out to be a sting operation, and my cousin and the girl were subsequently arrested.

I called around looking for him, and I found out that he was locked up in Alexandria city jail. When I asked what he was charged with, it was then I learned that he had a federal charge of transporting a minor for the purposes of prostitution.

One of the worst feelings in the world was having to explain to his father what exactly we had been into. I figured the police would be coming to arrest me any day, and I just hoped that my cousin kept his mouth shut long enough to give us a chance to fight the case or get away. But there was no escaping what was coming.

My whole world slowly began to unravel; I didn't get along with either of my kid's mothers, and I knew the police were watching so I had to be careful about sending my girls out to work. As I said before, I had long since been fired from my old job; I couldn't do what I needed to do in the streets and be at work every day. Besides, at the time the street money was much more lucrative. I ended up leaving the German girl too, after discovering that she had been prank calling my son's mother. That hurt at the time, not because of how I felt about her so much but because I needed the income she was bringing in. I was doing bad, and at that point I really didn't care about anything. I went to the one place I knew I could always go when things got bad-my grandmother's house. I would sit around and talk to her all day and try to figure out my next move, that is when I wasn't getting drunk or smoking weed. I was depressed and I felt like I was all out of options.

One afternoon, my grandmother and I were sitting on the porch having a conversation about who knows what, when all of a sudden an all-black SUV drove past with the window slightly cracked.

Even though the windows were tinted, you could make out that the driver was a white male, mid-thirties, with a baseball hat pulled down low on his head. I'll never forget my grandmother looking at me and saying, "Boy, that looks like them people". This was too funny to me at the time; I thought she had absolutely no idea what she was talking about.

When the truck rolled back past the house again though, I stopped laughing. I could tell that my grandmother was right, and

144

I felt the end was coming. I went into the house and made sure I got rid of anything tying me to any of the women. I erased all the files from my laptop with special software that I had, and I made sure I didn't have any old hotel receipts. After a while I relaxed a little, and when my uncle came over I told him I would meet him up the street so we could smoke some weed together.

As I left out of the house and proceeded to walk up the street, I was surrounded by cars. It was then I noticed FBI vests and badges, and I was subsequently placed under arrest. My truck was parked in my aunt's yard next door, and they asked for permission to tow it without a warrant. I gave it to them, because the last thing I wanted was for them to get a search warrant for my grandmother's house. I didn't want to put her through that or my aunt either for that matter.

My grandmother was standing in the front yard crying and screaming the whole time they were arresting me, and I begged the FBI to hurry up and take me to jail so that my grandmother wouldn't have to keep seeing all of this. I tried to act as confident as I could, but I knew I was finished. I remember being in the police van trying to figure out my next move. With everything else that was going on, it occurred to me I never did pay those traffic tickets off. With where I was headed, I would soon wish that traffic tickets were my only problems.

HATE

One of the incidents that forever changed my view on violence was my brother being shot during the summer of 1996. I had just graduated from high school a few months before, and my family was preparing to move into a house in a brand new suburban Maryland neighborhood development. My brother and I were still in the weed business, and we had a pretty steady clientele because we usually had product. According to him, a girl he had sold to several times before wanted to buy a pound or so of weed. As he approached her door, two masked men approached and demanded he give them the weed. He wrestled with the men, and after a struggle one of the men shot him in the shoulder. That incident made the reality of our choices hit home in a way it never had before. I was used to the haters by now, especially the type of hater unique to the DMV.

But the life and death consequences of this lifestyle I had chosen never became more real to me than the day I saw my brother bleeding from a bullet wound. One thing I do know about street life is violence is necessary in order to maintain boundaries. Without fear of violence, people will bring violence to you in order to impose their will. It was with this mindset I considered my brother's current situation. I was convinced the girl had set him up, and I wanted to get revenge. My brother wanted to leave it alone though, and no matter how I felt there was nothing I could do if he wasn't willing to do anything. Shortly after that, I bought the only firearm I have ever legally owned.

I was in the store one day and after casually walking past the sporting goods section, I decided I would purchase a gun. I was only 18, and although I had been carrying a pistol for years, I couldn't purchase one legally.

Instead, I decided to buy a shotgun I liked. I already had other guns at my disposal, but I have always liked shotguns ever since I shot them at Boy Scout summer camp. I installed a pistol grip on it, and kept it loaded with alternating deer slugs and buck shot.

I think at that time I was still fascinated by guns; I personally know guys who have military grade firearms in their house right now, and even though it was only a shotgun I felt proud to have a new gun, especially one that could fire such a large and powerful bullet.

One day after my parents and I had moved into our new house, my father discovered my shotgun next to a wad of money in a pair of pants I had on the ground.

We had a big argument about that, and I ended up moving out again. If I'm honest though, I know I never wanted to shoot anybody. I would never tell anyone if I had actually shot or shot at someone, but I will say I did want any potential threats to understand I would shoot them if that's what it took to protect myself. I used to have a small .25 caliber pistol that I would carry with me everywhere. I liked it because I could tuck it in the top of my timberland boot comfortably and still move around. It wasn't big and bulky, and even though it was a small caliber weapon it would serve its purpose in a pinch. I remember my older cousins laughing at me one day about how small it was, so I decided to go and get my shotgun and put it in the house we were in. I was so young and stupid back then. I'm very fortunate my older cousin had good sense in terms of how he conducted himself. He didn't get involved in all of the drama that was going on in the neighborhood, he stayed away from the go-go, and he advised me to do the same. I spoke earlier about the violence that stems from the go-go, and my cousin made it clear he wasn't out here for any of that.

The neighborhood had a pretty well-known reputation at that time, not only as a weed strip, but also because the lead rapper from one of the most popular go-go bands was from around there. I guess this made the neighborhood somewhat of a target for other neighborhoods, but I never got involved in any of that. I also knew there were some real shooters around there, who had a reputation in the streets for "putting in work".

I definitely witnessed my fair share of shootouts, and I knew all of that made it harder to make money. This lifestyle continued to claim lives, and I continued to witness death and violence all around me. Willie Wonka was one of the first people I met when I started coming uptown. Early on when my cousins refused to let me hustle with them, I would wait until they left and buy wholesale crack from him. He let me stand outside with him and hustle, all night if I wanted. Willie Wonka was probably the most outgoing person out of all the guys my cousins hung around on a daily basis. He liked talking slick to people, and he always had something to say. As the story goes, he was somewhere in SE shooting craps and talking loud as usual one day. I guess somebody didn't like what he had to say, so they shot him.

That is one of the main reasons why I have always stayed away from gambling in the street. I've gone to the casino a few times before, but I refuse to shoot craps or play poker anywhere else. Never mind the fact I don't like to lose money, but I have seen quite a few people lose their life over a craps game through the years.

There are rules inside of rules when it comes to gambling in the street, and just like anything else in the apprenticeship of sin, the consequences for not understanding those rules can be deadly. I think most people fail to realize how dangerous shooting craps is in the street because of the easy target you and your money become. Most of the time, guys are standing around with their head down concentrating on the dice.

I know several guys who have told me they made a career out of robbing neighborhood dice games, mainly because it's fairly easy to surprise the participants.

Most guys try to stay alert at first, but as the game gets more intense and the weed and drinks start flowing, it becomes much easier to get "caught slippin".

Another thing a lot of guys fail to consider is how shooting craps "opens doors", or exposes them to people in a way they normally wouldn't be exposed.

Suppose, for instance, that a guy that you are shooting craps with begins to talk slick to you. He gets inside your head, or he may think that you are soft and this is his way of trying you. That may seem like a trivial thing, but perception is a big deal in the street. I explained earlier about wolves and sheep, and one of the techniques wolves use is testing how far they can push boundaries. You could decide to talk slick to the guy back, and maybe that will be the end of it, or maybe it escalates.

Maybe the guy was hiding behind that to start something with you because of something else, or maybe someone "put a battery in his back", or encouraged him to try you for one reason or another.

Maybe now you feel like this guy is trying you, so you decide to do something to him. Maybe this guy feels like he needs to show off for the people standing around, or maybe you feel like you need to make a point because people are watching you. Maybe somebody else hears how he is talking to you, and now they feel like they can try you too.

All of these subtle nuances of person-to-person interaction in the street exist already, but my point is that a craps game adds an opportunity to create a problem, especially since money is involved.

Even if you only gamble with people that you "know", the dice game gives them an opportunity to try and calculate how much money you have, or how "long" your money is. Maybe you've been hustling hard lately, or maybe you're buying and selling more drugs than they are, and they feel some type of way about it. Maybe they feel like you shouldn't walk away from the dice game while you're up on them, because you can stand to take a loss. Maybe they don't say anything right then, but maybe they help set you up to get robbed later on.

I know that some may think that I'm being extreme in stating that someone considers all of these possibilities, but I personally know people who have experienced each and every one of these scenarios.

Some of them are dead, and others are in prison right now. In retrospect, I'm glad that I had some older men that were able to point out some of these pitfalls to me early on.

I think that a lot of the problems that we see continue to plague black neighborhoods is due to the absence of older men who have lived through the apprenticeship and can pass this type of wisdom on to the next generation.

It's not a matter of being scared; I carried a pistol and I knew that I would use it to protect myself. It was about avoiding problems, especially unnecessary problems, in order to get some money. I had to learn that everyone didn't want to get money though; some people said that they did, but their actions proved otherwise. Some people just liked being in the middle of a bunch of conflict, and they felt like their violent nature would earn them respect. I tried to avoid these types of people at all costs, if it was possible. That would prove to be increasingly difficult in another part of my apprenticeship, however. Nothing brings home the life and death reality of street life like being incarcerated. Prison is a world unto itself, with its own hierarchy, rules and social structure.

My first real experiences with prison life started in D.C. Jail. D.C. Jail has always been a violent place, and in spite of all of the efforts to clean it up, at the end of the day you still have a bunch of violent men concentrated in one place. After I was sentenced in 1998, I arrived at D.C. Jail very much unaware of the rules. I stayed to myself for the most part and tried to mind my own business. I saw a few people that I knew from the street, but I always looked at things like I was on my own. It didn't take long for me to begin to witness the violence. There was a guy around my age that arrived shortly after me. He wasted no time in getting into everything, and I knew that he was headed for self-destruction.

One day, we were all watching the Washington Redskins play the Dallas Cowboys on TV. For those that don't know, this is the biggest rivalry in Washington, D.C. as far as sports are concerned. D.C. has a lot of Redskin fans, but there are also a lot of Cowboy fans in the city as well. Anyway, this guy felt the need to be extra loud while the Cowboys were winning.

I'm not sure if he had placed a bet on the game or not, but with all of the noise that he was making I sure hope so. I saw the way some people were looking at him, and right away I knew that he was in trouble.

After the game was over, I saw the guy standing and talking to someone, when all of a sudden two guys started to come at him with knives in their hands.

I'm not talking about the crudely fashioned pieces of metal that you usually think of as a prison weapon; one guy had a hookbill knife with a handle and locking back, and the other guy had a butcher knife straight out of the kitchen. The victim tried to hold off his two attackers by wrapping his t-shirt around his arm as a shield, but he was fighting off two armed men.

They pushed him backwards over a table and began to stab him repeatedly, and by the time that the prison staff responded the victim was on the floor unconscious and bleeding severely. To say that there was a lot of blood everywhere is an understatement, and it was a clear reminder of how things could get ugly very fast. On the surface it may seem like the incident happened over a football game, but I think everyone knew that it was about more than that. The guy who got stabbed had opened a door and he wasn't ready to handle what came through it. I saw a guy from my neighborhood a few days later in the hallway, and I was glad that he offered me a knife. For the most part, prison has a very few simple rules to follow if you're trying to stay out of conflicts. One of the most basic rules is pay your bills. This ties in to what I mentioned before about gambling and what people perceive. Allowing someone to owe you implies a certain level of trust and when that trust is violated, there has to be consequences. Sometimes this can be a test as well.

Some people don't pay what they owe because they don't have it to pay for one reason or another; in other situations people don't pay simply because they don't fear any consequences. I have seen several instances of drug dealers coming to D.C. from New York and trying to set up shop with their drugs, especially in the late eighties and early nineties.

They would try to gain a stronghold over a particular neighborhood or area by flooding the streets with their product and by "fronting" a lot of the young drug dealers' work.

Of course, none of the men who grew up in the area want to see an outsider come and take over their neighborhood.

Some of these "Out-of-towners" were robbed and killed outright, some were extorted, and some were given the "soft press". A local guy might go to the out-of-towner and ask him to front him some work. The out-of-towner would usually comply, because again he is trying to expand his customer base. Maybe the local guy would pay him once or twice, but then the soft press would begin. Maybe his money would start being short, or maybe he wouldn't pay at all. Or maybe the local guy would start bringing other guys to the out-of-towner, asking him to front them work too. Eventually the out-of-towner expects to be paid, and that's when the problems begin. Once the out-of-towner tries to put his foot down, he is usually threatened or robbed.

Some out-of-towners may try to use force, but unless he has family or real "street soldiers" with him that can help him stand strong, he usually leaves town or gets killed. Most of the time you hear about a drug addict being murdered, it is about an unpaid bill. There are exceptions to the rule of course, but usually violence happens to real drug addicts because of theft or nonpayment.

A lot of older drug dealers are very hesitant to front younger guys anything, not out of fear, but because the cost of dealing with not being paid is not worth it. All of these dynamics transfer to the mentality of prison commerce.

There are three main sources of prison commerce: food, whether it be items sold at the commissary or perishables stolen from the kitchen; gambling, whether it be sports betting or casino style games; and drugs.

As for food, most commissary items are "resold" among prisoners with a markup in order to recognize a profit, and prices vary according to supply and demand for items stolen out of the kitchen. In either case, it's very easy for someone to run up a large tab. The very nature of the "store" hustle depends on credit, which makes the nature of the business much more susceptible to issues of nonpayment.

As for gambling, there are two types of games: cash in hand and credit. I've never seen a problem in prison when gambling was done by cash in hand. "Cash" is not really cash, by the way, it's usually whatever item that inmates have assigned value to. Postage stamps and mackerel are the most common in federal prison.

Credit games are always the largest source of controversy, whether it be an argument about how much to pay or when, or something else related to the payment of debt. All the gambling related violence that I've ever seen in prison involved credit.

Drugs, of course, are always a source of controversy. The same principles I mentioned earlier about drugs apply even more so in prison.

Most guys are willing to be lenient with a store bill, or even to give you a discount on a gambling debt, but if there is one hard and fast rule in prison it would be do not play with someone's money when it comes to drugs.

Of course, if you are a wolf you shouldn't even try to sell drugs in prison; I've seen a few people get their drugs taken or their lockers emptied simply because they weren't tough enough to be in the lifestyle that they were involved in. Respect is a big issue in prison, and so men tend to be hypersensitive about issues related to respect simply because no one wants to be seen as soft. Manners are a huge thing-saying excuse me if you bump someone, waiting in line instead of cutting the line to talk to your friends, and using a respectable tone of voice all seem like trivial matters to people on the outside, but behind prison walls a failure to mind your manners can cost you your life.

Another very similar rule is mind your own business. This rule may sound fairly easy, but it is the one that is violated the most often and leads to the most conflicts. Because prison is such a closed in environment, a person will see a lot, hear a lot, and know a lot that has absolutely nothing to do with them.

Failure to mind your own business will cause you to be in a situation you didn't intend to be in; this is another one of those rules that is important in the street but twice as important in prison. I'm not necessarily talking about snitching either, or reporting someone else's activities to the police.

Honestly, I have seen very little violence in prison behind that and even people who have that in their background can make it through prison with little to no problem. The largest source of problems that people seem to have as far as minding their own business is concerned, revolves around homosexuals and homosexual activity.

There are quite a few people who profess to have a problem with it, but the truth is that it has been a reality of every prison that I've ever been to. However a person may profess to feel, it's undeniable that homosexuals, especially the effeminate type, have a certain dynamic that they bring to prison. There is a large misconception that there are a bunch of men raping each other in prison which is far from the case. There are so many willing participants in homosexual activity that no one needs to rape anyone for sexual gratification. I know that rape is supposed to be about power and not sex, but all I'm saying is that I've never witnessed it. Besides there are so many "transgender women" in prison now that have feminine features, men that are into that are lining up to get with them.

Between the new surgery techniques and the hormone therapy that prisons are now required to give transgender people, it becomes easy for some men to forget about the fact that this person was born a man.

There is some debate amongst prisoners and society alike about the cause of homosexual activity in prisons. Some men say that everyone who participates in it has a natural inclination towards homosexuality, and that if you do it in prison then you would do it in the streets. Others argue that the lack of access to a woman for an extended period of time is what drives some men to seek this physical intimacy from another man, and they simply suffer from the lack of self-restraint.

Whatever the case may be, I have seen a few incidents of violence that involve homosexuals. The first incident happened at D.C. Jail. There were two people involved in a homosexual relationship, one masculine and one effeminate.

The effeminate person would walk around with a bed sheet tied around his waist like a dress, and make some type of makeshift lip gloss out of Kool-Aid and Vaseline. It was not uncommon to see men grab this guy's butt as he walked past, guys that you never would have thought were gay. I was shocked initially, but I kept my mouth shut because it was none of my business. One day, some guy decided to say something to the guy's "boyfriend", and they began to argue. What the guy didn't know is that the "boyfriend" had been incarcerated for most of his life, and had been in multiple fights and stabbings before.

A short while later the two men squared up in the middle of the tier. The gentlemen who had started the argument had a small ice pick type of weapon that he was swinging erratically, while the boyfriend circled just out of his reach. When the guy attempted to stab the boyfriend he side-stepped his thrust, took the ice pick from him, and began to stab him with his own weapon repeatedly. Another incident happened at the beginning of my current sentence in federal prison.

Again, the situation was pretty much the same. Someone decided to say something disrespectful to a feminine homosexual, and when his boyfriend found out about it he confronted the guy about it. I guess the guy decided that he was going to make a scene in front of his friends because he was being confronted by a man involved in homosexual activity. He began talking extra loud, which real convicts consider as an attempt to get assistance from the police and is known as a "check in move". The guy continued to talk loud and gesture, and as soon as he finished the boyfriend pulled out a long icepick and began to go after the guy. The guy who had been talking so tough immediately turned to run, and he was trying to escape being stabbed so badly that he attempted to climb a razor-wire covered fence.

Of course prison politics come into play in terms of how violence occurs as well. Most prison relationships are based on an alliance of some sort; because no man is an island, everyone needs someone to watch their back and protect their common interest, a wolf pack to run with.

Most jails are local, and alliances are segregated by neighborhood; although gangs are now quite prominent on the east coast, the majority of jails in the DMV area still follow this trend. Federal prison is different however. In the federal prison system, alliances are based on your state.

Your "car" or the group of guys from your state are the ones prison politics deems responsible for you. That means that they are supposed to help you to get acquainted to the prison, help you to get basic supplies, and let you know how things work. They are also responsible for maintaining order according to the mandates of prison culture.

That means that they are supposed to check your paperwork to see if you're "hot", or that you are not cooperating or have not cooperated with law enforcement. At lower custody level institutions this is rarely practiced, but in higher custody institutions this rule is heavily enforced.

Prison rules dictate that if someone is discovered to be hot then their car is supposed to make them "check in", or go into protective custody in order to avoid violence.

These barbaric rules are part of the prison experience, and no matter how much a person may not want to be involved in any of that, it is necessary to understand how it all works in order to survive.

In other parts of the country it's necessary for all black people to become part of one car, due to the large number of Mexicans. No matter what the situation may be, there are certain expectations placed on you as a part of a car, especially where violence is concerned. The main expectation is that you are not supposed to allow a member of your car to get jumped without coming to his aid. Some cars believe in giving someone a "fair one", or allowing two people to fight one on one.

As for people from D.C., there has always been a standing agreement across all federal institutions that no one is supposed to fight one on one.

Men from D.C. have a long-standing reputation for being exceptionally violent, and part of that came from the understanding if you fought one guy from D.C., you had to deal with the whole car.

There are exceptions made for guys who are into their faith, especially Muslims. Muslims have their own community; in most prisons they function somewhat like a car, and some people have even been known to become Muslim just for protection. I remember one incident in particular when the imam, or leader of the Muslims, got into an argument with a well-respected guy from D.C.

It happened in the chow hall. Normally people tried to avoid getting into a conflict in the chow hall, because you can be charged with inciting a riot, and again it is considered a check-in move. Anyway, the two men had words back and forth until it reached a boiling point. All of a sudden, it got really quiet, and groups of Muslims and guys from D.C. began to walk outside. The guards caught wind of what was about to happen, and the whole compound was on lockdown for nearly a month. That incident was one of the few times guards were able to intervene before things got out of hand, but I have witnessed several instances of all-out brawls erupt with no warning or notice. That's how things usually happen in prison; violence erupts suddenly, and people are left trying to sort out what happened after the fact. One of the forms of violence I have found to be most disturbing over the years is violence against women.

I know that may sound odd coming from a former pimp; the popular perception is pimps are required to slap and beat their women in order to achieve compliance and maintain discipline. Again, this idea has been reinforced by scripted dramas and comedy sketches alike, that make light of this barbaric practice as entertainment.

While it is true there are some involved in the business of prostitution that practice this outdated method - known as "gorilla pimping", there is very little respect for anyone who practices it. More often than not, the men who do it wind up losing all of their women, or going to prison for a very long time. On the other hand, I would be less than honest if I said I have never put my hands on a woman who worked for me. I tried to avoid it at all costs, but in certain situations it becomes unavoidable. I have been attacked by women who worked for me on more than one occasion.

I'm sure part of the rage they were physically expressing was born out of frustration caused by the lifestyle we were in, and all of the things that came with it. But I know another part of it was a test to see how I would respond to their open disrespect.

There are a lot of women who have become increasingly comfortable with putting their hands on people, especially men, in an aggressive manner. I don't know if it is born out of a sense of empowerment, a cultural shift, or a progression in the effect of the apprenticeship of sin and hate.

One only need to look at daytime TV or reality shows to confirm this as truth; it has become culturally acceptable for a woman to smack, push, kick, and hit a man to express her anger. Men dare not respond in kind, however.

In fact, most women use to their advantage the fact men are now prosecuted much more easily for domestic battery. There have always been women who have become so accustomed to the violence in disfunctional relationships they begin to seek it, as an affirmation of concern and love.

But this open aggression towards men has now become the new normal. Not only has the culture of violence in our society affected our relationships, it has distorted the roles of men and women and the reality of how we were made. This reality is ever present, and has become a permanent part of my experience as a black man.

I had no choice in learning how to navigate in its waters; although I willingly put myself into certain situations where its power was more immediate, I could not opt out of this mentality on my own.

The culture of hate continues on, and the effect of the apprenticeship of sin is still very present in my life. This hatred is what I face every day as my reality, and at this point it influences all I know about the world.

SEX

By the time I graduated high school, my sex life was out of control. I was having sex so often and with so many different women, I am truly blessed I never contracted HIV or any other STD. I don't say that with pride or to brag about my sexual conquests; the reality is I practiced a very unhealthy sexual lifestyle for a significant period of time.

Towards the end of my junior year in high school, I met the woman who would later become the mother of my oldest son and middle child. She had a dark complexion and a thick, slightly heavyset build, with a beautiful smile and bright brown eyes. She had a strong work ethic about her as well, and ever since I've known her she's had a job of some sort. She has always had a very sassy attitude and a sharp tongue to match.

At that point in my life I didn't mind dealing with a woman who had an "attitude problem"; I think in some ways I equated that way of behaving with my definition of a strong, black woman. Although my mom wasn't like that, my aunt and my cousin displayed that same attitude at times.

Even though she could be moody, she was extremely loyal and didn't require much from me.

We rarely went on any dates; our relationship mainly consisted of phone conversations and spending time at our parents' houses. We would watch TV and have sex, and at that time that was enough for me. We began to grow apart as time went on, and eventually we broke up.

I think I should point out that during this relationship I still had lots of other women I was dealing with, and as I sit and try to recall that point in my life there are so many random faces and episodes that flash in my mind. As I said before I have never been truly monogamous, although I have been in relationships that were supposed to be monogamous.

I have always believed in having a "main girl", or the one you actually care about and do things with, like buy a present for and spend time with during the holidays.

Ladies, if you ever want to know if you're the main girl, it's easy to figure out: Christmas Eve and the day before Valentine's Day are "side chick holidays".

Even though I have always believed in doing whatever I want to do, I was hurt by our break-up. Whatever it was we had it was comfortable, especially for the lifestyle I was living at that time. Our breakup happened right around the time I started hanging out and selling drugs uptown full time, and in a lot of ways the absence of that relationship made me behave more recklessly.

Like I've said before, I've never had a problem meeting women, but the abundance of cash that comes with dealing drugs combined with my sexual appetite helped me to be extremely promiscuous.

Not that I was paying for sex from these women or buying them expensive gifts, but I was able to eat out and party with these women without concern about the expense.

I was having sex with women I knew from the neighborhood, women I'd met on the street, and women I'd met through friends. Most of my days were spent selling drugs, and most of my nights were spent partying or at a hotel with some random woman. I went on like this for about six months after breaking up with my then girlfriend. One day, one of the girls from around the neighborhood introduced me to the girl who would later become the mother of my other two children. Our relationship started off fairly easy; we would go out all over town to different establishments, smoke weed, and of course have lots of sex. I can't say our relationship had much substance, but then again at that time I wasn't really looking for substance. I think at the time I might have just been looking for some steady female companionship.

In spite of all the people were around me, I was lonely in a way and wanted someone to share my life with.

That's not a popular sentiment to express, both as a black man and as a former pimp, but nothing reveals the honesty of this truth like men in prison. I have never seen so many "married" men in my life. Everybody claims they were a player in the street, but when the loneliness of prison sets in the truth starts to come out. As for me and my then girlfriend, I would soon find out just how shallow our relationship was.

One day, one of my cousins revealed to me he had run into her over at a house in the neighborhood and had been flirting back and forth with her.

I didn't really care because I had lots of other women I was dealing with, but my ego was a bit bruised simply because of the amount of time she and I had spent together. It was also embarrassing. One of the big no-noes for black men of my generation was "trying to make a ho into a housewife".

Plus, my cousin is a few years older than me and was getting more money than me at the time, and although I didn't want to believe it I had to accept the fact I meant nothing to this woman. If only I would've stuck with that. I sucked up my pride and went on with my life, and even though I felt like I got played I was too much of a player to hold onto negative feelings about a woman. I continued to have sex with a lot of different women, and I resolved not to open up to another woman any time soon.

After a few months had passed, this woman started contacting me again telling me how sorry she was about all that had happened and how she had been confused. She admitted she had allowed my cousin to "do some things", but she claimed she didn't allow things to go any further.

Of course I didn't believe that story; it was hard to believe she would go that far with my cousin and not have intercourse with him.

But the more I thought about it, I realized I really didn't care. I had decided to keep on having sex with her; because she had a car it made sex convenient, and as long as she remained available whenever I wanted her to be, my cousin and I could share her. Our relationship changed once I was arrested though.

While I was in the halfway house, she made every effort to be as supportive as she could be, and she went the extra mile to show me that she was serious. She brought me money, food, clothes, and chauffeured me around every chance she got. She made herself totally available to me, and that meant a lot to me at that time.

Between all that I was going through with my case, and the support this woman was giving me, it was hard not to once again believe our relationship meant something.

Over time, I convinced myself what had happened in the past didn't matter, because what we had now was real. We had grown closer through this test, or so I told myself. We became an official couple, and I tried to spend every available moment I could with her. I was released from the halfway house, and outside of going to work I was with her. I thought we had grown closer, and I can honestly say that, for that period of time, I was almost completely faithful. I had sex with a few random women in between, but they were only random women I met with my brother rather than any "side piece". We practically lived together in my parents' basement, and her being with me all the time became normal. Over the next few months we stopped using protection and she became pregnant. The good times we shared wouldn't last, however. I went off to begin serving my five-year federal prison sentence when my then girlfriend was two months pregnant. I tried to spend every moment I could on the phone with her, and all I could think about was what was happening with her and the baby growing inside of her. Prison by itself wasn't all that stressful; I was at a minimum security institution, and the place didn't even have a fence around it. My biggest stress was worrying about what was happening with my then pregnant girlfriend.

She had begun living at my parents' house, and at this point I was still trying to hold on to the love I thought we had, especially after my daughter Zhane was born. I was excited to be a parent, but sad to be so far away from my first child.

Things started getting worse and worse between my daughter's mother and me. She started going out more and more, enjoying her social life. She became more distant, and I could tell something was going on.

Some of the older guys had been advising me to let go a long time ago, and that I would only be making my time hard by worrying about what she had going on out in the world. I began to feel the pain of the distance and of betrayal, a pain like no other I had ever experienced. Eventually she confirmed what I already knew in my heart. She told me she had a new "friend", and she was moving out of my parent's house. I distracted myself by diving into my music, writing raps and playing the piano.

I had an old friend who went to college not too far away from the prison, and so I poured my attention into her and our "long lost" relationship. I was determined to fill that void I felt in my heart, but it proved to be increasingly difficult from behind prison walls.

I didn't have alcohol and weed readily at my disposal to numb the pain of my emotions; although they were certainly available, I wasn't willing to risk greater consequences over temporary emotions. I also couldn't use casual sex as a distraction like I had for most of my life.

I had to suffer through it, and I vowed that I would never give that much of myself to any woman ever again.

Soon I learned to master my emotions and to be comfortable in my solitude, and that would later become an important lesson in the mastery of this part of my apprenticeship of sin.

I came home from prison very bitter; I felt like my daughter's mother had abandoned me when I needed her the most. We began to deal with each other and have sex again, going back and forth in our disfunction like so many young couples do. Our relationship would never be the same again, though.

The time we spent apart had ruined any chance that we may have had to form a real relationship, and no matter how many times we tried to fix it we would never be able to make it work. Initially, I went back to what I had always done-having sex with lots of different women. I had a few different relationships, and although some were more meaningful than others, I never even considered being faithful. One of my cousins introduced me to the world of online dating, which at the time was a new fad. There are thousands of websites dedicated to online dating now, but back in the early 2000's it was still a relatively new concept in the black community.

I couldn't believe that meeting women was now as simple as posting a few pictures of myself and writing a few lines. I was in pretty good shape from all of my prison workouts, and my skin was clear from the time I had spent away from drinking and smoking weed. I have always been a fairly, decent writer, in fact, prison helped me to sharpen my communication skills through all of the letters that I wrote to women. Now that I had hundreds of women available to me with just a few clicks of a mouse, I felt like a kid in a candy store. I began meeting and having sex with women from all over the DMV area. I enjoyed the whole process of meeting new women online, and I would spend hours searching through profiles for women that I wanted as if I were shopping.

I found it much easier than meeting women at a bar or club, where a man usually struggles to make awkward, shallow conversation inside of a noisy, crowded atmosphere. I started meeting women from all different backgrounds, nationalities, and age groups.

I could control the atmosphere on the internet; my words set the tone for all future conversations, and I determined when and how to approach and deliver my thoughts. My page was the bait, and if they liked what they saw and read, then the hard part was already done. All I had to do was continue to stimulate their mind long enough to get them in the mood to move further. By the time I got their phone number, it was almost guaranteed we would be having sex sometime in the near future. We may go on a few dates, but most of the women I met on the internet would have sex with me within the first two encounters. One of my most memorable experiences with online dating came about through a Thai woman I'd met.

She lived in suburban VA and worked as a nanny for a wealthy white couple, but at night she loved to party. We would meet up at some of the bars in her area, and we always had a good time.

She introduced me to a few of her other friends, who were all gorgeous Asian women.

I'd had sex with more than a few women outside of my race before including Asian women, but there was something that I found to be exotic about her. I don't know exactly what exotic is anymore, but at that time she was it. She also liked to smoke weed, and eventually she introduced me to a few other friends who wanted to buy some as well. A few requested that I bring them coke and ecstasy. That was pretty much the extent of our relationship, and besides having sex and partying we really didn't have that much to talk about. One day I met up with her and a group of her friends at an Asian karaoke bar. I brought along a few guys that I knew from my parents' neighborhood, and introduced them to some of her friends. We had a great time that night. We drank lots of tequila and laughed at the old Asian men singing karaoke in a language that we couldn't understand.

A few of the guys with me would put on the background tracks to the Asian songs and rap over them, and the Asian women thought that this was the best thing ever.

I don't think that an evening like that would have been possible for me without internet dating, not because I couldn't meet women of different nationalities, but because I probably would have never given myself the opportunity to meet and date women outside of the very small world that I traveled in. My internet love life was creating problems for me in other areas of my love life however. I was still in and out of a relationship with my daughter's mother during this time.

I've figured out that I can be a bit sentimental when it comes to relationships, and I tend to hold on to what is familiar even if the relationship is unhealthy. Despite all of my promiscuity I love very hard, and although I may not love very many people or fall in love very often, when I do love someone I'm all the way in it. At times I even found a way to convince myself that I could make our relationship work, regardless of my infidelity and all of

166

the issues that we had. We shared a child together, and because we got along easily it becomes simple to mistake the nostalgia of the past and the shared experience of parenting as real love.

You start lying to yourself about why things don't work, and how things could be. I even proposed marriage at one point, and for a while we called ourselves being engaged to one another. I was never faithful to her in spite of all of this, and although I may have gone a week or two without dealing with another woman I never tried to be a one woman man.

About a year after getting out of prison, I ended up reconnecting with my old girlfriend from high school who is now the mother of my oldest son. Again, I felt comfortable with her because of what we had in the past, and it was easy to hold on to that. Her timing was great at the time when she reached out to me, because I really needed someone stable in my life then.

Looking back on it all, I know that was the one quality that attracted me to her the most, the stability and consistency she provided me. She was supportive of all of my dreams, and she did her best to help me achieve my goals. She knew how to organize my life in the way that women do, and she began to handle more and more of my affairs for me. She even co-signed for me to get a car. After living in chaos and disorder for so long, that felt good.

I had opened up to her about the problems that I had in the past with my daughter's mother and her selfish ways, and I guess she figured that "fixing" me and all that was wrong in my life was the way to my heart. She was partially right; that type of concern was what I needed at the time, because I was miserable.

I hated my job, I was struggling to make ends meet without breaking the law, and the situation with my daughter's mother only complicated things further. I was drinking a lot, and I had no idea where my life was headed.

In a lot of ways my then girlfriend took me in and helped me get myself together, and although I didn't always act like it, I appreciated her concern for me. She made it clear that she felt like I never belonged with my daughter's mother in the first place, because she and I should have never broken up.

She also made it clear that she wanted the one thing that my daughter's mother shared with me: a child. She had gotten pregnant by me when we were younger, and I know that part of her always regretted having an abortion. I knew that the last thing I needed was another child, but I felt like she had done so much for me and given me so much of herself that I owed her this.

We stopped using protection, and she eventually became pregnant. As her pregnancy moved further along, our relationship got worse and worse. We were sharing an apartment, and although she wasn't necessarily hard to get along with I know that added to the stress.

Between the depressed funk that I was in, the drinking and running the streets that I was doing, and her pregnancy hormones, we argued more frequently.

Outside of having sex, we barely communicated with each other. I looked for any excuse to stay out all night, any small thing that I could blow up over. That was mostly due to how miserable I was with myself, and my promiscuity was an attempt to alleviate the symptoms. I never stopped having multiple women, and now I was ready to take my online dating to the next level. At some point I had discovered websites for swingers.

In my mind, I had mastered the challenge of having sex whenever I wanted, and now I was looking for something else to excite me and fill that void that I felt.

I dealt with a few women who were bi-sexual, and I experienced a few threesomes with a few of them. I would take pictures of some of our encounters and post them on these swinger websites. Other couples would respond, and we would hook up and exchange partners. I remember that for Valentine's Day, me and another one of the women that I had a relationship with hosted one of these parties.

By this time I had stopped staying at the apartment my pregnant girlfriend and I had shared, and I was pretty much spending all of my free time partying and chasing women.

I met this other woman through her mother, who was a co-worker of mine at my job. She was not only one of the most gorgeous women I had ever dealt with; she was fun to be with and into trying this lifestyle with me. Our relationship was more sex than substance back then; like me she came from a good family, but she was trying to figure a few things out for herself and was looking to have fun along the way. That was perfect for what I wanted out of a woman at the time, and so we began to explore the world of sexual promiscuity together through threesomes, orgies, and swing parties.

On this particular night, two other women that we had had sex with in the past were looking to have some fun as well. One of the women brought a guy with her; he seemed cool enough, so it was all good. After he and I smoked some weed and we all drank lots of alcohol, the party got underway. Early the next morning, I stumbled in my parents' house drunk and exhausted. After laying down for about ten minutes my mother woke me up and told me my girlfriend was about to deliver the baby. I drove to the hospital dead tired, still drunk and reeking of alcohol. I remember my girlfriend and her mother screaming at me because I kept nodding off, but I couldn't manage to get it together. I managed to sober up a little eventually; enough to witness my girlfriend have a C-section. I'm sure they must have informed her that it was necessary at some point, but I don't remember.

Finally, my son Pili Jr. was born. I was proud to have a son, a namesake at that, but I still didn't slow down with what I was doing. My older brother only helped to make things worse. He had been working as an "exotic dancer" at the local clubs, and needless to say that meant access to a lot of women. I was pretty bad when it came to womanizing and having multiple women, but my brother made me look like a virgin.

I would hang out sometimes with him and some of his dancer friends, and there were so many women around that were ready and willing to have sex that it still seems unreal. I'm not just talking about young, impressionable twenty-somethings either; although there were enough of those around too, there were plenty of college-educated women with careers and families to choose from.

Some of them were even married, but that didn't matter. Nothing made me realize the truth behind the allegation that there is an abundance of women, in proportion to the number of available men like hanging out with my brother. Womanizing was the one activity that my brother and I could always bond over, no matter what else we had going on in our lives. It was as much a pastime to us as playing basketball or going fishing.

I could share numerous stories about all of the times that we passed around women as if they were objects to be used for our sexual pleasure. My brother also turned me on to a local swingers' organization that he belonged to.

Up until that point I had experienced all of the same activities that happen at a swinger party, but I had never been to an actual party full of people who were into casual sex as much as I was. My brother told me that I would need to bring a woman with me in order to get in, so I invited one of the women I had enjoyed threesomes within the past.

Although neither one of us was by any means shy and were both comfortable naked in front of other people, we were a little nervous going in just because we didn't know what to expect. A woman greeted us at the door of the house, and at first it appeared to be like any other house party I'd ever been to. There were snacks and lots of alcohol, and there were people standing around making small talk. As we walked downstairs to the basement, we saw how different things were though. There were about 15-20 women and men walking around either partially or totally naked. The host welcomed everyone to the party, explained briefly that we were free to do or not to do anything that we wanted, and said that we should remember to respect each other's boundaries.

After that, the party officially began. There were rooms sectioned off for different activities; one room for watching porno movies together, another for oral sex aficionados and another strictly for women to "play" with each other. Soon there were naked bodies everywhere, and everyone seemed to be enjoying themselves. A girl that my brother had introduced me to before started a conversation with my date, and pretty soon they were off to the girl-on-girl room together. I had sex with more women than I can remember that night; sometimes my brother and I shared, and sometimes by myself.

Again, these were not horny, impressionable young adults simply experimenting with their sexuality; in fact, I was probably one of the youngest people there. Besides me and my date there may have been three or four other people who were under thirty, and no one was under twenty five. There were a lot of married couples, and some of them were in their sixties and had been together in the lifestyle for thirty plus years.

These were hardworking, intelligent, educated black people who had made a conscious choice to enjoy this lifestyle. That was the first experience that ever made me feel like being promiscuous didn't have to be a shameful, dirty thing. Seeing all of these responsible people taking control of their body and their sexuality was empowering to me. All of these experiences helped to shape my transition into being a "pimp".

I'll be the first to admit that I have a certain disdain for the title pimp, because in my mind it has become synonymous with a bunch of idiotic mannerisms and behaviors that I have never participated in.

My transition was based on two separate but equally important factors. The first and probably the most important was coming to understand myself and who I was as a man.

I had been exposed to this alternative lifestyle, and I knew that once my eyes were opened I could never be satisfied with an ordinary relationship again.

I had already begun to scratch the surface in a sense; I had begun hosting parties for various female strippers that I knew. Between the women I had met in my various trips to strip clubs in the area and the women I met through my brother, I knew a good deal of women who were already in the life. The financial incentive was definitely a motivating factor as well.

I received a small fee for coordinating parties and events for the women already, so this was in a sense a natural progression.

There was a woman who worked at an underground strip club that invited me to come and see her all the time. The first two or three times I came I paid at the door and tipped various dancers, but after I met her I always got in for free.

I had no inclination to be a pimp back then; I would sell my weed and ecstasy pills to dancers and strippers in the club, and have sex with one of the dancers while I was there. I went back to dealing with my daughter's mother at some point doing this whole process. By the time my son Zhalil was born, she and I both knew our relationship was hopeless.

I had fully transitioned into my new lifestyle; I was all the way in the game, and the "square" relationships we shared had no place in my life. I craved a new type of relationship, one where everyone understood I was in control. These women gave me the power to decide every detail of their lives, and it was like a drug to me.

This power upended everything I thought I had been taught a man was supposed to be in a relationship-humble, compliant, and a provider. These women longed to be controlled, to provide me with whatever I wanted, and to do so they were willing to use their bodies at my behest.

I understood the progression; from my childhood years and the experimentation I had done thru my teenage years and the exploration that came with it, to my adult years and the manifestation of all I had seen and done.

I needed a way to express who I was and my sexuality in a way that was real to me, a way that was a natural extension of what I believed, who I am and what I wanted in a relationship.

This newfound power was the culmination of my sexual experiences, and my transition into a pimp marked the fulfillment of my apprenticeship of sin in my sexuality.

HYPOCRISY

I have found prison to be one of the most spiritual places I have ever experienced, at least in my very limited life travels.

Not only because of the searching and seeking that most people do in moments of despair, but also because of the exposure to various beliefs, ideas, and viewpoints you can receive. When I first arrived at D.C. Jail in 1998, I was surprised to find so many expressions of spirituality. There were a lot of guys who held bible study, read the bible openly, and professed to be in studies to join the ministry. There was a communal prayer that inmates held nightly on the tier, and all the men held hands as they closed their eyes in prayer.

There was also an older African lady who would come and hold bible study with all of the men right on the tier, and everyone would sing songs with her and talk about the bible. I found a few moments of peace in these bible studies, but I was dealing with so many emotions at the time I didn't know how to truly be at peace. By the time I was transferred to federal prison, I was mad at the world. I was angry at "the system" and how it had treated me, and I wanted the world to know it.

I also told myself I was done with religion; the pastor from my cousin's church promised to write a letter to my judge and come to court for me, but in the end he was nowhere to be found. Plus, I questioned where God was when I got this unfair sentence for my first adult offense.

I felt like God "let me" go to prison for my first adult charge, even though I personally knew several people who stole, robbed, and murdered, but never spent a day in prison. I couldn't understand it, and so I chose to believe what I thought about God was a lie.

One day, one of the men who was at the prison invited me and a bunch of other young guys to the Nation of Islam service. I had vaguely heard of the Nation of Islam, but I knew little about what they believed. My exposure to their organization was limited to what I saw in the movie about Malcolm X and the men I saw around D.C. selling newspapers, bean pies, and incense.

I had even attended the Million Man March with my brothers and my Dad, but I still knew very little about the organization and what they stood for.

When I arrived at the service I was greeted by several well-groomed men; their boots were shined, their pants were creased, and they had on bowties over their well-pressed shirts. The service came to order with one of the men reciting a short prayer. Then one man introduced himself as the student minister at the prison.

He began to talk about the condition of black America, about how oppressed we were and how we had learned to re-create this oppression in our homes and our communities.

He began to explain to us that this oppression was designed for use against us by white men, whose ultimate aim was world domination. He then related that concept to current events that were happening, and, also to the circumstances of our current incarceration. Then we watched a video of Minister Louis Farrakhan that further explained some of these concepts.

I watched the video with awe, excited by the prospect of building this uplifted black community the minister spoke of, and grateful there was this body of people that seemed to be so passionately concerned about my current condition.

I left the service energized, and I was given a book to read titled *Message to the Blackman*, written by Elijah Muhammad. Immediately I was floored by some of the statements made in this book.

In the book's foreword, Minister James Shabazz states "Muhammad is exposing Negroes for the first time to a brutal appraisal of their actual standing in the American community and what they can expect in the future from a system that under various disguises still grips them in mental, physical and moral slavery and after one hundred years of alleged freedom from the clanking shackles of southern plantation servitude continues to lull them to sleep with false promises of a bright tomorrow which never comes."

For a black man in the prison system, those words seemed to jump off the page and slap me in the face.

I had never considered my condition, not from the standpoint of my status in the "American community" that Mr. Shabazz spoke of. I began to question if I was in fact free, or if indeed I had been "lulled to sleep". I certainly didn't feel free, especially after receiving a prison sentence for my first charge as an adult.

It was bigger than that though; I mean, regardless of how I felt about the fairness of my sentence, at the end of the day I had to acknowledge the fact I had broken the law.

But how did this system, this culture I was born into, influence my decision? No preacher at any of the churches I had ever been to addressed these subjects, and I certainly hadn't read any books from any religious organization that spoke on the condition of black people.

Equally shocking was the demand that black people "throw off the shackles of the white man's Christianity and return to Islam, the religion of our ancestors". Now at that time I knew very little about black history. I knew very little about any type of history, except that which was taught to me in school. Even though my high school was pretty much all black, history was still taught from a Eurocentric point of view.

What little time was dedicated to black history, usually only during black history month, was dedicated to common names like Rosa Parks, Martin Luther King, and maybe Frederick Douglas. No one taught us anything significant about these activists' lives or the times they lived in, and they certainly didn't teach us about the God of our ancestors.

In the first chapter of the book, titled "Allah is God", Mr. Muhammad poses the question "can God be a mystery God and yet send prophets to represent Himself?"

He goes on to ask, "Who is that mystery God" and "can one teach that which he himself does not know?" These were deep, life-changing questions for me.

As I said before I grew up Roman Catholic, so I was used to a priest stating every Sunday to "let us proclaim the mystery of faith".

The concept of God as a mystery was a part of my spiritual fabric, and for the first time in my life I found myself struggling to defend something I thought I believed in.

Although it would have been much easier to put the book down and retreat into one of the Christian services the prison offered and where I would have been more comfortable, I could no longer run from the reality that was being placed right in front of my face.

I was a blind follower; beholden to that which had been installed in me since birth. Before I was old enough to choose, I had been baptized into this mystery, and now I had to decide if I would continue to hold on to it. Mr. Muhammad states "if one teaches a thing that he himself does not know, he can be charged with lying to the people". He also points out the dictionary defines the word mystery as "something beyond human comprehension". I decided to check that out for myself.

The first definition for mystery that I came to is "a religious truth that one can know only by revelation and cannot fully understand". I decided to reject this definition of God, and now I had come this far I needed to figure out who God really is.

Mr. Muhammad states "God is a man and we just cannot make Him other than man, lest we make Him an inferior one; for man's intelligence has no equal in other than man." As much as I liked this newfound teaching, this was one of the places I had to draw the line.

I knew I was no longer comfortable allowing religious organizations to classify God as some holy magic trick to be manipulated at their personal discretion, but I was also unwilling to believe God was a man. I would not substitute one falsehood wrapped in religious authority for another, no matter what the person's skin color happened to be. I was uncomfortable with a lot of the assertions made about the creation of man, of white people, and about an integrated society.

I was being torn between a social consciousness that I liked and a theology of divinely inspired segregation and discrimination that I couldn't subscribe to. For example, I was excited to read some parts of Mr. Muhammad's program for self-development.

I agreed "we just cannot depend on the white race ever to do that which we can and should do for self."

I believed we needed to "pool (our) resources", "make (our) neighborhoods a decent place to live", "spend (our) money among (ourselves)", and "build an economic system among (ourselves)". I was uncomfortable however, with how Mr. Muhammad defines white people. I had heard the term "white devil" before, but I did not understand the teaching behind it before reading this book.

Mr. Muhammad states "Allah has said to me that we are living in the end of the world of white rule, a race that Allah has made manifest to you and me as being real devils".

Up until this point, I thought that the term "white devil" came about as a result of all of the malicious deeds that blacks had suffered at the hands of white society, from slavery to the civil rights movement, all the way up to the present day.

I never imagined that Mr. Muhammad taught that not only did God sanction the creation of white people as devils; they were the product of a science experiment by an ancient scientist named Yakub. I could not accept this as truth; despite how angry I may have felt, I refused to subscribe to racist views. It almost seems silly to say I personally know a lot of good white people, people who have helped me and showed genuine concern for me and my family.

I say it seems silly because I've never been in a position where I found myself defending racial equality, but it has always bothered me that most white people, when accused of espousing racist views, will quickly reference the number and quality of relationships that they have with minorities.

But a relationship with someone doesn't always mean that your belief system works to further the interest of the other party, and in fact it may be quite damaging to those you hold as friends.

After all, domestic violence is usually found in the midst of a so-called loving, romantic relationship.

I guess that another part of me has also operated under the assumption that most people find being not racist as normal, and so I empathize more now with white people who try to define the quality of their convictions by their relationships with minorities, especially after being challenged to articulate my position on this issue by what I was being exposed to.

In spite of the racist world system I do still believe exists, I could no more blame the entire Caucasian race for all blacks had experienced than Caucasians could blame other ethnicities for all they found wrong in the world.

To do so would make just as culpable of the same bigotry I claimed to hate.

In fact, Mr. Muhammad makes a lot of the very same claims that have been traditionally aimed at black people in furtherance of racism, such as having a history of walking on all fours like beasts, living in caves and treetops, and being turned into monkeys, apes, and swine.

I had begun to participate in the services more and more, but I quickly became hesitant when I became familiar with these teachings.

I found myself at a crossroads, one where I felt my choice was to love my people and the upliftment of blacks at the expense of racial tolerance, by subscribing to and sanctioning a doctrine founded on racism.

I decided to stop attending the NOI services, although I had been changed by all I heard and read. I was intrigued by the religion of Islam however.

I had been invited to Jummah services several times by some of the men in the Sunni Muslim community, but up until that point I had no interest.

One day, I was talking to another guy from D.C. who was a Sunni Muslim, and after he explained a few things about what they believe I decided to attend their service. I already believed in God as an omnipotent, omniscient, omnipresent being with no equal. Muslims focus on this as the cornerstone of their faith. Tawhid, or monotheism, is the belief in the unity and oneness of God.

According to Sayyid Muhammad Rizvi, in his book *Islam: Faith, Practice and History*, "(t)awhid is the first part of the kalimah - the formula of faith in Islam. It says: La ilaha il-lal lah, there is no God but Allah". He goes on to explain the Sifat, or positive and negative attributes of God. Most of these I had been taught to believe since birth, with one major exception: as-sharik, or the attribute that "God has no partner or colleague".

This distinction was the biggest difference between my Christian upbringing, which was founded on the co-existence of God and

Jesus as Father and Son, and my newfound path in Islam, which forbids associating anything with God.

Another large distinction that came with Islam was the belief in the teaching and prophecy of Muhammad. Born in 570 AD, Muhammad was proclaimed to be the messenger of God at the age of forty. Muslims believe that the Quran, the prophecy that was revealed to Muhammad, is a miracle.

In her book, *What Everyone Should Know About Islam and Muslims*, Suzanne Haneef says that the Quran "was revealed to the prophet over a period of twenty-three years during the interval between his fortieth year and his death in numerous parts which bore an intimate relationship to the events through which the prophet and his community, the first Muslims, were passing at the time". I also learned about the five pillars of Islam; the declaration of faith, prayer, fasting, poor-due, and pilgrimage. After I gained a basic understanding of what Islam was about, I made my shahada, or declaration of faith. I was now considered to be a part of the Muslim community. I attended Jummah weekly, and I made my five daily obligatory prayers. I even began studying Arabic, in order to learn how to read the Quran. I enjoyed the sense of community and brotherhood I felt amongst the Muslims, but I also began to have some issues with my newfound path. I began to get frustrated with how much of my time Islam required. Between prayers, studying, and being in community with the other Muslims, I began to feel like I was losing my identity. I had to admit to myself I only wanted a little bit of religion, not this life altering process that Islam had become in my life. Mrs. Haneef describes this attitude of a good Muslim as taqwa, or God-consciousness.

She says "it refers to the constant awareness that one is always before God and that He knows everything concerning him, even his most secret thoughts.

This attitude produces within one such an intense love for God that he wants to do only what is pleasing to Him, such great fear of God that he tries to avoid doing anything which he dislikes, and such a keen consciousness of God that he never for a single moment imagines Him being unaware of what he does or that he will not be held accountable for all his intentions and actions." She also talks about the amount of faith that a person possesses, and the way that they express that faith.

She states "Islam makes a distinction between a person who submits to God's guidance by obeying His laws (a Muslim) and one who has the deep inner certainty of faith (a mu'min: one who possesses iman, faith, a believer), and indeed the difference is very significant. A Muslim (submitter) may obey God's laws without real depth of faith, while a believer both possesses this faith and acts on it." That is where I was at that time. I started off desperately trying to be a mu'min, to become the most devout follower of this new teaching I had discovered. I told my family and friends about my conversion, about all that I was learning and reading. But I never felt a real connection to God through any of the rituals that I was performing. Although I understood the words that I was praying, I didn't understand why I couldn't just say them in English. I began to feel like my prayers were a chore rather than an expression of my faith. I felt like I was becoming someone I didn't recognize, and that I began to lose a part of myself.

I started becoming less and less involved in the Muslim community, and eventually I stopped making my prayers altogether.

One day as I was practicing the piano, the director of the Christian choir approached me and asked me if I would assist them in preparing for a concert that they were putting together. I spent most of my evenings in the prison band room, and I had been practicing blues and gospel chord progressions.

I informed the choir director that I would try and find a musician capable of helping him, but that I couldn't do it personally due to my faith. He said he understood, and I began asking some of the other musicians at the prison if they would agree to help the choir.

Two of the musicians who I felt were competent enough refused to do it, and the only musician who was willing to do it was not very qualified at all. As they began to practice, I watched as the musician stumbled over notes and missed cues repeatedly.

I had never felt so torn in my life; on one hand, I had become a member of a faith group that expressly forbids me to participate in this activity. Yet for the first time in a long time, I felt myself being drawn into a closer experience with God.

I had heard people speak about having an encounter with God or an experience with the power of the Holy Spirit, but up until that day I couldn't really understand any of that, not in the way a person understands something through a shared experience.

To this day it still feels odd trying to put that feeling into words; the best way to describe it is that it felt like God pushed every thought, every input from my senses out of my consciousness. For the first time in my life, I heard God speak directly to me and ask if I was going to stand there and keep watching. Again, I want to point out I am very critical of so-called religious experiences. I have seen religion manipulated and twisted for personal gain so many times over the years that I will gladly own my cynicism.

But I can't deny that on that day I heard a voice inside my head speaking to me; I have since heard that same voice several times and I believe it to be God.

Some may attribute it to stress, schizophrenia, an imaginary friend, or whatever it is that they believe in, but nothing makes you believe hearing the voice of God is possible like a personal experience. In any event, I decided to jump in and help the choir with their concert. I started off by showing the piano player a few chords, and by giving the choir members a few notes. After a while it became apparent the only way the choir would have its concert was if I played for them.

After giving it very careful consideration, I decided to do it. I knew it would alienate me from my newfound Muslim community, but I had to do what I believed God wanted me to do.

Besides, after hearing what I believed to be the voice of God I really didn't care about what anyone else thought. The concert ended up being a success, and a lot of the inmates and staff were very pleased. The leaders in the Muslim community were not pleased at all though. They asked to meet with me, and they told me that as a Muslim I couldn't do those types of things. I had had enough, and I told them I was no longer a Muslim. The same men who had been so close to me now would walk past me without even speaking to me. I did start playing the piano for the church on Sundays, and I tried to learn all I could about church music. One weekend, a woman came to the prison to do a music workshop with the choir. She played the piano and sang, and she began showing me different piano techniques to use. After practice, she began to talk to me about becoming a minister of music when I returned to the streets. I thanked her and told her I would consider it, but I never really gave it much thought. I was released a few months later, and I fell into my routine. One day, a relative asked my mom to ask me if I would consider playing the piano for their church. At first I was apprehensive, but when she mentioned that the church would pay me I figured that I would at least give it a try. I played at that church for a few months, and was offered a job at another church. I continued to hone my skills over time, and as I got better and networked with more people the job offers continued to pour in.

At one point in time I was making $500 a Sunday, and although I wasn't the highest paid musician around I felt like that wasn't too bad for something I had picked up in prison.

My lifestyle did not reflect what I appeared to be on Sundays, however. I was still selling drugs and smoking weed, and later I began pimping.

I even brought some of the women who worked for me to church sometimes; I'm sure the people at the church wondered who these women were, but they never said anything to me about it. Often I would show up to service late, hung-over, and sometimes even reeking of alcohol. I've also met women in church who would later come to work for me. I've been to a church where a woman flashed her tongue ring at me from the choir stand, and I let her perform oral sex on me in the parking lot.

I've been introduced to a lot of women through churches I traveled to-grandmothers, mothers, aunts, sisters and cousins have all either tried to get with me or introduce me to a relative of theirs, and on more than one occasion I took them up on their offer.

As the saying goes, I was at church but I wasn't in church. God seemed so far away from all that was going on with me, and very few pastors, ministers, and evangelists at the various churches seemed to genuinely care about my life or any of the things I was going through. I got fired by one or two churches, and I slipped further into the streets.

Eventually, I stopped playing for churches altogether. In Matthew 6:24, Jesus says, no man can serve two masters: for he will hate the one, and love the other; or else he will hold on to the one and despise the other. I had made it clear what I was going to serve: fast money, the fast life, and all that came with it. And I was determined to hold on as tight as I could, for as long as I could.

DISFUNCTION

I don't think most people in America really understand what it feels like to be on the business end of the criminal justice system. I'm not talking about the broad complaints that are hurled at law enforcement on behalf of the black community as an attempt to win political favor; rather, I am referencing the specific practices and policies that are being brought to bear on mostly black and brown, young Americans.

Some may feel the concept of fairness is subjective and is dependent upon your social status, economic background, race, etc. Others compare and contrast our policies with those of other countries as a barometer of equality.

But whatever your stance on this issue is, I think one of the greatest tragedies in America today is the manner in which our criminal justice policies are practiced.

I have witnessed many promising young lives permanently altered as a result of these policies, including my own. According to the 2015 U.S. sentencing guidelines manual, Congress enacted the Sentencing Reform Act of 1984 in order to "enhance the ability of the criminal justice system to combat crime through an effective, fair sentencing system." In order to understand the goal of the act, we must consider how Congress defines a "fair" sentencing system.

The manual goes on to state Congress "sought to avoid the confusion and implicit deception that arose out of the pre-guidelines sentencing system which required the court to impose an indeterminate sentence of imprisonment and empowered the parole commission to determine how much of the sentence an offender would actually serve in prison.

This practice usually resulted in a substantial reduction in the effective length of the sentence imposed, with defendants often serving only about one-third of the sentence imposed by the court." This gives you somewhat of a better picture of how Congress defines fair.

Now in my mind, it is clear the author of the guidelines manual - and by extension the agencies represented by it - have a clear bias from the outset as to how sentencing should be handled. After all, is there an objective way to quantify "confusion and implicit deception"? Furthermore, who were the parties that were confused and implicitly deceived? Was it the courts, the defendant, the American public, or a combination of all of the above? This narrative paints a partial picture of the prevailing mindset of Congress at that time, and it set the stage for what was to come. With this bias in mind, you can see how the Commission shapes the argument for the sentencing scheme these policies created.

By using language that describes the new model of sentencing as "effective" and "fair", and by claiming these policies will create "honesty in sentencing", one must naturally assume sentences enacted outside of these policies were ineffective, unfair, and dishonest. And what were these so-called deceptions Congress sought to remedy? According to the guidelines manual, the injury occurred when courts were allowed to "impose an indeterminate sentence and empowered the parole commission to determine how much of the sentence an offender actually served in prison." If we examine this statement, we can see how misleading it actually is. There is nothing indeterminate about any prison term I have ever heard of.

Prior to this legislation, courts typically imposed sentences within a range of specific possibilities, which allowed for objective review of offenders past history, mitigating circumstances, and relevant conduct post sentencing, in order to determine how much of a sentence was actually served.

This concept benefited not only offenders who were given a clear path to return to society through the incentive of rehabilitation, the parole commission also served as a de facto judicial review process via their parole powers.

This concept of checks and balances is the cornerstone upon which our county was founded, however, Congress sought to remove this layer of protection from citizens convicted of crimes. With the aforementioned in mind, Congress references the "substantial reduction in the effective length of the sentence imposed, with defendants serving only about one-third of the sentence imposed by the court" as a negative consequence.

This demonstrates how polarizing this sentencing scheme is. The distinction is clear: there are legislators who view sentences imposed outside of the parameters of the Sentencing Act of 1984 as confusing, deceptive, and unfair, and therefore wish to see offenders serve a higher percentage of their actual sentence, and those of us who are of a different mindset.

The Commission addresses this "philosophical problem", by stating that "most observers of the criminal law agree that the ultimate aim of the law itself and of punishment in particular, is the control of crime."

The commission describes the two differing approaches to achieving that end as those who believe "punishment should be scaled to the offenders' culpability and the resulting harms", and those who believe in sentences based on "practical 'crime control' considerations" that will "effectively lessen the likelihood of future crime, either by deterring others or incapacitating the defendant."

Again, we can see the implicit bias in the rationale behind this new sentencing scheme: on the one side, the commission makes the offender the focus of the argument, and on the other side the commission cites the reduction of crime as the main factor. This is the adversarial mindset that plagues the criminal justice system.

Somehow, the prevailing school of thought in the application of criminal justice came to the conclusion that examining an offender's conduct at every stage of the process of their involvement was counterproductive in moving towards the common goal of reducing crime.

I will expand on this paradigm a bit more later in the book as well, but for now I want to explore this conflict a bit further. The Commission divides the two approaches into categories: real offense versus charge offense sentencing. The Commission argues that the problem with "real offense" sentencing lies in the difficulty of crafting "a sentencing system tailored to fit every conceivable wrinkle of each case, because the system "would quickly become unworkable and seriously compromise the certainty of punishment and its deterrent effect".

In considering the aforementioned alternative, though, we must ask ourselves how then does this process become unworkable? For years, we have entrusted our judges with the power to determine a sentence. It has always been a complicated process, with an assortment of factors, circumstances, emotions, and issues all influencing the decision. This, in my opinion, is how it very well should be. Crime has an impact on the lives of everyone involved-the offender, the victim, and the community. Maintaining law and order is the foundation of any civil society, but most people have varying opinions about what that means. In the "black community", these varied opinions actually helped to create some of the "get tough" policies that we see in place today.

On one hand, criminal justice advocates have been critical of the effects that sentencing schemes have had on black and brown men for as long as I can remember.

On the other hand, most of this legislation came into play at the same times that crack ravaged black communities all across the country. Hard working, law-abiding black people were made to feel like prisoners in their own communities. I spoke on some of the violence and crime that I witnessed in my younger years, and I remember the period of D.C. being known as the "murder capital".

The result was that family members of some of the same people who were perpetrating a lot of these crimes began to cry out for the government to "do something". At the same time, politicians quickly learned that a "tough on crime" agenda was a surefire way to win an election.

More and more politicians began to tout their records on criminal justice as evidence of their electability; most were former prosecutors, who had become assistant district attorneys after completing law school, and had built their careers on the backs of the "criminals" that they prosecuted.

How, then, did the Commission determine a solution? The guidelines manual states that it took "an empirical approach that used as a starting point data estimating pre-guidelines sentencing practice.

It analyzed data drawn from ten thousand pre-sentence investigations, the differing elements of various crimes as distinguished in substantive criminal statutes, and data from other relevant sources in order to determine which distinctions were important in pre-guidelines practice.

After consideration, the Commission accepted, modified, or rationalized these distinctions." This is where the problem lies. We have already established the biased view from which the Commission started.

I believe it to be nearly impossible for a group of people to take an objective set of facts and determine a "one size fits all" sentencing scheme, especially when there is a bias towards a certain end.

The Commission claims that its categories are "relatively broad and omit distinctions that some may believe important, yet they include most of the major distinctions that statutes and data suggest made a significant difference in sentencing decisions". What are these distinctions that the Commission chose to overlook? The best example can be found in the guidelines policy on departures.

Under this system, courts may only depart from a guideline specified sentence when it finds "an aggravating or mitigating circumstance of a kind, or to a degree, not adequately taken into consideration by the Sentencing Commission in formulating the guidelines that should result in a sentence different from that described". Some of the factors, such as race, sex, national origin, creed and religion are properly banned from consideration.

Other factors however, are the exact type of mitigating factors that most rational people expect the court to be able to consider. The most relevant factor that courts are not allowed to consider is socio-economic status. This is the one factor that disproportionately affects minorities all across the country. There is ample evidence to suggest that poverty is directly correlated to crime; in fact, the federal government has itself published numerous studies over the years that corroborate that fact.

There is also plenty of evidence that minorities are more likely to live in impoverished communities than are whites. This is one of the reasons why we see the racially biased levels of mass incarceration that exist today. While the Commission appears to attempt to remove bias from its mandates, the courts are barred from acknowledging the economic disadvantage that discriminatory practices have created in communities of color. Young men and women who come from communities where crime had become a way of life face a "double jeopardy" of sorts, from the harm done by communities incapable of nurturing its members into productive citizens, and a court system that refuses to acknowledge the trauma of that experience. Included in that mindset is the Commission's prohibition on considering, "lack of guidance as a youth and similar circumstances" as grounds for departure.

Although this factor has the potential to affect all, as most statistics show minority communities have the highest concentration of broken homes and families, which results in the misguided youth that we see today.

One only needs to look at the juvenile criminal justice system statistics as proof; however, the Commission chose to ignore these facts in its "empirical approach". Other factors, like coercion and duress, are also prohibited factors, but it is far beyond my level of comprehension as to why.

For most of my life, I have understood coercion and duress to be not only mitigating factors, but as the cornerstone of an affirmative defense.

In fact, I would argue that courts have found these to be relevant factors not only in determining a sentence, but also in determining both mens rea and guilt.

I mentioned post-sentencing rehabilitative efforts in my earlier discussion about the parole commission; however, it is worth repeating that the Commission has given specific guidance to the courts that it may not consider any effort that an offender has taken to rehabilitate themselves when determining a sentence. Another factor that courts may not consider is "Physical Condition, including Drug or Alcohol Dependence or Abuse". Out of all the factors I have mentioned so far, this is the one I had the most personal experience with. While I was waiting to be sentenced on the conspiracy to possess with intent to distribute charge I got back in 1998, one of the motions that my lawyer filed was for a departure from the guideline sentence based on "diminished capacity".

According to the guidelines in place at that time, "if the defendant committed a non-violent offense while suffering from significantly reduced mental capacity not resulting from voluntary use of drugs or other intoxicants, a lower sentence may be warranted to reflect the extent to which reduced mental capacity contributed to the commission of the offense, provided that the defendant's criminal history does not indicate a need for incarceration to protect the public."

As I mentioned earlier, I was enrolled in mental health treatment after catching a charge as a juvenile a few years prior, and was subsequently diagnosed with ADD as well as depression. I was subsequently prescribed medication, which I took a few times before quitting and returning to marijuana. This was the foundation of the testimony given to the court by the doctor who had previously treated me. I was instructed to get a diagnosis from him by my lawyer in order to argue my case, but this would ultimately prove to be unsuccessful.

Although the doctor testified that in his opinion, my depression was the trigger for my criminal activity and corresponding drug use, the court found I didn't satisfy the requirements mandated by the guidelines, and denied my motion.

After I had exhausted any option for departure I faced a guideline range of 87-108 months, but because I pleaded to a "lesser charge" which only carried a maximum sentence of five years, that became my guideline sentence.

According to the guidelines manual, "nearly ninety percent of all federal criminal cases involve guilty pleas and many of these cases involve some form of plea agreement."

The Commission later said it "expects the guidelines to have a positive, rationalizing impact upon plea agreements for two reasons.

First, the guidelines create a clear, definite expectation in respect to the sentence that a court will impose if a trial takes place."

The second reason the Commission states is "the guidelines create a norm to which the courts will likely refer" in the plea bargain process. According to the Commission, these new procedures make honesty in sentencing "easy to achieve".

The commission declares "the abolition of parole makes the sentence imposed by the court the sentence the offender will serve, less approximately fifteen percent for good behavior. It is this "honesty", combined with harsh mandatory minimum sentences written into criminal statutes that bring about a ninety percent rate of guilty pleas. But what has been the result of this new sentencing scheme?

Per an editorial published in the *BNA Criminal Law Reporter*, Mary Price and James Felman point out that "on October 31, 2012, the U.S. Sentencing Commission issued a comprehensive report, 'Mandatory Minimum Penalties in the Criminal Justice System'".

This Commission, although comprised of different members, is the same legislative body that wrote the original guidelines and all of its subsequent versions. And what did the Commission find in its report?

According to Price and Felman when the Commission first examined mandatory minimums in 1991 it reported to Congress that "honesty and truth in sentencing.... is compromised [because] the charging and plea negotiation processes are neither open to public view nor generally reviewable by the courts"; the "disparate application of mandatory minimum sentences...appears to be related to the race of the defendant"; "offenders seemingly not similar nonetheless received similar sentences" which creates "unwarranted sentencing uniformity"; and "since the power to determine the charge of conviction rests exclusively with the prosecution for the eighty-five percent of the cases that do not proceed to trial, mandatory minimums transfer sentencing power from the court to the prosecution". This disaster we now see is exactly what the adoption of this new sentencing scheme was supposed to eliminate.

Many changes have come about since the guidelines were first adopted; most notably, in 2005 the Supreme Court's decision in United States v. Booker shifted the sentencing guidelines from mandatory to an advisory role.

This was a partial acknowledgment of some of the problems these policies created; however, it did not resolve many of the most serious issues.

Despite the well-documented miscarriages of justice that were reported in 1991, the Commission, and by extension Congress, has done very little to rectify the myriad of problems that still exist, even in the face of United States v. Booker. As the editorial notes, the 2012 report demonstrates how the injustice has continued.

Among the most egregious: "certain mandatory minimums apply too broadly, are set too high, or both to warrant the prescribed mandatory minimum penalty for the full range of offenders who could be prosecuted under the particular criminal statute", "the 'structure and severity of mandatory minimum penalties' do not account for mitigating circumstances that might justify a lower sentence", and "'factors triggering the mandatory minimum' do not always 'warrant the proscribed mandatory minimum penalty' when considered in light of "the individualized circumstances of the offense or the offender".

The editorial also points out other statistics contained in the Commission's report, such as: since fiscal year 1990, not only has there been an increased reliance on statutes carrying mandatory minimum penalties (excluding immigration offenses) but defendants now are convicted of violating statutes that carry longer mandatory minimum penalties"; "while the percentage of offenders convicted of violating a statute carrying a mandatory minimum of five years imprisonment declined between 1990 and 2010, the percentage of offenders convicted under laws carrying ten years of imprisonment increased from 34.4 percent to 40.7 percent during that period"; and "as of September 30, 2010, 111,545 offenders in BOP custody were convicted of an offense carrying a mandatory minimum penalty, a 178.1 percent increase from 1995".

I included this data to provide a backdrop for my experiences. Like most people, I assumed when I was arrested in 1998 I stood a chance of receiving leniency from the court, due to my youth and lack of criminal history.

I was a first-time offender, in fact, and I had no idea the court would even consider sending a first-time offender to prison except for a violent felony or in the most extreme of cases.

My lawyer quickly informed me that I was mistaken. I couldn't understand why my case was even being prosecuted on the federal level. The amount of crack I was charged with had a street value of roughly one thousand dollars, which is not very significant.

Had the police decided to show up two days earlier before I cooked it, I would have been eligible for probation for the exact same amount of drugs. This was during the time that crack had a one hundred to one ratio to cocaine as far as the sentencing guidelines.

I was amazed when I went to prison and met so many men that had been caught with "half keys", or a half of a kilogram of powder, and had received roughly the same sentence that I had. Several changes to this policy have happened since then, and as of this writing the ratio stands at eighteen to one. Even at that level it is unfairly applied and affects mainly poor, black men.

I was also given a mandatory minimum sentence of ten years on my second charge.

Despite everything that I knew about the law after doing time before, I learned just how easy it is for the federal government to make a case against someone, and now I truly understand just how much power federal prosecutors have.

As the editorial points out, "we observe the use of mandatory minimums in particular throws into high relief the impact of prosecutorial discretion to make fact driven distinctions between offenders that have preset sentencing outcomes.

Discretion remains in the system, but it has simply been transferred from judges to prosecutors, who essentially determine the sentence in such cases".

This injustice continues for black men all across the country. Despite it all, this is the path my apprenticeship took my life on, and although I may not have understood all that was involved I could not change the disfunction I had chosen for myself.

Chapter IV

RETIREMENT

{POVERTY, HATE, SEX, HYPOCRISY, DISFUNCTION}

POVERTY

So the big question, I guess, is what does it all mean? That is the question that has plagued me from the start, as I began to conceptualize this book. There are millions of people with a story to be told, some experiences worse than others. As I said earlier, writing this book ended up being much more autobiographical than I originally envisioned.

I started with a grandiose vision that I would share my opinion of all that is wrong with the world, and my "fresh" perspective is what the world needs right now.

But I didn't believe any of the words written here or that I intend to share in the future could carry the authenticity I hoped to convey without providing the context of my experience. That being said, I will share one of my main motivations for completing the project - the desire to retire from my old lifestyle, and all that comes with it.

When I am eventually released from prison I face a lot of challenges - supervised release, life as a registered sex offender, parental responsibilities, and the demands of every day existence, just to name a few.

One of the most pivotal issues that will ultimately determine my success or failure will be my ability to monetize my skill set. The challenges of the "global economy" make that a daunting task on its own, but for a black man who is a two-time convicted felon and a registered sex offender, I fear what waits on the other side of the door for me. I refuse to sit around and do nothing, however.

I have very strong convictions about what it means to be a man, and one of the biggest of them is that a man must take responsibility for his life, his actions, and the choices he makes. In pointing that out, I have no intention of trying to elicit pity for myself or the current state my life is in.

Let me be clear: I have been a fool, a damn fool. I made a lot of horrible decisions over an extended period of time, and although I had plenty of opportunities to make better choices I refused to do so. I created this mess for myself, and as a man I can admit that. The white man didn't do it, my family didn't do it, I did this to myself. I can't even say I benefited from my life of crime, because even though I had some enjoyable experiences, I'm going home from prison flat broke.

Before I get further into my views on any other point, I believe that an honest assessment of all that has been discussed thus far is a necessary point from which to start.

I've met a lot of other men in prison that have had to face that same reality, and although most don't have the courage to admit it publicly, there are quite a few of us who have nothing to show for their time on this earth except the children they fathered and the destruction they left behind.

Although the concept of hard work, self-reliance and pulling oneself up by the bootstraps is an ideology commonly attributed to political conservatives, I'm sure they would be surprised to learn a large majority of young black men hold these principles at the core of their convictions.

I believe the most important thing for any man to do, but especially one in a situation similar to mine, is to be proactive in preparing for the future. I want to examine that idea from a few different points of view. The main thing I have done to prepare myself is to seek an education. This may seem like an obvious step, but for a person who is behind prison walls this is no easy feat. In fact, I think that most people would be surprised to learn just how difficult it is to learn while you are in prison. Prisoners are ineligible for federal Pell grants, and without them college is next to impossible for most people.

Some state prisons and a few federal prisons have contracts with local colleges that are willing to provide classes to inmates, but the availability and extent of these classes varies from prison to prison.

I was able to complete an entrepreneur certificate program through Kent State University, and an associate's degree in Paralegal studies through Ashworth College.

The certificate program was funded entirely by the federal prison that I was in, and even though I'm grateful for the opportunity I wish that I had been able to do more. My associate's degree was funded entirely by my parents, and the school that I selected was chosen exclusively because of its relatively low cost and flexible payment options. Inmates are not given access to the internet, so most of the new methods of learning are currently unavailable. I was unable to pursue my bachelor's degree for this very reason, in fact. The few schools that still offer correspondence courses via print charge inmates full tuition, which makes college unaffordable for all but a select few inmates.

Even the guys who may have a few dollars left from "the streets" are unwilling to spend that much money, especially when they don't have the same level of income anymore. Besides, it's hard to view a degree as a worthwhile investment, especially with the last bit of money someone may have, when the job market is so uncertain for "squares" who have college degrees. There are a lot of inmates who have accepted their fate as second class citizens, and are content with the idea of working low paying, labor intensive jobs. I believe that's why it's easier to get staff to purchase exercise equipment for inmates than it is to get vocational training. There are other men like myself who refuse to accept this fate, however.

For those like me, we understand the only path that will provide us the opportunity to shape a meaningful future and the pride that comes with it is entrepreneurship.

That is the main purpose of this book, and my main focus in all of my efforts to be proactive in moving towards a positive direction.

I wrote this book partly as a networking tool, as a chance to share a part of who I am, to help shape and redefine my brand from all the negative attention the apprenticeship of sin has brought me. It is, in a lot of ways an open letter requesting assistance from those who are able; a plea for help, of sorts, with the hopes that someone like a hedge fund manager, venture capitalist, or fellow businessman will at least consider giving me an opportunity to present some of my ideas to them. I live, sleep, eat, and breathe business and finance. I spend most of my day reading newspapers, magazines, books, and articles related to some aspect of business.

I understand business plans and balance sheets and a host of other business related subjects, but it all means absolutely nothing if I never have the opportunity to use what I know. I don't use the term "given the opportunity" to imply I am looking for a hand-out.

I am looking to expand my network beyond those entangled in the apprenticeship of sin, and so I desire the opportunity to meet people in the world that at times seems so far from the reality of what my reality was.

I know I can provide ROI (Return on Investment)on any of the business plans I have created. I would venture to say most black men who have ever been involved in the business of crime understand ROI in a way that most CEO's would never understand.

I am still amazed when I read about start-up companies that the term "burn rate" is actually an accepted practice; in fact, this is an industry-wide statistic that measures how fast start-up companies run through someone else's money, and some of these businesses are given millions of dollars just to "try something out". Many VCs (Venture Capital) invest in a hot new startup without ever feeling confident there is a clear path to profitability.

For black men from the street, this is a foreign concept; ROI and profitability are life and death concepts, especially when other people's money is involved.

For me, I would love to sell as many copies of this book as possible, but I would rather it provide me the opportunity to meet people capable of helping me to achieve my goals. I know that may sound strange to some, but you have to consider the context. A few years ago, I wrote to the SBA and inquired about their requirements for some of their loan guarantee programs.

To my surprise, I learned that I am not eligible to be a principal on any loan backed by the SBA until I am completely finished with my supervised release.

I've tried to rationalize this; after all, the SBA can't very well recover assets from someone who is locked up. But this argument fails to hold up. What's the difference between a guaranteed loan to a person that gets arrested and isn't on parole and someone who is? Aren't they both still in jail?

This policy basically guarantees that men like myself who are looking to start a business when they get out of prison are unable to do so, at least not by using traditional financing sources. That means even if I wanted to return to doing electrical work and wanted to do so as an independent contractor or under my own company, it would be difficult for me to secure financing for a truck and tools.

That is one of the hundreds of added regulations that make becoming a productive citizen after being incarcerated increasingly difficult. That is also one of the reasons why I need to meet people who are capable of helping to open this door for me.

In the past, I would have tried to find a way to make it happen on my own in the only way that I know, but I can no longer allow my pride to keep me from doing whatever it takes to become who I envision myself to be.

I also understand that there are thousands of other black men who continue to become entangled in the criminal justice system, simply because they lack the access to the capital that it takes to own a piece of their community.

What I think most people involved in the rehabilitation side of criminal justice fail to realize is that most people who were selling drugs don't want a government handout, per se. They don't expect the government to provide the income that they and their family rely on.

As noble the intentions of most people involved in this type of work are, the failure to understand the desires and the mindset of this generation of black men, in particular, has led to valuable resources being misused and ultimately wasted.

For those of you who truly want to help lower the recidivism rate, and help black men who are getting out of prison become productive, please pay very close attention to what I am about to explain to you.

The number one thing all of the non-profits, NGOs, organizations, agencies can do right now is provide resources and capital to those of us who aspire to create businesses, and then get out of our way. In my opinion, most black men who were involved in criminal enterprise were trying to achieve a life free from government handouts and poverty.

Many watched family members go to work and devote their talents to companies that treated them as second class.

Some grew up with older family members who were involved in the enterprise of crime, and while everyone is aware they are breaking the law, criminal enterprise becomes the family business due to many of the reasons I mentioned. Whatever the catalyst was, once they became involved in the streets, the money that came with it afforded them some opportunities.

Opportunities to wear expensive clothes, drive expensive cars, eat expensive meals, and so on. Although it is possible to save money, most men don't, at least not in the way they should. Most men know the government can come and take their newfound wealth at any given moment, so they try to enjoy as much of it as they can. Others simply can't see far enough into the future to believe in something worth saving for. Some just get caught up in enjoying the feeling of economic freedom, and the pride and respect that comes along with it.

This is the lifestyle you hear about in all of the most popular rap songs, the tales of opulence and machismo. It is that feeling, the longing for that lifestyle that is responsible for the actions men commit that ultimately return them to prison. Although I have no idea what the future holds for me, I can say I have never been unable to find a job when I wanted one. I may not have been able to find a job I liked or even a job I wanted, but I have always been able to find some type of employment. Most men mature and develop their business acumen, much in the same way people in the corporate world do. That means learning to save money, expanding their networks, and becoming more frugal as their responsibilities increase. Even so, the hardest part of retiring from a criminal lifestyle is accepting the pittance companies tell you that you are worth to them per hour. Not only is it a matter of pride, often the paycheck is not enough to meet basic expenses.

Even as my skills increased and my paycheck grew, I still hated the limitations that came with being an hourly employee.

I have accepted the fact I will have to get a job after I'm released, but I do intend to work for myself one day.

I believe that to be my purpose, not only because of my own desires, but because I believe that to be the only way to create true wealth for my family and my community. As much as I regret some of the things I've done for money, I don't regret any of the lessons that I've learned along the way.

I want to take all of the knowledge that has been passed down to me on both sides of these walls, and create a success story from it. In the Dec/Jan. 2015/16 issue of *Esquire Magazine*, Richard V. Reeves points to some staggeringly sobering statistics about the economic status of black America.

Namely, he states "seven out of ten black kids raised in middle-income homes will end up lower down", or in the bottom two levels of five income brackets, by the time that they reach adulthood.

He also points out other equally sobering statistics: sixty-six percent of black children live in America's poorest neighborhoods compared with six percent of white children; black Americans are twice as likely to be unemployed as whites, the same ratio that existed in the 1950's; and in 2013, the average net worth of black families was $11,000. Entrepreneurs haven't done much better either; according to economist Robert Elton, firms less than a year old have almost halved from fifteen percent in the 1970's to eight percent today, as stated in Reeves' article.

This is the reality of the world I will be returning to after prison. I spoke earlier about the economic incentives of selling drugs, and I think some points are worth reiterating, especially in the context of the statistics that I just mentioned.

I've heard the statistics on recidivism quoted frequently, but I don't think anyone who hasn't actually sold drugs understands just how easy it is to get started. One of the most attractive parts of selling drugs, especially at the "street level", is the low barrier to entering the market.

As everyone knows, the one thing that has been constant since the war on drugs began is the demand for product. Getting high is part of the American way of life, and there will always be someone who is willing to fill the demand. As I mentioned earlier, I personally have started off with twenty dollars worth of crack and turned it into over a thousand dollars in a single night. Once a person returns from prison, his or her ability to sell drugs increases exponentially. Prison is the best networking tool ever invented for drug dealers. Prior to going to prison for my first offense, my network was limited to the drug dealers I knew from the D.C. metro area.

After doing time in federal prison, my network expanded to men all across the country, men who I ate with and exercised with every day. I have been approached several times by men who like my character and wanted to do business. During my current sentence, one of the ways I have attempted to rehabilitate myself is by teaching myself Spanish. I'm not fluent as of yet, but I can hold a conversation and watch TV programs with a decent level of comprehension. Again, men were watching me and trying to figure out my intentions.

One day while I was sitting in the Spanish TV room, one of the Mexican guys struck up a conversation with me. He was an illegal immigrant who had been caught crossing the border with drugs, and was going to be deported once he finished his sentence. We began to hold conversations over the next few months, never about anything too serious but just polite conversation. One day, when we were talking, he asked me what my purpose was for trying to learn Spanish.

I explained I was trying to increase my skill set, and I planned to do some work as an immigration paralegal. He said "ok", and we continued talking about other things. A few days later, the prison put a Mexican guy in my cube; this particular prison was set up as an open dorm, in rows of two and three man cubicles.

Anyway, I began talking to him over the next few months I'd give him food and help him out whenever I could. He was also an illegal immigrant who had worked as a drug mule, and so he had nothing other than what he made in prison.

He began working in the kitchen, and would steal food to sell so that he could buy a plane ticket back to his state once he was deported, or at least that's what he told me. One day out of the blue, he asked me if I remember the conversation I had with the other guy about why I wanted to learn Spanish. I told him that I did and I wondered where this conversation was headed. He told me that some of his people had been checking me out, and that they would like to do business with me.

He then told me about a "friend" of his who could fly a plane to a small airport right outside of D.C., and that if I had someone willing to pick them up, then he could set things up for me. Apparently, this is something that he and his friend had done several times before, and now they were looking for someone they trusted. I immediately said no.

I didn't know if this was a set-up move for the police or not, but I wasn't going to ask enough questions to find out.

I was curious about what happened to the previous guy who they had meeting the plane at the airport before they asked me, but I had no intention of dealing with them so it didn't matter. Over the years, I have been approached several more times by men awaiting deportation with offers to do business. Most offered me drugs, although a few offered me women after learning I had been in the prostitution business.

Almost all of them were willing to deliver a load of product; with nothing more than my word as an assurance they would get paid. All of this from prison. Is it possible that some were government informants, who were looking to gain favor with the government by setting someone up? Sure. Do I believe at least a few of them only wanted to do business, with a black man they felt relatively comfortable with? Yes.

Even without meeting new contacts, most drug dealers who are released have earned the respect of doing time, especially if they didn't "snitch". Most of the other drug dealers they know who are willing to help them "get on their feet" offer little cash, but will readily offer to front them some drugs.

For a man facing the conditions I mentioned before, with little or no assistance from the agencies that are responsible for his post-release supervision, it is easy to see how a person returns to a life of crime. I also want to speak about the economics of prostitution.

I'll be the first to admit that out of all the topics that I've touched on so far, this is the one I have been the most reluctant to talk about in detail.

I pleaded guilty to sex trafficking of a minor, and to most, the fact that I was involved in prostitution, especially with young women who were underage, make me a horrible person in their eyes. Additionally, I will have to put my face, my name, and my address on the sex offender registry - what I call the creep list - for the rest of my life.

Again, I'm not looking for pity from anyone; I accept how this charge stigmatizes me, and I have no desire to plead my case or argue any of the facts of my case that I pleaded guilty to here. However, I will say the government has very little to do in order to secure a conviction.

I was two days away from going to trial, but after considering how little the government needed to do, coupled with the possibility of life in prison, I pleaded guilty.

Consequently, I hope as part of my efforts to be proactive I can be included in some of the work that is being done with the victims of sex trafficking, as well as the policies and regulations that are being proposed for prostitution as a business.

I do feel I can bring a level of honesty to the conversation that most are unable to share, partly because I have the actual experience, but also because I'm aware people already view me as a horrible person. That being said, we need to examine some fundamental truths. From a purely economic standpoint, the business of prostitution has an even lower cost of entry than selling drugs. All that is required to get started is a body; and while condition and presentation may affect the profit margin, these things are not "deal breakers". Pretty much anyone can find someone willing to pay them for a sex act as the old saying goes, "18 to 80, blind, crippled or crazy."

That was one of the deciding factors I focused on when I got started. I appreciated the fact that the women were a "reusable commodity" in a sense.

That's not to say I thought of the women as chattel, but the reality is sex and the persons performing the act generate recurring revenue without depleting any inventory. This is the difference between selling drugs vs. prostitution as far as business opportunity is concerned.

The same factors that make service-oriented businesses more attractive as start-ups than product-oriented businesses apply to criminal activity as well, in some instances. This is also one of the reasons, as law enforcement officers have noticed, that you see a lot of former drug dealers turn to the business of prostitution.

But considering these factors only describes the benefits pimps receive; the question most people usually ask is "what makes these women decide to give you all of their money?"

I'll explain some of the psychology of the relationship between a pimp and his women (even though the industry term for these women is "hoes", I refrain from using it out of respect) in a later chapter. For now, let's examine the issue from a purely financial standpoint.

It may seem like a foreign concept to most that a woman would decide to give all of the money they earned to someone else, when they were the ones who did all of the work. But if you really consider it further, that is the way most of America earns a living. Most Americans get up and go to a job every day, where they work in exchange for a salary and benefits.

There are also people who work as independent contractors, but the freedom of working independently comes with the added responsibility of covering all of your own expenses.

Each of those options comes with a host of underlying issues, and one only needs to look at all of the proposed bills in front of legislatures around the country to confirm that, especially in the face of this new "gig economy" that has come with the change in business structure and technology over the last two decades.

The prostitution business works in much the same way; a woman understands that when she chooses a pimp, he becomes responsible for every aspect of her daily life. He is the doctor, the babysitter, the HMO administrator, the chauffeur, and everything else that she needs. What she eats, how she looks, and what she does are all reflections of the pimp she is with.

That is why appearances are important in the prostitution world; not only does a pimp have to keep his women looking attractive in order to obtain clientele, a pimp knows that his stable is his best marketing tool in terms of attracting future "employees". While it is important for a pimp to look good in order to be attractive to women, a good pimp knows that any women considering working for him will want to know how she will be treated.

She will want to understand what she gets in return for her service, in much the same way that anyone who is considering employment for a company will review the benefits package.

I've "acquired" several women through other women who were working for me at the time; some would go and actively recruit, while others had associates who were curious about this new lifestyle and the "make-over" that came with 'choosing up' with me.

What was their incentive, aside from the emotional aspect? The women who were most committed to me and our lifestyle understood that increased revenue benefited everyone on the team. I've also encountered women who wanted to remain as "independent contractors".

They were willing to use my advertising model, and wanted me to provide them with transportation, in exchange for a split of the profits.

I would always explain to the women that doing it my way was more beneficial to them, because as independent contractors they would be responsible for all of their own expenses, including food, appearance, hotels, and so forth.

The women who were good at math usually conceded; often their resistance was more about a reluctance to concede control rather than a financial decision. Other women were more stubborn, and I would have to allow them to actually try it their way. In the "world" of pimping this is considered a big no-no, but I understood that sometimes the best way to gain trust is to let someone bump their head.

A few of the women who started off this way turned out to be some of the most dedicated to me later on, and although others chose to walk away altogether I understood that it was a "part of the game".

It is important to understand at least some of the financial aspects of the prostitution business, aside from the emotions that some may have, in order to truly understand those who are involved in this lifestyle. Of course, the added dynamic of underage women presents other issues. For some pimps who actually desire and seek these girls, younger women command a higher premium because they are more desirable. Often they are in prime physical condition, which makes customers willing to pay more.

It's also much easier to retain younger, impressionable women for much longer, which means young women offer the promise of more recurring revenue long-term. But what makes a young woman choose to prostitute herself, at least from a financial aspect? First, we have to understand the impact that this global economy has had on the U.S. labor market overall.

As technology has replaced the need for significant numbers of low-skilled employees, positions that were typically occupied almost exclusively by teenagers are being filled by adults who need the income to support families.

When you add in immigrants, who are typically low skilled workers, teenagers are finding that the entry level job market has become increasingly competitive. American culture is also centered around consumption, and teens are the target of billions of dollars in advertising revenue to persuade them to purchase the latest and the greatest in products. The result is that you have a low-skilled person with a high appetite for consumption of goods, and who often lacks the vision and the discretion to make informed choices. Some of the young women are dealing with a myriad of family issues as well. And, although some come from families dealing with substance abuse or other types of abuse, I've encountered lots of teenage girls who are looking to escape the "confines" of parental control.

In fact, one of the best things that a parent can do to ensure that their child will turn to a criminal lifestyle is telling them "if you don't want to follow my rules, you have to find somewhere else to live". That is music to some pimps' ears - not only does that pimp acquire a low-skilled employee with an appetite for consumption, their tumultuous family situation leaves them desperate for all that a pimp has to offer.

That's not to say that every teen who gets involved in prostitution is desperate, I'm simply trying to open parents' eyes to the role that they play in this issue.

I personally know pimps who target bus stops, shelters, receiving homes, and any other locations that vulnerable woman and girls are likely to frequent. What exactly does a pimp have to offer? Apart from the emotional aspect, a pimp offers these girls and women the ability to meet their immediate needs.

Food, clothing, and shelter is part of the cost of doing business as a pimp. Supply is high due to the factors I listed earlier, and competition from organizations looking to rescue those being trafficked is scarce.

Ask anyone who tries to provide services through NGOs or non-profits, and I'm sure they will immediately inform you of the overwhelming demand and budget constraints.

Simply put, if pimping and prostitution is your business, business will be good for the foreseeable future. So what can be done to fix some of these problems? The first thing that needs to happen is that America needs a collective reality check. We can't legislate these problems away, by locking up scores of pimps simply because it satisfies our need to put a face on the bad guy. That solution didn't work for prohibition, it hasn't worked for the war on drugs, and it isn't working in the sex trafficking industry. In fact, I heard on the news that Amnesty International is now calling for legalized, regulated prostitution.

This obvious step would provide women the safeguards and protection of government services, and would provide those who are inclined to profit from this business a chance to legitimize an industry that has existed since the beginning of civilization.

Second, we need programs that provide funding for young people to create enterprise in their communities. As a young man, I could find a basketball league or a football team just about anywhere. I even found a few low paying jobs when I really tried. No one ever explained to me that the skills that I was learning through criminal enterprise could be applied to something that I wouldn't go to prison for.

Imagine if communities of color began to put more time into encouraging our young people to become capitalists, instead of trying to distract them from reality with false promises of becoming superstar athletes.

While it is certainly possible for young people to become world class entertainers and sports figures, that is not the reality for most of the young people affected by the apprenticeship of sin. We also need to have targeted, detailed business plans to provide impoverished communities an income alternative to criminal behavior. I was watching the movie, "The Godfather," one day, which I consider one of the best stories ever told on film.

I had never really thought about it before, but the catalyst to all the conflict that erupted in the movie centered around the drug trade.

There is a scene in the movie where all of the bosses sit down to discuss a solution to the war that is going on between them, and one of the bosses stands up and outlines his proposal and how they should regulate the drug trade amongst their organizations. This boss wants drugs kept away from kids, and away from schools, but the focal point of his solution is to keep the drug trade in the black neighborhoods, because "they're all animals anyway". As popular as this movie is, I wondered why I never heard about any outcry from activists about this. Although this movie is fictional, from what I understand it's based on real life events.

Whatever the case, no one can deny the fact that most open air drug markets are typically in African-American and Latino neighborhoods.

It would also be fair to say that drug trafficking is a major source of income for many young men in these neighborhoods, regardless of how the drugs arrived there.

If there is truly going to be a change in these neighborhoods, there must be consistent, focused economic investment in the people that reside in these neighborhoods. Typically, economic investment has meant opening new mega-stores or new commercial developments. While those investments are good for the businesses, it does little to help the people in the surrounding community.

The idea is that these new businesses create job opportunities, but in reality, they are just another venue for people in that community to purchase and consume goods and services that they did not create and have no vested interest in.

This is the type of change I would like to help bring about, because the reality is as long as things continue the way they are now, thousands of young men will learn the same twisted ideas about what it means to be successful. They will be conditioned to be poor, to spend first and to save later.

They will learn to traffic illegal substances and seek their fortune outside of the law, because they will never learn how the system works.

Our girls and women will have no choice but to use their bodies as a readily available commodity, and will use that commodity as an instrument of commerce not because they want to, but because we have left them no other option.

They will learn this apprenticeship of poverty, because those of us who came before them refused to show them another way.

I refuse to stand by and abandon my family and my community to that fate, and I pray that this book provides me the opportunity to affect change.

HATE

I don't think I understood how much I hated myself before I came to prison. I'd like to think I didn't, because I took fairly decent care of myself, but after some deep reflection on the issue I realized I had learned to hate who God had created me to be. I spent so much time trying to change into what other people thought I should be or look like that I became afraid.

Afraid of what people thought, of what someone might do to me, and afraid of someone seeing who I really was, I spent some time watching the "Star Wars" series through a study that one of the chaplains put together for all of the inmates.

I had watched them all before at home, but I never examined the morality of the different characters' journeys through their imaginary world.

This time was different though, because it was the first time I could actually relate to the humanity of the struggle Darth Vader went through. I know on some level we all have a gift, an ability that was given to us for some purpose.

Regardless of your theology, this quest to understand our individual gift has been the source of angst for humanity since the beginning of time, and there have been countless volumes of prose and poetry dedicated to that journey.

What is it that fights on the opposite side of that struggle? Every emotion given to man! Sometimes it's doubt which causes us to be unsure about the purpose we were created for. At other times, it is our pride which makes us believe we are not as fragile and vulnerable as we really are.

Our fear is also against us, fear of what lies ahead and of the reality of how little control we have. Most often it is our anger that fights against us, charging our bodies and minds with rage over all we think and feel. It was in contemplation of these emotions I began to consider the journey of Darth Vader and the power of the dark side. The dark side, as the movies demonstrate, is the polar opposite of the force. Where the force is used to build, the dark side is used to destroy. One is clearly for good, and the other for evil.

But vary rarely is humanity that simple; although Hollywood has led us to believe people fall squarely on one end of the spectrum or the other, that is not reality. Life is a complex journey through some variation of the emotions I referenced earlier, and our responses to them dictate the level of faith we really have in our personal morality.

Very rarely are people on the team with the green or red light sabers; more often than not, we switch sides back and forth in the middle of the fight. But I do believe it's possible to learn and experience one side of this spectrum of morality more frequently and intimately than the other. For Darth Vader, his fear motivated him to become something he swore to destroy.

He believed he could gain control over something greater than himself by allowing his fear to manifest as anger. This is the part of his journey I could relate to the most. I was born and raised to do good works, things my family and community could be proud of. But I was afraid. I was afraid of the people around me, the people that looked like me and talked like me, but didn't act like me. I was a good person surrounded by an evil mentality, both at school and in my neighborhood. Eventually, this evil began to persuade my thoughts. I believed in order to control how others perceived me, I needed to become like the evil I saw. Rather than view the morals that had been instilled in me as boundaries designed to keep me safe, I began to view them as obstacles that hindered my progress.

Like me, Darth Vader did not arrive at these conclusions without influence or persuasion. In the "*Star Wars*" saga the Sith Lord was the clear antagonist, and he manipulated the emotions of young Anakin Skywalker with the goal of getting him to serve his own interest. Again, real life is rarely that cut and dry. Sometimes our villain is a class member or the guy who lives around the corner, and attempts to bring out the worst in us. Sometimes our villain is a family member, who betrays the trust that the relationship implies in order to tear us down further. More often than not, our true villain is ourselves.

We vilify ourselves by imagining an alternative version of ourselves that is based on the expectations of others. In our mind this new self will be better, stronger, faster, more attractive and well-liked by all. We suffer, because even the noblest parts of this imagined self are not immediately present in our lives. Maybe we allow all the opinions of others to devalue our opinion of our current self, and so we lash out. We lash out at others with the rage of our pain, fueled by our fears and with the intent of letting the world see how we feel. Sometimes our rage is an effort to hurt others as an expression of righteous indignation, with the mistaken belief that our actions will bring us empathy or a sense of justice. In some instances, we choose to turn our rage inward. We inflict wounds on ourselves far greater than any adversary could ever dream of, in places deep down in our psyche. We believe if we suffer enough, someone will accept our penance and grant us the happiness we feel we deserve. This too is a part of choosing the dark side. In the "*Star Wars*" saga, we learn the power of the discipline of the dark side lies in the ability to express your hate.

As young Skywalker transformed into Darth Vader, we see his natural abilities were influenced by the decision to use them not through the disciplined, focused way of the force, but through the unbridled destructive way of the dark side. As Darth Vader channeled his anger and hatred through his gift, his ability to use that gift for destruction increased. I came to understand this concept to be the crux of my apprenticeship of sin and hate. I've had time to do an honest assessment of my life, including my accomplishments and failures thus far. As I mentioned earlier, I wasn't a successful enough criminal to achieve the wealth and notoriety others have seen.

That is the reality of most of the men involved in a criminal lifestyle, in spite of the false appearances and braggadocio that has become synonymous with it.

In examining that reality, I began to wonder why that was the case; I certainly had the mental faculty and discipline to do so.

But as I considered my past as objectively as possible, I realized it was my unwillingness to do whatever it takes to be "successful" as a criminal.

Like Darth Vader and the dark side, the apprenticeship of sin requires you go further than you've gone before. You do things you've never done and swore you would never do, in order to be truly successful. I remember there used to be a pregnant lady who came to the crack house my cousins and I sold drugs out of. She usually had one of her other children in tow, as she shamelessly rang the doorbell.

I couldn't sell her crack, or rather I wouldn't sell her any. One of my cousins told me I was "tripping", because she was going to buy it from somebody else anyway. As much as I knew that to be true, I still couldn't rationalize this woman was going to smoke crack while she was pregnant. I'm not just talking about a few weeks pregnant either; she was visibly pregnant.

Maybe that was the good down inside of me fighting to the surface of my conscience, or a sign from God I really didn't have what it takes to be successful in this lifestyle. I still remember that incident like it happened yesterday. Years later, I was hanging out in my old neighborhood, when the same woman came walking through with her now teenage son. He is developmentally disabled, undoubtedly from his mother's constant drug use. I have come across lots of children who are "crack babies" since then.

I know some of the psychotic violence and the myriad of social ills we see are directly affected by the hundreds of black children who were born with cocaine in their veins.

The knowledge I was complicit in destroying lives that way bothers me. I've done some basic study on the chemistry of the brain, enough to understand what happens to developing brains when they are fed crack. Of course, I wasn't at a place in my life back then to look at it that way. Yes, I did refuse that woman, but

I have sold drugs to other people who I probably shouldn't have; People who were too old, too young, too sick, and too poor. I've exchanged drugs for merchandise I know was stolen from someone else, some of the items likely stolen from children. I've exchanged drugs for food that was meant to feed a family for a month. I've also exchanged drugs for sex with women, and I've even made some degrade themselves for my personal amusement. It gets easier after a while; just like anything else, you can get used to the dark side. Part of my lack of success is also due to my desire to live a "normal" life. Prior to my first incarceration, I never wanted to leave the block.

I'd sleep on the floor in the crack house, waiting for someone to ring the doorbell.

I had an all-black military flight suit I wore over my clothes; I liked it because it had big pockets for my money, and I could run around in it without getting my clothes underneath it dirty, which was important in case I decided to go out and party later on.

I used to call it my "work outfit". After getting arrested and going to jail, I told myself I was done selling drugs. I was twenty years old and expecting my first child, with no idea how I was going to support a family when I came home.

I did get a chance to meet drug dealers from all over the country though, and according to the rules of the dark side that was exactly what I was supposed to be doing, trying to find a "connect". This was my opportunity to meet someone who could supply me with whatever I wanted, if I was bold enough to try my hand at selling drugs again.

The only catch to that was I would have to be willing to subject my family to the possibility of me going back to prison again. In spite of all I had done, I loved my family and I know they loved me. I couldn't imagine putting them through that again. I was surprised by how many guys talked openly about going to sell drugs again when they got out. That's pure insanity, for a person to contemplate the same course of action that brought them to prison in the first place.

You either have to be comfortable doing time in prison, unconcerned about the effects incarceration has on your family, be totally disconnected from the reality of consequences, or a mixture of all three.

Some people had no relatives they were close to, due to various issues in familial relationships, or because they had "burned all of their bridges" and everyone pretty much gave up on them. Whatever the situation was anybody else faced, I couldn't imagine putting myself through that again. They say insanity is doing the same thing and expecting different results, and I was convinced I was in fact a sane person. But the power of this apprenticeship, of the dark side, was a lot stronger than I was able to understand at the time. I got out of prison and lived a pretty normal life, but the dark side and all I had learned began to creep in ever so slowly.

It started by hanging out with some people I had no business being around, in places I had no reason to be in, and eventually led to me doing things I shouldn't have been doing. It happened so gradually, over an extended period of time.

I compromised everything I wanted to become little by little, until one day I was right back where I started. I rationalized my insanity by telling myself I was doing the wrong thing for the right reasons. This was for my family, for my kids. It becomes easier to engage in self-destructive behavior when you create some fictional higher purpose as the objective of it all. Besides, as long as I wasn't on the block every day like before, I figured it wasn't as bad.

Before I knew it smoking weed became selling weed, and selling weed became pimping. When I really sat down and considered the time I spent pimping, I know for a fact my success was limited by my inability to be as ruthless as the lifestyle demands. Pimping requires a man to be the master of all of his emotions;

show me a sympathetic, sensitive pimp, and I'll show you a broke pimp. The relationship between a pimp and his women requires a mix of respect, discipline, and unrequited admiration.

Pimping is a mastery of the dark side, of the apprenticeship of sin. It is the transition from the role of Darth Vader to that of the Sith Lord. A pimp must understand how to use the dark side in order to train others and manipulate their will.

All women are attracted to different qualities and are usually inclined to choose a pimp who exemplifies those qualities, but whatever a woman's inclination may be, she must understand a pimp is only concerned with his money. Any attention and affection she receives will be directly related to the income she contributes and even then it remains in the pimp's discretion how much or how little she receives. She is not entitled to anything; as the saying goes "you stay to pay, you don't pay to stay."

Pimps must maintain absolute control over their women, and at no time should anyone under a pimp's control get the idea there is a democratic process.

Nor can a pimp allow a woman to believe he is more concerned for her than his money. A woman must understand her total submission to the will of her pimp is required at all times and in all things. Again, this was not my natural inclination, but like all other parts of this apprenticeship I got better at it over time. The women who worked for me bought into the vision of what I was attempting to put together, at least for a while. Like any other part of the apprenticeship, challenges began to surface that would require me to go further into the dark side. The biggest challenge would come in playing the role of disciplinarian.

Pimping requires a woman to submit, and when boundaries are tested a pimp has to enforce consequences in order to maintain control. There were always issues that had to be dealt with at one point or another, in part because of the amount of women I had with me at times, but also because of the complexities of my relationships with these women. Some of these women had been with other pimps before, but most of my women were "turn outs", or new to the lifestyle. Some of the women only knew me through the lifestyle, while others knew me through family or through social settings. This made certain women feel as though the rules were different for them and they deserved special privileges. Others believed they weren't getting the attention they deserved and I was showing favoritism.

Some just tested the boundaries to see what I would do. I refused to yell, argue, and scream though; I didn't like doing that in any of my previous "square" relationships either, although it probably would've made the relationships better. I certainly wasn't going to bring that into pimping, because I believed by responding emotionally I was teaching the women to act up in order to get my attention. Sometimes I'd figure out some "punishment" for my women, but more often than not I made it clear if you weren't willing to do what I wanted, then you could just leave.

I definitely wasn't willing to put my hands on them in order to make them comply.

There is a big misconception that violence is a part of every pimp's toolbox; while it is certainly true there are pimps who operate this way, most pimps I have met believe if you have to beat your women, then it's not pimping anymore.

That's not to say I have never put my hands on any of the women, but it was never done as a method of discipline. There were only three incidents I can recall putting my hands on women who worked for me in a violent manner, and in each case it was self-defense.

In one case I was defending someone else, but in the other two incidents I was attacked by a woman who became enraged about some issue we had, and decided to lash out physically.

I know it may be hard to believe, but there are quite a few women who believe violence is a part of a "normal" relationship between a man and a woman.

Some of these women came through their own apprenticeship, and grew up in a household where they were witnesses to or victims of violence and abuse. Others have been in abusive relationships early and often enough to become comfortable with the "love hate" dynamic that usually exists.

But surprisingly, it has become increasingly common for women, especially women of color, to physically attack their male companions as a way of expressing their anger. If you look at the way relationships are portrayed on daytime and "reality" TV, this point is reinforced almost daily. In fact, it has become culturally acceptable in a sense, to see women smack, punch, kick, and otherwise attack a man. This is a trend in relationships that has developed over the last twenty five years or so.

But it certainly wasn't always like this; in fact, at one point in time it was considered normal for a man to beat his woman as a means of correction.

As the women's independence movement grew and domestic violence became a hot button political issue, women understood and began to manipulate the fact men face serious legal consequences for putting their hands on them.

While I agree these safeguards are appropriate and necessary, the reality is some women have exploited this shift, in both the law and public perception.

Somehow, the popular perception has become that a man is just supposed to take it when a woman hits him, and somehow it's "cute" because women are physically weaker than men. At no time is it culturally acceptable for a man to hit a woman though; even if it's in self-defense, the odds are if the police show up, then the man is going to jail.

In some areas the police will now take both parties to jail, but more often than not men are the ones who face consequences when a dispute between them and a woman turns physical. Whatever the case, I was not going to put my hands on the women who worked for me, even in situations where I knew it would've been the best form of discipline and would've made maintaining order much easier.

I also believe bullying is much more taboo in the black community than it is in other cultures. Earlier I explained my views on how I was taught to perceive the issue.

I think black culture has very defined ideas about what manhood is supposed to look like, and we see that manifest every day as far as bullying is concerned. It's very hard for young black men to receive empathy from the community in this area.

One of the reasons is that blacks have been suffering at the hands of someone else for so long there is a certain indifference to seeing others in pain. We marginalize the experience of others due to the sheer volume of hate that surrounds us.

Another reason has to do with our unwillingness to accept weakness in our men. Masculinity has always been defined by a certain amount of bravado in all races and cultures, and for black men this concept is prevalent in every stage of a young man's development.

From our parenting style to the way we interact with one another, black men are hesitant to accept what we perceive as weakness. There has been a lot more acceptance and understanding over the last decade or so, as topics like cyber-bullying and suicide have become more prominent in mainstream culture.

One of the main areas we see this in is LGBTQ rights. If there is any issue the black community has maintained a majority conservative view on, it would be that of homosexuality. Because of the prominence of Christianity in the black community, most people's views are somewhat intertwined with the teachings of the faith.

That doesn't mean homosexuality isn't present in the black community, however. I know I personally grew up seeing homosexuality in and around my community.

I spoke earlier about the transvestite prostitutes who plied their trade both in the neighborhood where I lived and on the street where my family attends church.

There were openly gay camp counselors at the recreation center where I attended summer camp, and I also had two uncles who were gay. One of my uncles was an officer in the Navy, during the era when "don't ask don't tell" was firmly in place.

I was too young to really know my uncle Billy; he spent a lot of time on deployment, and most of my memories of him are of the visits we made to his hospital room as he lay dying from complications of AIDS.

This was during the late 80's, when the awareness of the AIDS virus was just beginning to spread and was still considered a "gay" disease. I had much more interaction with my uncle Mickey, my other uncle who was gay.

He had a long career with the federal government, and although I didn't really understand what he was into when I was young I knew he was always with his "friend". I never thought about it as them being gay, I just figured they were good friends like Bert and Ernie on Sesame Street.

They even babysat me and my brothers a few times; I remember my father seemed to be unusually tense every time they came over, but he never said anything to me directly about how he felt about their lifestyle.

As I got older I learned a lot more about my uncle Mickey, like the fact my family didn't care much for his partner because he was a deadbeat. I also learned my uncle used crack. My mother had to pay his bill before, including one to a very impatient drug dealer, and this made my father furious. I've also given drugs and money to my uncle; sometimes I sold to him, but more often than not it was a gift.

I considered it an act of charity, especially after learning Uncle Mickey was also dealing with complications of the AIDS virus, and eventually he passed away from them. I always felt like my

Dad didn't agree with my uncles' lifestyle, and I'm sure it must have been hard for him to navigate that relationship.

He was never openly rude and he even seemed as welcoming as he could be, but I have seen plenty of other people that were openly hostile towards homosexuals. Homosexuals have always been somewhat of a target in prison, and I've witnessed how complicated that dynamic can be.

Most people consider homosexuals to be an easy target; in the caste system of prison, homosexuals are only slightly above "cho-mo's", or child molesters, who are on the bottom of prison society.

That's not to say all homosexuals are "soft" however; I've witnessed a few incidents that ended badly for people who forgot picking a fight with a homosexual is still picking a fight with a grown man.

In fact, I would venture to say most black homosexuals have a decent amount of fight experience under their belt. From what I've been told, most have had to endure the punishment of male family members who thought they could beat the gay out of them, and that toughening them up would make them less gay somehow. They have also had to fight for most of their life, due to violence that is routinely targeted at them because of their sexual preference.

During my stay at one prison, I became cool with an openly homosexual guy from D.C. I'm not homophobic at all, and so I didn't have a problem with talking to him.

I think after being in the "adult entertainment" industry, I've seen just how wide the range of sexual preferences and activities is, and so just because someone is open about their preference doesn't mean he was the only one who enjoys something some wouldn't consider "normal".

The biggest issue I had was what other people had to say because I chose to talk to and be friendly to homosexuals. In one particular incident, I was sitting at a table I shared with another guy inside of the TV room. Prison is very territorial in that way, and the cultural norm is men have certain areas they claim to control. So it was with this table; although I shared this table with another guy, he believed himself to be in control of the table. Anyway, my homosexual associate and I were having a conversation at this table one day. Out of nowhere, this other guy comes up to the table and begins yelling and demanding I not talk to this "fag" at the table.

Now this was problematic for a few reasons; one, because no man has the right to tell another man what he can or can't do; two, because he was yelling; and three, because he had just disrespected me and my associate. I responded to his statements in kind, letting him know I was free to do whatever I wanted to do whenever I wanted to do it. After a few words were exchanged, he invited me to the bathroom to fight.

I told him I was on my way, and proceeded to get a shank one of my homies had. My homosexual associate also retrieved a weapon, and was stationed at the front of the bathroom ready for combat. Before things escalated any further, one of my homies had a relationship with the other guy and mediated the situation. As I approach the end of my prison sentence, I'm thankful that he did; things certainly could have gotten out of hand very fast, and in prison the reality is at any moment a situation can turn violent. It seems crazy to think someone would risk killing or being killed, simply because of their dislike of someone else's sexual preference. The sad truth is that it happens every day in America. Although several laws have been enacted to ensure people are treated fairly regardless of their differences, it's impossible to legislate hate out of the hearts of men. In the struggle to reverse the trends that create the apprenticeship of hate, the biggest struggle remains societal acceptance of individuality.

I spoke earlier about my belief that this struggle is much more pronounced in the black community than it is for the majority of white society. Part of it is the hyper-masculinity I spoke of earlier.

Education plays a role in that hyper-masculinity, as the idea of physical prowess being tied directly to your self-worth is reinforced by parents, teachers, coaches, professional athletes, and the media. Children learn to believe athletes are the ultimate success story, and because they constantly see the praise that is heaped on them, this becomes their ultimate desire.

Even on a much smaller scale, some parents make more time for basketball practice than math problems. Teachers are coaxed by coaches into letting a few bad grades slide for the star quarterback. This furthers the apprenticeship of hate, as those who are not athletically gifted feel scorned in favor of those who are. It also contributes to a culture in which men view all interaction with other males as a physical competition. White society has typically been more forgiving of its members; although the concept of "nerds" and "jocks" has been part of mainstream culture for years, technology has made a new generation of "nerds" into the new cool kids. Black culture has not received the education and benefits in this changing dynamic, thus a lot of black men are stuck in this old paradigm. I think one of the biggest developments I see in terms of minorities moving towards more acceptance of individuality is the change in rap music. Rap has begun to change into something much different than it was twenty-five years ago.

I grew up in the era of "gangsta rap", when the crack epidemic was at its height and the rap music being made reflected that lifestyle. At that time, it was a new thing; no one had ever made music that spoke so openly about the apprenticeship of sin in all of its various forms. The idea that record labels would have to begin putting parental advisory stickers on records was unheard of prior to gangsta rap. The music was violent, misogynistic, and full of contempt for authority and mainstream society. Rap began to change from party themed dance anthems into tales of street life and wanton disregard for human life.

By the time I reached high school, it was pretty much impossible to have a career as a rapper if you weren't talking about the apprenticeship. This was the backdrop for my own foray into the world of recording rap music. My raps were based on the reality of my life at that time; I wrote about what I was actually doing, what I was seeing, and how I was living. During that time, credibility was everything.

One of the worst things that a rapper could be accused of back then was being a "studio gangster", or someone who was portraying a lifestyle they weren't actually living.

Things began to change, however. Rappers began to have greater commercial success if they featured R&B singers on the hooks. Eventually, that led to rappers singing hooks themselves. As time progressed, rap became more and more commercial.

Catchy hooks similar to the jingles used in TV commercials began to replace the lyricism that the music once stood for.

The music took on a softer edge, as the music returned to the club and the artists who made these songs spoke less about the apprenticeship.

Rappers who wouldn't have stood a chance at success during the height of gangsta rap now had the ability to shine, as street credibility became less important to the sources of the music.

I'll admit I had a hard time adjusting to how "soft" rap music had become; not so much because I enjoyed the ignorance I was living in, but because I believed rap music had a responsibility to tell that story.

I felt as crazy as some of the lyrics were; rap was the only opportunity to present the reality of the apprenticeship to some who otherwise would never hear our description of our experience. Once rap became commercialized, the lyrics and the subject matter lost its artful mastery of lyrical skill and wordplay. But as I thought about it, I'm sort of glad that rap has taken this step to become broader. As a father, I like the fact that every song my children listen to isn't a direct reference to the apprenticeship. Although there are still plenty of songs that speak about this experience, it's possible now for a rapper to have success without being "hood certified". Besides, there is no authentic "hood" experience. This facade is part of the larger problem that the apprenticeship of hate and sin has created.

We have to begin to create a culture that does not force young men to define their worth in their ability to destroy one another. We have to be able to demonstrate emotional health through compassion and basic human dignity. We can no longer promote the savagery that has claimed the lives of so many.

The opposite of hate is love, and we must first learn to love and appreciate ourselves, in spite of all of our flaws and faults. Our culture must allow us the space to be different without being excluded.

We can no longer afford to allow our ethnicity to box us into a pre-defined way of life that traps us in a social slavery worse than any that an outside influence could bring to bear on us.

We must find value in each other, and learn how to communicate with each other in ways that are not hostile and threatening. We have to allow the free exchange of ideas and the concept of "agree to disagree" to become part of our culture, to be cool.

There must be more voices that speak out to end this apprenticeship of hate; not through marches and speeches after the effects of the apprenticeship of hate and sin are visible and present, but in our daily lives and actions. We must teach our children the wisdom we have acquired through the destruction that the apprenticeship has brought into our lives.

We cannot ignore the parts of the apprenticeship that threaten our lives and our children's' lives daily, but we must put our minds and our hearts to ending the hatred we have learned to feel.

We can no longer allow the dark side to be our resting place, if we are truly to end the hate and destruction we practice.

We must choose to exercise our power to change our future, lest we enroll the future generations in this apprenticeship of hate and death.

SEX

Out of all the areas in my life that I have gained a new perspective in, I would have to say that relationships and sex prove to be the most challenging.

After all, no one can really plan out matters of the heart; the whole process involves a bunch of factors outside of any one individual's control, but relies instead on the consent of two or more individuals.

In my quest to understand my sexuality better, I have tried to examine my past experiences in terms of being healthy or unhealthy, and while the conclusions I have come up with are certainly subjective I do believe some of my views are shared by some people with similar experiences.

Again, because I am aware that my being classified as a registered sex offender makes me a horrible person in a lot of people's eyes, I will use the freedom of an already ruined reputation to express some pretty unpopular points as articulately as I am able, with the hopes that at least something I say will influence the discussions and the decisions of policy makers.

With that objective in mind, let us now consider the current state of sexuality as practiced in American culture. For as long as I can remember, there have been discussions about the increasing expressions of sexuality in our media.

Every generation seems to push the envelope slightly further, and as the youth seek to enjoy the hedonistic delights of human flesh, the older generations of parents and grandparents choose to disregard their past in favor of regulation, modesty, and control. Sometimes this is done out of a genuine parental concern, a desire for young people to benefit from the wisdom of past mistakes and failures. In other cases it is a religious or moral

230

authority that causes these behaviors to be offensive. Some of these older people believe America is living in a "troubling time" and we as a nation have "lost" our identity.

I speak on this concept a bit further in a later chapter, but I feel the need to point out one of my favorite scriptures here.

In the book of Ecclesiastes, King Solomon says, The thing that hath been, it is that which shall be; and that which is done is that which shall be done: and there is no new thing under the sun. Is there any thing whereof it may be said, See this is new? it hath been already of old time, which was before us. (Eccl. 1:9-10 KJV) I'm always amazed by how many so-called Christian conservatives choose to overlook this wisdom. Although images of sex and sexuality are much more readily available due to the changes in technology, the reality is that people have found various ways to express themselves sexually since the beginning of time. Most cultures around the world have a clear expectation and definition of what sexual maturity means; in fact, most cultures view coming of age as a cause for celebration. America, however, has chosen the path of shame and hypocrisy. Let us first acknowledge the facts: a woman is sexually mature when her menstrual cycle begins. Her reproductive organs have begun to function in the fashion for which they were intended: pro-creation. All other issues aside, we must begin any conversation about sexuality with that fact in mind.

The reason being is that most who seek to dictate the morality of this issue would have us to believe that it is wrong for young people to satisfy their desire for sex, at least outside of the confines of a committed relationship. Biology tells us differently, though. With that in mind, let's examine the cultural and social aspects of sexuality.

Throughout most of history, women became mothers in their teenage years; in fact, I read somewhere that it's believed that Mary gave birth to Jesus around the age of fifteen.

Women were considered "old" to be having children if they had not married by the age of twenty, and some cultures considered this a sign that something was wrong with her.

Between advances in medicine that aimed to curb the high rate of death during childbirth that young mothers were experiencing, the women's rights movement, and the changes in society and income when it comes to providing for a family, the concept of what's normal has changed.

But what we consider normal in America is far from normal in many other parts of the world. Some would argue that the Bible and/or Christianity is the source of the cultural norms that we see in place today, but that argument would be false as well. While I choose to defer from going extensively into the facts about the reality of marriage during biblical times, I will simply say that it is a far cry from what we consider marriage to be today. Our concept of marriage and relationships isn't even consistent with practices and norms in place half a century ago.

Our idea of marriage is based on Eurocentric principles conceived in social experiments that have been created over the last century. Our beliefs about relationships have more to do with property rights and money than they do with civility and human dignity. Where, then, does that leave our teens? We know for a fact that sexuality is a large part of the images that companies use in their marketing strategy towards young people. Sex is implied or referenced in almost every program, commercial, song, and book that they are presented with. But how are they allowed to express that sexuality? That is the crux of most of the problems that we face. I know that for me, sex was a huge rite of passage among my peers. Even at fourteen years old, you were definitely the butt of everyone's jokes if it became public knowledge that you were still a virgin.

Most young men made every decision with consideration of how it would affect the opposite sex from the way they dressed, smelled, walked, and talked.

We learned to spend much of our time and energy in our quest for sex. Our women faced an entirely different set of hurdles, though. As I said before, I believed sex to be an obligation for women when I was growing up.

American culture has painted a picture of culturally acceptable sexuality to be a bunch of men who behave like sexually repressed idiots, constantly chasing behind morally pure women seeking the perfect marriage, or behind a savvy temptress who plays coy at all times in order to bring men into some level of compliance. Women must never publicly acknowledge that they actually enjoy sex, but instead women must always seek love and the security of a committed relationship.

This has begun to change, however, and as women have become much more willing to take control of their sexuality the rules of what we now consider normal has begun to clash more and more with the outdated models of old.

Even as a child I recognized the hypocrisy of what was being taught versus what was actually being practiced.

Although these paradigms have proven to be unrealistic statistically, there are still some who try to hold on to these outdated rules of sexuality.

Divorce rates are estimated to be around fifty percent, regardless of whether the couples are regular attendees of a weekly religious service or not, and over the last forty years we have seen marriage rates steadily decline.

As women gained financial independence the "necessity" of marriage became obsolete, and when combined with the other factors I mentioned we began to see more single women and single parent homes where the woman was the head of the household.

This is especially true in the black community, as the number of available black men continues to be scarce due to a lot of the social ills the apprenticeship of sin has caused. So most young women enter into this newfound world of sexual maturity confused, ashamed, and unsure of what is expected of them. Parental expectations are at odds with all that is happening in society, and so an already confused young adult begins to view the structure of parents and church as out of touch with reality. Eventually hormones and peer pressure win, but instead of enjoying the support of family the young adult stumbles through this process feeling alone. This opens the door to the possibility of several different types of unhealthy relationships, one of which is abusive relationships.

I spoke earlier about the changing dynamics in male/female interaction in relationships, and because young people mirror a lot of what they see, abusive relationships become a part of their apprenticeship. Young men have no clue how healthy, open communication is supposed to work, because they have been apprenticed into the belief that like most ways in which they try to express themselves, their sexuality is wrong.

They may have no idea what a healthy relationship looks like from a male perspective, and so they try to use movies and TV as clues like I did.

Others are dealing with anger issues in other areas of their life, and so they lash out at their partner with no fear of consequences from an absent father figure.

Some young men simply seek power and control over another, much in the same manner that power and control has been exerted over them.

Young women barely have a grasp on their own emotions, and so they have no idea how to interact with a romantic interest who has no control over their own emotions.

Because they fear the judgment or reprisal of the people that they love, many suffer in silence. Some young women choose to build relationships with older, more mature men. In most cultures, it's quite common for younger women to be in romantic relationships with men several years older than them. These older men seek the tenderness and beauty of young flesh, and the allure of a "fresh young flower". Younger women are drawn to the maturity and stability that older men bring to their life; even in America, this is how relationships have been formed for years.

Teens, especially teenage women, have sought out these relationships with older men, and if you watch any of the most popular movies that have been made over the last fifty years that chronicle teenage romance, you will find this to be true.

From adventures with fake ID's to slumber parties with young women talking about their romantic encounters with soldiers, it's all in there. But there was never a clear understanding about what is actually acceptable, and the ambiguity left room for problems. For example, just how young is too young?

State law varies on the age which a person is able to give sexual consent, but many states have now adopted the federal policy that the age of majority, eighteen, as the age at which one possesses the capacity to consent legally.

But how realistic is that, and where does that leave those who are under the age of majority and those involved in a relationship with them? In most states, sixteen is the age at which you can operate a vehicle on your own. We trust sixteen year olds to operate a machine which is capable of killing multiple people if handled incorrectly or irresponsibly.

In fact, a sixteen year old can be prosecuted under the law for vehicular manslaughter and/or homicide; that doesn't include all of the other crimes for which a juvenile can be tried as an adult. Many young black men experience this fate on a regular basis, and up until recently it was possible for them to receive a life sentence. Yet our legal system says that they lack the capacity to consent to contracts and sex alike. Although no one likes to acknowledge the obvious, this hypocrisy in our legal system does much more harm than good. By creating this legal "grey area" of teen existence, many teens feel the need to conceal much of their behavior in order to protect themselves and those involved with them from the penalty of law. Furthermore, most states have adopted into their laws the federal policy of "strict liability". This policy basically means that if you are involved in any type of sexual activity with a minor, the government does not need to prove as an element of the offense, that you had knowledge that the "victim" was underage.

That means that it doesn't matter if you were shown a fake ID or told a lie about their age (which many young people admittedly do), if you were involved with them, you're guilty.

Advocates say that strict liability is an important tool for those looking to combat sex crimes against minors, but by giving such broad discretion to prosecutors and not considering individualized circumstances, those involved with underage men and women are charged with serious crimes for conduct that by most standards is quite normal. This defeats the purpose of these so-called legal safeguards, because although prosecutions may increase, the community is not made any safer, and the reality is that young women will continue to seek relationships with older men, and vice versa. I had a discussion with someone about the alleged sexual misconduct that R&B singer R. Kelly was involved in years ago.

As noted in the February 2016 *GQ Magazine* article titled The Confessions of R. Kelly, Kelly settled a lawsuit in 1996 with a woman that claimed they had sex when she was fifteen years old, and in June 2002 R. Kelly was indicted for making child pornography after a video surfaced that showed a man that was alleged to be Kelly having sex with a young woman and urinating in her mouth.

Police are reported to believe that the girl was as young as fourteen at the time this alleged incident took place. Many say that R. Kelly preyed on a young, vulnerable victim, and that if he did commit these acts then he is some sort of sexual predator. Kelly went to trial and was found not guilty by a jury in June 2008.

I have no desire to argue the finer points of Mr. Kelly's alleged actions, but I wanted to use this high profile incident to bring to light a few points.

Although fourteen is quite an impressionable age, our legal system chooses to put teens in a victim role when it is legally convenient. If this same teen had encountered Mr. Kelly on the street, robbed him, and killed him, this same teenage victim would now be capable of forming the intent necessary to commit capital murder. How can someone be capable of committing a crime against an adult for which they can be treated as an adult, but yet be incapable of consenting to sex with that same person? How can we say that you are old enough to make life and death decisions with a deadly vehicle, but too young to decide what to do with your own body?

As the father of a teenage daughter and an uncle to a host of nieces, I certainly understand how emotional and irrational teenagers can be.

Please don't misconstrue any of my statements to be in support of grown men having sex and urinating on fourteen year olds; In no way do I agree with or support that, for my or anyone else's family. Yet I'd like to believe that my daughter has the maturity as a teenager to decide whether or not she wants to have sex with a celebrity and allow them to urinate on her.

As harsh as that may sound, I know that my daughter will face much tougher decisions on a day to day basis than whether or not she wants sex and a "golden shower" from some singer that she likes or from anyone for that matter, and that if she does in fact have sex with them and/or choose to sit still for said urination, I have to at least consider the possibility that my daughter wanted to have sex and/or get urinated on.

I'm sure that statement disgusts some people, who define this way of thinking as "victim blaming".

Many defend their position by claiming that turning an abuse of power into a matter of emotional choice robs the victim of dignity and compassion that they deserve.

The abuse of power as a means to victimize is very real in many situations, but it cannot be the de facto explanation for all behavior. To those who think this way, I counter that you are a large part of the problem.

You and your hypocrisy create the conditions that rob young people of a safe emotional space to explore their sexuality and express themselves, as they try to "figure it out".

Sex and sexuality has a component of trial and error attached to it, like most things in life, and while it may make us feel good to identify someone as an abuser or predator to appease our sense of morality, the truth is that sexuality is a complicated issue.

You want to know if what I'm saying holds any truth to it? I challenge you to hold a conversation with some teenagers in your family. Ask them if they would have sex with their favorite celebrity. I'm sure most of you will get a quick "no", simply because you are one of the last people on earth any teenager wants to be honest with about anything to do with sex.

That is an issue in itself; most of the people likely to read this book are not the type that a teen would be willing to talk to about being sexually active period, but for those of us fortunate enough to have relationships with young people willing to tell the truth, most will admit that they would more than likely have sex with their favorite celebrity.

Next, ask if they would allow them to urinate on them. Almost all will give you a quick "hell no", and it's not because they're lying either. Some may tell you "yeah, for the right price", but in reality I know plenty of rational adults who would answer that question in the exact same way. For those of you involved in psychotherapy, I challenge you to compare and contrast your views with Erikson's theory of psychosocial development.

I'm not suggesting that we readily accept teens having sex with grown men as "the new normal", nor am I suggesting that every situation is the same. I'm simply trying to acknowledge something that most people refuse to admit, consider, or talk about. Where you stand on this position has a lot to do with your ability to bring realistic solutions to the table.

I remember my high school years, and how many grown men driving flashy cars were waiting outside of the school to pick up their young girlfriends, and if you are honest with yourself, that is probably your experience too, especially for those who went to school and graduated any time before the year 2000.

We can run from the truth and pretend that it doesn't exist, but attempting to further criminalize and penalize human sexuality will not make it go away. It is critical that people understand these truths, because it is the foundation on which underage prostitution is built. I spoke earlier about the financial incentives of prostitution, but now I want to look at some of the cognitive, social, and biological motivations behind the women who choose to participate in this lifestyle.

In examining this issue, I want to examine two closely related theories of behavior motivation. One explanation of people's motivations is that they are a product of their cognitions, or of their thoughts, expectations, and goals. Under this theory motivations are divided into two categories: intrinsic motivation and extrinsic motivation.

According to different studies, "intrinsic motivation causes us to participate in an activity for our own enjoyment rather than for any concrete, tangible reward that it will bring us. In contrast, extrinsic motivation causes us to do something for money, a grade or some other concrete, tangible reward". Most people, in trying to examine prostitution, seek to understand the woman's extrinsic motivation, especially when a pimp is involved. They try to calculate the tangible reward that the woman receives, since a pimp requires that his women surrender all of their profits to him.

What most people fail to understand is that most women are motivated not by an extrinsic reward, but by an intrinsic one. As other studies note "we are more apt to persevere, work harder, and produce work of a higher quality when motivation for a task is intrinsic rather than extrinsic". Another popular model of motivation and the underlying human behaviors was developed by psychologist Abraham Maslow. Maslow's hierarchy of needs "suggests that before more sophisticated, higher-order needs can be met, certain primary needs must be satisfied." This hierarchy is usually displayed in a pyramid, with the basic needs at the bottom and the higher-level needs at the top.

At the bottom of the pyramid are the physiological needs, which include water, food, sleep, and sex; safety needs, or the need for a secure environment come next; love and belongingness, and the need to obtain and give affection are above that; esteem, or the need to develop a sense of self-worth is next; and at the top is self-actualization, or the state of self-fulfillment.

With these two models in mind, let's examine some of the dynamics of prostitution. Obviously one of the biggest incentives a pimp has to offer is the ability to meet a woman's immediate physiological needs.

For women and girls who lack these basic needs, the pimp presents an attractive option; not only is the pimp able to meet these needs, more often than not, the pimp is able to do so in a manner that the woman is attracted to.

I think it's also necessary to point out that Dr. Maslow lists sex as a physiological need, in the same category as food, water, and sleep. I'm sure that if you took a survey, most people wouldn't consider sex to be a physiological need. Certainly there are people who abstain from sex, some for most of their adult lives. Yet Dr. Maslow acknowledges in his theory the point I made earlier about the biology of our sexual nature, and regardless of your moral beliefs I think that it's naive at best to disregard this truth when confronting the issue of sex trafficking.

Too often those who work with victims of trafficking choose to approach teenage sexuality with kid gloves, and bring solutions that are unrealistic and unfulfilling, especially when these so-called experts have access to information that I pulled out of a basic psychology textbook that contradicts their whole model. Indeed the statistics confirm this to be true; according to one 2005 study, slightly more than half of women between the ages of fifteen and nineteen have had premarital sex, more than double the number of women in the same age range who reported doing so in 1970.

I will expand further on the sexual aspect of prostitution later, but I wanted to be clear about what well-published studies have shown to be true regarding sexuality, especially that of young adults. While a woman's physiological needs certainly have extrinsic value, understanding their relationship to the intrinsic value that a woman places on them is necessary in order to better understand the relationship between a pimp and his women.

Next, we examine the safety needs of these women. This is a large part of a pimp's incentive to his women. Most women who choose to work for a pimp do so because of the world he creates for her. He is responsible for housing her, feeding her, and clothing her, much like a parent for their children.

But a pimp provides a woman a measure of protection in the streets as well; not only in the course of their line of work, but in all of her affairs. The pimp is responsible for her legal matters, medical bills, as well as transportation to and from any and all activities.

While this is attractive to a lot of women who consider this lifestyle, it is especially attractive to young women who are underage. For them, the pimp is able to provide them the relative safety that they once felt with a parent. The pimp is also able to serve as an intermediary in certain matters that their status as a minor prevents them from handling themselves. I spoke earlier about parents who choose to evict young people, especially those who are underage.

Some believe that they are standing on principle by doing so but, in reality, these parents are the fuel that keeps underage sex trafficking alive and well. At 14,15,16,17, even at 18, what is a young person who has no job, no money, and nowhere to live supposed to do? Not only are they affected by the emotional issues they have with their families, now they have to figure out how they will provide for themselves. These needs, along with the need for love and to belong are what make prostitution and the lifestyle associated with it continue to grow. The need for love and belongingness is next in the hierarchy, and is based on the need for affectionate relationships.

While it is true that an affectionate relationship between a pimp and his women looks a lot different than the "traditional" definition, the underlying motivation is the same.

A pimp uses affection as a tool, as the incentive that keeps his women loyal and motivated.

Many come from broken homes or broken relationships, and so the pimp serves as father figure, lover, and friend all rolled into one. I think most people misjudge how powerful the needs for affectionate relationships are. Let's sidetrack and consider the reality of relationships in America today.

I spoke earlier about the divorce rate being fifty percent, but the amount of single parent households has increased to almost twenty-five percent, compared with thirteen percent in 1970. In fact, nearly sixty percent of all African-American children and over thirty-three percent of Hispanic children live in a single parent home.

These statistics show that traditional relationships, as America has defined them, have been failing much more frequently over the last forty years or so.

This dynamic has affected not only the adults in these relationships, but the children raised in them. I could spend a fair amount of time dealing with this subject alone, but I will consider it sufficient to state that broken relationships are the new normal. Understanding this paradigm shift is important when trying to deal with the mentality of those involved in a life of prostitution. One of the most often asked questions I get from people who find out that I used to be a so-called pimp is how I convinced women to come and work for me. Most people are surprised by the simplicity of my answer: I told these women the truth. We live in a culture that contains falsehood and hypocrisy in most, if not all, of our major organizations.

Our families, our communities, our churches, our schools, and our government are all founded on some noble concept that ultimately failed to be displayed in real life.

That is part of the foundation of the apprenticeship of sin as well. In order to become a master of the apprenticeship of sin and elevate to the level of instructor, you must first be willing to acknowledge to the world that this hypocrisy exists.

Again, that's one of the main reasons why this book ended up being much more of an autobiography than I intended.

I felt it was important to show my progression through the apprenticeship subjectively, in order for readers to have context for the solutions I present. This is also the reason why the truth is such a powerful tool in a pimp's hands. I spoke earlier about the alleged R. Kelly incident as a starting point for a discussion about sexuality and teenage responsibility.

In a lot of ways, the truth that a pimp speaks serves as a validation of this point, because while most of society continues to preach about the value of the broken system of relationships I referenced earlier, a pimp is able to offer these women and girls a lifestyle that allows them to navigate the reality of their experiences.

These women have seen the fighting and the bickering that comes with broken relationships, and they have witnessed the lies and deceit men use to fulfill their sexual needs.

Most have experienced the prying eyes and thinly veiled sexual advances of men as their bodies began to signal sexual maturity, and have felt the disappointment of abandonment that comes after allowing men to use their bodies and give nothing in return. I've had clients for my women who were doctors, lawyers, politicians, policemen, pastors, and almost any other position of trust that you can think of, and pimps must use the truth to prove himself more honorable and trustworthy than the men that these women encounter who live contrary to their position and power. The pimp offers the woman a "red pill, blue pill" choice, similar to that seen in the movie "*The Matrix*".

The options are presented as a choice between returning to the blissful ignorance of societal norms, or learning how to use that truth for their benefit. The pimp shows the woman that she can regain power over her sexual presence, by demanding that men compensate her for the privilege of using her body.

She understands that men have always sought to use a woman for sexual purposes, and that the only thing she can control are the terms and conditions of how that happens.

Society has told them that a committed relationship is the only situation under which sex is appropriate, and then it does everything it can to prove that concept false.

The pimp puts this concept into a new perspective, by pointing out the fact that every woman is trading herself for something of value from a man, whether it be a wedding ring, the promise of family and the stability of combined income and the care that comes with it, or the spoils of romance.

The pimp then offers her a relationship based on truth, on terms and conditions that are clearly defined. The pimp demands her service and her loyalty; her body is the vessel through which she will generate revenue, and her mind will be made available to the pimp for the purposes of the apprenticeship. In return the pimp will offer her a love based on this new reality. She understands that the pimp doesn't love her; instead, she understands his love to be for the fruits of her labor.

To some this sounds crazy, but for some women the path to the affection they seek is unambiguous in a relationship with a pimp, and that makes the longing that she feels for a connection of some sort, longing that is a natural human desire, seem attainable. She learns to crave the affection that a pimp gives in exchange for her income, and over time she begins to thrive under this clear-cut system of expectation and reward.

As I mentioned earlier, most women choose a pimp who exudes qualities that they would seek in a "normal" relationship, and as the women begin to adjust to the lifestyle they become more emotionally attached to the pimp.

Most pimps maintain a household or "stable" of women, and part of the learning curve for the women is learning to share the affections of their pimp.

All the techniques that a pimp uses are rooted in psychology, with names like systematic desensitization, operant conditioning techniques, and dialectical behavior therapy.

Over time a woman begins to find her self-worth and esteem in her ability to function in this system.

Esteem is fourth in Maslow's hierarchy, and according to his theory this is the level at which women involved in prostitution will seek to determine their value to a pimp.

Self-actualization, the fifth step in Maslow's hierarchy is closely related to the esteem stage, because as women seek to define their worth in this new way of life they strive to become the best prostitute that they can.

They understand that the pimp places value on their ability to provide income, and that in order to be seen as more valuable they must be willing to do more, to provide more.

As the pimp continues to reinforce these ideas, the women under his control begin to compete for his time and attention. Because the pimp is only one man and therefore constrained by the limitations of availability, his women value the attention of a pimp as a precious commodity. This too is a tool available to a pimp in administering this apprenticeship. The women learn to deal with these emotions in a different way.

They become desensitized to meaningless sex with strangers, and to the jealousy associated with sharing a man with multiple women. Of course, this lifestyle takes an emotional toll on these women as well.

Some women adapt mentally to this way of thinking more easily than others, and more than a few women use drugs and alcohol as a coping mechanism. Society treats them as outcasts, because they don't conform to the idea of what they think women are supposed to be. For many, this causes feelings of regret and shame. The threat of injury from a wayward john is also a source of stress, and some women are beaten, robbed, and raped despite the protections of a pimp. Legal troubles are also a large source of stress. There is a fine line between legal escort services and illegal prostitution, and law enforcement officers constantly pursue women involved in the latter.

This is only a small taste of the reality of those involved in prostitution, and because most of the people who are involved in providing counseling have never been personally involved in the lifestyle, they are unable to function in their roles as counselors as effectively as someone who has.

So, what then, are the solutions to this large and growing problem of human trafficking? For starters, we have to change the way that we deal with sexuality in America.

We can no longer use tired ideas and methods and hope that our young people will somehow evolve into this romanticized ideal that has proven to be elusive in most of our own lives.

I'm constantly amazed by how many of these "professionals" who dole out sex and relationship advice are either single or in unhealthy relationships themselves.

Until we give our young people the freedom to command and control their sexuality outside of the collapsed framework of past ideals, those who are willing to tell the truth are able to exploit that truth for their own personal gain.

We must empower our young women as their bodies mature into womanhood, not absent of restraint but not pressed into the shadows either, by their desire to protect the men that they choose to deal with from the rule of law.

We have to accept the change in our culture, in order to acknowledge that there is no new thing under the sun.

Prostitution has been around since the beginning of time, and in the same way that we have acknowledged the hypocrisy in areas ranging from homosexuality to marijuana use, so too must we begin to expand our approach to human sexual behavior in America.

These common sense techniques are necessary, if we truly want to end the apprenticeship of hypocrisy and sin in our sexuality.

HYPOCRISY

My current spiritual path is the result of several experiences I've had during my current incarceration, and although the process hasn't always been pleasant I'm grateful to be at this place in my journey.

My spirituality is one of the biggest reasons I decided to write this book, and as I seek to put in place some of the changes that I've outlined. I believe sharing my journey in this way makes that more real.

I have met some amazing brothers along the way and had the chance to hear some amazing stories, about both the pain caused by the apprenticeship of sin, and about the wonderful grace and mercy of God. Throughout my time in prison I have been involved in the protestant Christian services as the music minister for the inmate choirs.

At the start of my sentence I decided to throw myself wholeheartedly into building a closer relationship with God, and I was determined to become what I thought a good Christian should be. At the jail in Alexandria, VA where I was being held, the chaplain ran a religious program for Christians. Every morning we had classes where we would study various scriptures in the Bible, and afterward we would hold discussions about what we learned.

We also had guest preachers who came in and spoke to us, and sometimes we would watch videos made by different preachers and teachers about their interpretation of Christian doctrine.

This would also be the first time I actually studied the different church doctrines, and I began to learn just how far-fetched some of the teachings are regarding how Christianity is supposed to be practiced.

Although I had been to different denominations of churches before, I never really understood what the differences were between them, or why they mattered.

One pastor that came in taught on the different categories of demonic spirits, including what their names were and their functions.

We watched videos of a Dr. Ken Ham, who tries to explain the scientific reality of the story of creation as told in the Bible, including the age of the earth and dinosaurs. None of that by itself was too far from what I considered normal or reasonable at that time, but as I began to yet again attempt to embrace religion I ran into the same problems. In order to become a "true" follower, I was required to surrender more of the logic and reasoning that made me who I am. Once I was transferred to federal prison, this became more and more troublesome. The first institution I was sent to was medium security; there were a lot of men there with long sentences, and quite a few of them had life.

There are plenty of reasons to be humble and grateful every day, but nothing brought that reality into focus for me like seeing the word "deceased" written in the spot where the release date is supposed to be on some paperwork that one of the brothers in the church had. I think I needed to see that at that time, because it kept the reality of how valuable life truly is in its proper perspective. I can say that spending time with the Christian brothers at that prison was the first time I had ever witnessed that level of fellowship among people of any faith. There were plenty of men who had violent, troubled pasts, but it seemed like those were the men who were the most peaceful and humble. There was a true brotherhood amongst the men; we ate together, laughed together, played sports together, and prayed for each other's lives and families. The chaplain reinforced this bond with his teaching style, and although there were men from all different backgrounds, the chaplain's messages were generally uplifting and unifying. I tried to surround myself with people who were on the same path as me, and although I still had reservations about conforming to a lifestyle shaped by religion, it became a lot easier to do within a community of like-minded people.

My new lifestyle would not be without problems, however. As I became more involved in my spirituality, I found myself alienated from the rest of the guys from D.C.

I've never been one who fit in to any particular social group with ease, and although I can proudly accept I'm "weird" to some, prison social structure added to an already difficult situation. I spoke earlier about the politics of prison, and the way social and communal groups are organized.

My spiritual path put me in direct conflict with a lot of the expectations prison society placed on me, and that put me at odds with a few people who were determined to maintain those norms. Some couldn't understand why I chose to alienate myself in order to be a part of this other community. Christians in prison have a reputation for accepting "undesirables" into their fellowship, and so that made some people question my morals and principles. Muslims aren't given the same scrutiny Christians are in prison; I guess because some view the different doctrines in terms of masculinity, and so they view Islam as a religion that allows its followers to be "tough".

Whatever the reasons are, this struggle was one I faced both internally and externally. Initially I continued to strive to be this vision of Christian maturity I envisioned, but over time I found myself beginning to socialize more and more with people outside of the circle of Christians I was in.

Part of that was due to normal human interaction, but another part of that was because I wanted to maintain some sort of reputation. Over time, I began to talk and act like my old self and the people I hung around, and although I still attended church I was no longer concerned with trying to be a "super-Christian". There are positive and negative aspects that came out of that part of my journey. In some ways, I felt weak for allowing my environment and the people around me to influence my behavior. I guess some of that is natural, but in my mind I was supposed to be above the peer pressure.

I feel like grown men shouldn't care what others think, and I hated how this test of my faith exposed that area of weakness in my character. But I also considered how much of that was simply a part of who I am as a man.

As bad as I felt about not following the standard I had created for myself, I had to learn to accept part of my old self is who I choose to be as a man, and be honest with myself about that. I wasn't this perfect Christian. I still enjoyed the coarse language and dirty jokes I had grown accustomed to over the years. There were parts of the old me I hated, but there were also parts of my experiences that are tied to my identity.

I found that as I allowed people to see this side of me, people began to open up about their own personal struggles, and I began to understand the ministry of Jesus in a way I never had before. I began to accept people as they are and for who they are, because I could now accept myself for who I was.

I no longer saw Christianity as a rigid dogma with exacting standards, but instead it became a call to enter into fellowship with people who were broken, people like me. This understanding of God was the beginning of a transformation, but I had no context for it at that time.

A short while later I was transferred to a low security prison. This prison was further away from home, and when you combine the difficulty I knew the distance would cause my family in visiting me, the reality of my sentence, and the mental anguish that prison causes, I was miserable. I was struggling to find hope, and I was looking for something to feel good about. I continued attending church services, and I got involved with the prison choir again as well. There was another piano player working with the choir, and he had some techniques I was interested in learning. I became more involved with the church and the choir over time, but as always there would be challenges to come. There were a lot of rules and regulations the inmates had put in place for the members of the church ministry, and I really had no intention of dragging myself through any of that. I enjoyed the music ministry, but I didn't need any added stress at that point in my life. There were a lot of "people problems" going on much like you see in any group, and most of that worked itself out over time.

The biggest problem I had was with the doctrine that the head chaplain was teaching. The chaplain spent a fair amount of time teaching against the concept of the trinity, or one God in three persons. He taught that there was only one God, Jesus Christ, who was all three persons of the trinity. He supported his teaching with scriptures, and referred to both the Old and the New Testament as evidence of his position.

The main scripture he referenced was Matthew 28:19, Go ye therefore, and teach all nations, baptizing them in the name of the Father, and of the Son, and of the Holy Ghost. (KJV)
According to this chaplain, this was not authentic scripture; rather, it was supposedly added by those seeking to distort the truth. This version of Christianity went against all I was brought up to believe, first as a Catholic, and later on as a Baptist.
I had studied religion outside of a Christian perspective as well, but up until that point I had never really considered how that teaching came about.
After all, if what this pastor is saying about additions to the Bible is true, why should we believe it to be the "inspired word of God" at all? Now that my curiosity was piqued, I began to research this issue further. I began researching the history of Christianity, from before the adoption of Christianity as an official religion by Constantine, to the Council of Nicea, and beyond. I had never really considered Christianity and the Bible from a historical perspective.
In my experiences participating in other faiths I had heard about the fallacies of and additions to the message of Jesus the Christ, but I had never considered trying to research and gain an understanding for myself.
I'm always surprised at the number of Christians who have no idea how the Bible came about, or know little to nothing about Christian history at all. We teach our children all types of history in our schools - American History, world history, and even a little bit of black history. Somehow, the history of Christianity is not seen as having equal importance.
Out of all the documentaries, mini-series, and movies that have been produced - some which have been very successful at the box office - I have yet to see a major production about the history of Christianity.
I have a strong feeling this is by design, and although I'm hesitant to support a lot of conspiracy theories, I did have a strong desire

to discover the truth for myself. For the first time in my life I challenged my convictions by examining all of the evidence I had available without bias. Not only did I gain a different view on how the trinity came about, I began to view the Bible not as God's supreme authority handed down to man. Rather, I could accept it as spiritual guidance that was available for me to interpret for myself.

In my quest to prove the chaplain wrong I began not only to agree that the trinity is false, I also could see the falsehood in the way Christianity is widely practiced today.

Around the same time, I was sitting in my dorm reading a popular African-American magazine, and there was an article in there from a woman in ministry that detailed her perspective of some part of her spiritual journey.

I don't remember the specific details of the article, but I do remember that her views on spirituality made a lot of sense to me. I saw in the footnotes that she was a Unitarian Universalist, but I had no idea what that denomination believed. I asked one of the chaplains to pull up their belief statement and address from their website, and I was quite surprised by what I discovered. Unitarian Universalists, or UU's, didn't have any creed or set statement of faith per se.

There is no rigid set of beliefs that you have to accept before becoming a member, no strict dogma.

Rather, UU's "covenant to affirm and promote: the inherent worth and dignity of every person; justice, equality, and compassion in human relations; acceptance of one another and encouragement to spiritual growth in our congregations; a free and responsible search for truth and meaning; the right of conscience and the use of the democratic process within our congregations and society at large; the goal of world community with peace, liberty, and justice for all; (and) respect for the interdependent web of all existence, of which we are a part".

This was a huge shock to me because of what I thought religion was. Up until then, I had no idea that there were faith groups that not only allowed you to question and reason, they encouraged it. I had been conducting "a free and responsible search for truth and meaning" for a long time, but it had been on my own and without the support of a community.

I was excited to find a religious tradition that allowed and encouraged me to be myself, without forcing me to conform to some historical standard, ritual, or custom.

I was free to develop my understanding of God and my belief system as I saw fit, not based on what someone else told me I should think. This discovery marked a total paradigm shift in how I saw God. I began to study more about this new faith, and I decided to become a member. I joined the Church of the Larger Fellowship (CLF), which is designed for UU's at large that are away from congregations for whatever reason. I also took part in the lessons provided by the CLF prison ministry, which helped me understand my newfound path by allowing me to explore its history and traditions.

One of the first things I found was that UU's were supporters of the civil rights movement, and during the 1968 protests in Selma, Alabama, two white UU's, James Reeb and Viola Liuzzo, lost their lives in the violence directed at supporters of the march. This was one of the biggest reasons why I decided to become a part of this organization. The UUA continues to speak up and speak out about social justice issues, from income inequality to voting rights to police brutality.

Many of the majority white UU congregations across the country have chosen to support the "Black Lives Matter" movement, and some have even hung banners bearing that slogan outside of their churches.

In an article titled Ferguson: Up to Our Necks, published in the quarterly UU magazine UU world, CLF senior minister Meg Riley speaks about her understanding of white superiority through the lens of her interaction with police and other first responders.

She tells a story of how she and her community reacted to first responders when they arrived in her neighborhood, and how safe and peaceful she felt in her choice to walk outside while they were present.

She then makes the observation "and yet, if I lived in a different neighborhood, one where primarily black people lived, I might not have walked out sleepily to find out why police were congregated near my house.

Rather, I might have chosen to stay inside, fearful not of criminals on the loose but of the police themselves." She goes on to proclaim, "I have been conditioned from birth to see whiteness as safety- white neighborhoods, white authority figures.

My lived experience, my conversation with people of color, and my study of history has shown me over and over that this is a wild and cruel perversion of the truth. But the cultural conditioning is strong. Unless I fight it every day, white superiority seeps into my brain in slow, almost undetectable ways." I had no idea that white people who thought this way existed, much less a white woman minister who was willing to not only speak publicly about this mindset, but to publish an article about it in a religious publication.

That was startling enough by itself, and the fact that I was reading those words while sitting at a desk in federal prison drove those words home that much further.

White superiority is the prevailing mindset at most prisons; this is especially true when the staff is majority white, but there is an element of it in every manifestation of authority, educational experience, and mainstream religious doctrine, regardless of the race of the person in charge.

I have felt the effects of white superiority at times among groups of mainly African-Americans and other minorities, simply because of the system of white superiority that is part of the apprenticeship of sin in this country.

I used to believe because I listened to a white priest every Sunday tell me about a white Jesus, whose depiction hung at the front of this black church, I might be included in the club.

After all I was "articulate" for a black child according to my teachers, and I even had a few little white friends. But no matter how hard I tried, I couldn't escape the mindset that was attached to my skin color.

The conditioning that comes from generations of being the proletariat means that subservience is automatic for some, and so many black people still unconsciously accept their place to be mentally inferior to whites.

I'm still amazed by how often I see black men debating some issue or subject, and when they begin to seek a mediator to determine who makes the valid argument; they will most often look for someone who is white.

I've seen people in search of answers walk past college educated black men in favor of white men who don't even have a high school education. Exceptions to this rub do exist, of course - sports, rap music, drugs, pop culture, and the like are all considered appropriate questions for black people to answer. This mentality of white superiority is ingrained into black people so deeply that in us, too, it begins to "(seep) into (our) brain in slow, almost undetectable ways", as Min. Riley says. We teach it to each other, by teaching each other how to talk on job interviews so that we please whites, how to talk to white police, and other ways that we are expected to allow white people to exercise the superiority that Rev. Riley speaks of.

As I considered all of his, I began to wonder why none of the churches I had ever attended spoke about these issues. In fact, the only time that I had heard race, social justice, and spirituality taught as issues that are interconnected was at Nation of Islam services.

Most of the black preachers I had ever listened to were too busy trying to make the congregation feel something; church and religion by extension, became a vessel of escape from the social issues of the day.

Civil rights was no longer an issue to rally around in the black church and so the community activism that was once a big part of these institutions has all but ceased to exist. Everybody wants to get paid these days, and most black preachers understand that you have to put on a performance if you want to have any success in the business of ministry. I continued to try and understand what being UU looks like for black people. I found that the UUA has a long history of black involvement in its affairs, some of it inspiring, and some of it quite troubling.

In spite of any statistics or quotas that were or were not met by the UUA congregations, I didn't want my racial identity to be the deciding factor in whether or not I would become a participant in this "chosen faith".

If I only sought to participate in activities with people who looked like me or came from the same background, I would become guilty of the same segregationist mentality that white superiority created. Furthermore, this would not be true to my values; regardless of how many negative experiences that I've had in participating in groups where the mentality of white superiority is present, I feel compelled to be a part of a wider community of people who want to openly address and face the problems that exist between us.

I would paint a less than honest picture if I made it seem as if I don't feel some racial barriers are artificially inflated by preconceived beliefs on both sides of the racial spectrum.

More often than not, race becomes less of an issue when groups of people from different backgrounds seek a common purpose in a structured environment with clearly established rules. In my experiences it is the grey area of social interaction that causes problems.

One of the things that has been the most difficult for me in my interaction with white men is that they have become used to black men deferring to their supposed intellectual superiority that the apprenticeship of racism has taught them to assume automatically. It feels at times as if I, as a black man, am required to constantly prove each point and qualify each statement that I make under a scrutiny not present in interactions between white men.

I first became aware of these dynamic years ago, as a young teenager, while participating in events with the Boy Scouts. I remember sharing this sentiment with my father who then explained to me that he had been experiencing this same mindset at work every day for as long as he could remember. At that time, my father was a civilian contractor with the Department of Defense, and as uncommon as it is to see a black man work in technology today, it was virtually non-existent back then.

On the other hand, I have received negative attitudes from black people as well; for espousing some of the same ideals that UU's affirm in their seven principles. I spoke earlier about the bravado and machismo expected of black males, from the beginning of their childhood. "Justice, equity, and compassion in human relations" is the polar opposite of what most men from black communities learn which the foundation is for a lot of the black on black violence that you see today.

Although these are basic humane principles, creating a culture and society where these principles are valued is the real challenge. That requires finding value in those who think, talk, act, look, and love differently than you.

Many people profess to be "open-minded" and to seek a "better world", but the reality is that overcoming the bias and segregationist mentality prevalent in much of the United States takes a conscious, continual effort that most people are unwilling to give.

In his book, *Darkening the Doorways*, Dr. Mark Morrison-Reed offers insight on the issue of diversity amongst UU's. As liberal as UU theology is, UU congregations have struggled to diversify, and although the UUA has made several resolutions to increase diversity, most congregations remain majority white.

Dr. Reed states that "we are caught in a paradox and that there is a perversity to our call for more diversity. We do not want change. Having found a comfortable religious home - no small challenge - we fear it might slip from our grasp.

While it is important to be a justice-seeking and openly tolerant community, we also yearn for stability, familiarity, and people like 'us', companions we can trust.

We want a religious home where we can come when facing life transitions and personal challenges, seeking solace from the emotional wounds an unpredictable world lays upon us.

If who we are now - the community that has nurtured us - were going to appeal to more people of color and Latina/Latino and Hispanic people, it would have happened. Indeed, we find it a challenge to attract people regardless of color or culture.

Intellectually, we understand the need for change. Emotionally, however, we don't want change, at least not too much. Reluctant to voice this heresy, we say we want more diversity. What we would actually prefer is a change of appearance rather than substance. We would settle for looking different rather than being different." This is the heart of the issue that not only I face in my individual spiritual journey, but that communities and organizations all across the country are trying to figure out. I choose to seek like-minded people who are willing to give the same tolerance and understanding that they ultimately would want for themselves.

I choose to identify with those who refuse to conform to some religious code, and I will not be held captive by the ideals of any community where I have no part in deciding its boundaries. This concept is part of a larger quest to understand my identity on my spiritual journey, as I seek to define what makes me a member of the black community other than my skin color.

I have an appreciation of certain foods and music, but does that make all those who do part of this community as well? I would submit that the idea of any community based on racial identity is a fallacy. Black people enjoy a variety of experiences, backgrounds, and ideals, and the very notion that a community exists simply because of a shared skin color is rooted in white superiority.

While it is true that African-Americans have a duty to honor the ancestors, heritage, and legacy of those who survived the white oppression of the past, that alone does not and cannot make us community.

Nor does the continual struggle for civil rights; by maintaining the distorted view that equality is a battle only to be fought by those oppressed, society allows civility to be distorted into the "us versus them" mentality common in our culture.

Therefore, I choose to define my community as a step towards retiring the hypocrisy of intolerance that is founded in the principles of religious authorities I no longer choose to accept. I choose to seek God for myself, and while I welcome the guidance of others along this journey, I reserve the right to decide what I internalize. I'm sure that it bothers some people that the UUA, as well as other faith traditions, have a long-standing history of supporting homosexuality.

As liberal as the so-called black community is supposed to be, homosexuality continues to be an issue of internal tension. In my opinion, this mindset exists for two reasons - one religious, and one secular.

In his book, *Moral Purity*, Aaron M. Shank lists homosexuality as one of the "specific moral perversions to flee from", alongside bestiality, incest, fornication, the "woman-domination movement", and others.

There are certainly a lot of Christians who share this view, and because black culture has roots in the version of Christianity taught to their ancestors by their slave-masters, many black people practice the same sort of religious discrimination that was once inflicted on their forefathers.

This is not a hard and fast rule though; it's one of the worst kept secrets in many black churches that there are quite a few men, many in music ministry, who practice homosexuality. In fact, there are quite a few very popular Christian music artists who practice homosexuality but, like most things in black culture, talent excuses hypocrisy.

Nor is it true that homosexuality is a practice unique of European culture; one cannot make the assertion the people referenced in the Bible were Asiatic without accepting the homosexuality referenced among them as well, and even the most pro-black scholars have to admit that homosexuality is referenced in writings and teachings on black civilization such as *The Egyptian Book of the Dead*. Other people simply think that the practice of two women or two men having sex with each other is just nasty.

Again, this isn't a hard and fast rule; most men, especially black men, are more tolerant towards homosexual women than they are men. Homosexual men, especially the ones who behave effeminately, are viewed as soft and weak. The crazy part of it is that so many of these so-called tough guys are the first ones who become involved with homosexuals behind prison walls.

As I said before my experience in and around the "adult entertainment" industry has allowed me to see things from a much broader perspective than most, and I've witnessed firsthand how deceiving appearances can be when it comes to someone's sexual practices compared to what they profess.

Nothing drove this point home more than witnessing some of the great lengths men go through not only to obtain sexual gratification in prison, but to hide their activities from other men. If you ever want a good laugh, ask a homosexual who has been incarcerated to tell you about some of their experiences. As far as homosexuality being nasty, I'll be the first to admit my struggle with certain things. I was in the waiting room, the other day talking with a friend of mine when an openly gay man and his lover began to tongue kiss as they greeted each other. I'd be lying if I said I didn't cringe a bit myself. Although I fully respect their right to show affection to one another in that way, there was something about seeing that physical gesture that I naturally found unappealing. I think that by acknowledging that fact I can deal with those feelings in a much more productive way, however. While I may not find homosexuality to be appealing in some regards, I can respect others preferences. Just because I choose not to eat certain foods like chocolate and pork, I can still go to a restaurant that has those items on the menu. I also think that my own hedonistic experiences have helped me to have a much more open mind to whatever it is an individual chooses to enjoy with his or her own body.

Relationships are difficult no matter what your sexual orientation happens to be. As I said before, I have never been faithful to just one woman. I've practiced polyamory for most of my life, even before I understood it the way that I do today.

As of this moment, I have no desire to attempt to form a monogamous relationship with one woman. I know how much pressure I've felt over the years to conform to that societal and religious expectation, and so I did what most men do who have no honest desire to be monogamous: I lied. I lied about who I was and what I wanted.

In *Quest*, a monthly newsletter published by the CLF, Erika Hewitt makes an interesting observation in her article titled "Secret Keeping". She states "the risk of keeping secrets about who we are is a splintering of the self. It can be exhausting. Anytime you keep a secret about who you are, you have to present to the world a substitute, inauthentic front that, unwittingly, snares other people into your false world. Keeping secrets about who we are involves manufacturing a false part of ourselves. Eventually, it can exact violence against the soul - or outrun our energy to maintain it."

I understand this "violence against the soul", even though most men find my preferred type of relationship culturally acceptable. After all, most men would love to live at least a part of the lifestyle I experienced as far as women are concerned, especially during my time as a pimp. It's just not acceptable for men to say that publicly, especially not to a woman they love or are in a relationship with. Polyamory has begun to slowly gain acceptance, as the lifestyle receives increasing media coverage through articles and TV series.

Although it is no longer thought of as being tied to the swinger lifestyle and sixties era free love, it continues to be taboo to a lot of people, especially in the black community.

I also enjoy dating women outside of my race. Interracial dating is much more common today than it was when I was growing up, but I still wouldn't go so far as to say that it's now a normal thing. Right before I was incarcerated, I became involved with a white woman from Germany.

Although she eventually started working for me, our relationship started off on different terms. I used to be very aware of how people looked at us when we were out, especially black women. I know there is a perception about black men being "mesmerized" by white women.

Some black women have been through their own apprenticeship of sin through the effects of racism and white superiority, and so the stereotypical blue eyes and long, flowing hair that white superiority has taught us is the only standard of beauty represents an attack on their worth.

This woman did in fact have blue eyes and natural hair that reached down to her waist. I received a lot of cross stares and dirty looks from black women, and I always wondered if these same women would have paid me any attention if it were not for the woman I was with.

I also experienced the same dirty looks when I would go out with a Chinese woman I was involved with, and again there is a perception in the black community about black men desiring something "exotic". I also remember how much nicer white people treated me when I and women of different ethnicities were in stores or restaurants together.

I'm not suggesting that D.C. is so segregated and racist that interracial relationships still invoke the same responses they did in times past, but I can't ignore the hypocrisy I believe still to exist in some people. Some may feel I'm hypersensitive and I view all things through the lens of race, but I can only speak to my experiences and the way I perceive them. Understanding my struggles with relationships this way helped me to gain empathy for homosexuals in a way I never had before, especially for those that are "in the closet". I choose to believe they too deserve a God and a community that allows them the freedom of being who and what they choose.

I have no problem with people who choose to believe that homosexuality, polygamy, whore-mongering, or anything else from their interpretation of the Bible is a sin that makes those who are unrepentant worthy of the fires of hell.

As I choose to exercise my freedom to find God, I have to respect those who disagree with me. I do think it is a part of the apprenticeship of hypocrisy that Christians in America by and large support freedom of religion under the first amendment, when it is clear the God of the Bible destroyed more people and civilizations for worshipping a "false god" more than anything else. Yet these so-called conservative Christians protest abortion, homosexuality, Obamacare, and plenty of other politically motivated issues, driven by their moral and religious beliefs. That, too, is their right, however.

My problem lies with those who continue to try and impose their religious morality on others, as if they are the only ones who are allowed to have an opinion. For those who would cite their God as their authority, my response is simple: I reject your interpretation of who God is.

If your version of the Bible, Torah, Koran, or whatever else you believe in tells you that you are empowered with some greater moral compass, good for you. When you believe this gives you the right to determine what I am allowed to do or believe, then I have a problem. Of course, civil societies need laws, which I will talk about a bit later. I'll be the first to admit even in my subjective view of morality, I have not always held true to my own standard.

But the path I choose at this point in my spiritual journey reassures me the God I believe in finds worth and value in everyone, and so I am obligated to try and do the same. In the Spring 2015 edition of *UU World magazine*, Nancy McDonald Ladd explores this concept. In the article titled "Universalism in Practice," Ladd defines Unitarianism as "one God, not three, not mediated by Jesus or any other prophet - but one God".

She defines universalism as "the unyielding belief that each and every person is endowed with an original blessing that calls them and claims them regardless of circumstance or even of worthiness".

She goes on to say "if each and everyone is endowed with inherent worth and dignity then humankind cannot be categorized, and thus whole groups of humankind cannot be dismissed. It is not just one kind of person or one category of persons who are offered every blessing of life and every dignity."

This is the standard I choose to embrace, as I seek to unlearn the poisonous doctrines of my past. My spiritual journey has taken me to places I didn't understand at the time, but were preparing me for this part of my journey. I have no idea how any of this will play out in my life outside of prison. I've never participated in a UU church before, so in a sense this is my version of "jailhouse religion".

I'm still involved with the Christian services as the minister of music as of this writing; one of the things I enjoy most about being UU is that I can attend any service or no service at all, without being untrue to what I profess to be.

I am able to find value in all traditions, all things, and all people. As a musician from a Christian background, I'm sure this part of me will continue to be present in any expression of faith I'm a part of.

But for the first time in my life I have clarity about what I am and where I want to be. I'm aware as I grow I may change my position on certain issues, but that doesn't mean I have to change my identity as a person.

I can enter into a relationship with as many women as I am able to be mature, respectful, and honest with, without fear of a burning hellfire.

I don't have to accept the doctrine of original sin; rather, I can choose to freely accept the blessing God has given to us all. Most importantly, I can choose to connect with and share my blessings with others, not out of a sense of obligation, but because I know is what I was created to do.

There is a joy in accepting my place in this journey, and I intend to hold onto it for as long as possible.

I've heard of people finding this sort of peace in the worst of circumstances, but secretly I always felt like it was a polite way to mask their pain.

I still very much feel the pain of my past failures; even though I've forgiven myself and done what I could to make amends thus far, I can't pretend that the real consequences of my actions don't exist. I can choose what to do about it, however.

I can choose to be a part of the solution, to do my best to ensure that the apprenticeship of hypocrisy is exposed for what it is, so that we may begin the apprenticeship of love and finding value in each other.

DISFUNCTION

I feel the need to start this chapter out with a point I've made several times before in this book, one worth repeating here as I begin this part of my discussion about the apprenticeship. I am a firm believer in personal responsibility. I believe one of the great injustices we have created in our current culture is destroying any sense of accountability of one's actions to others. The concept of being interconnected is lost, in favor of the idea that it's all about self.

We exalt fame and individual effort above all, and we have learned to devalue the importance of belonging to a community; not an ethnic group based on skin color or racial identity, but a real community.

Yet this ideal of individualism is illusory; when this self-serving value system results in a failure or deficiency of some sort, people who were once fiercely independent find a way to blame society, the media, the community, or some oppressor for all that is wrong in their lives.

While it is true there are systematic, organized methods of oppression embedded into most of today's' institutions, any realistic assessment of disfunction begin with a person's willingness to accept responsibility for all of their own shortcomings and moral failures.

That is one of the messages I hope to convey throughout this book; although I speak at length about some of the flaws found in the institutions that helped shape my journey, I pray my readers can discern my bad choices are my own.

In no way do I desire to further the notion all that is wrong with the world is outside of our control as human beings and the choices we make.

I cannot absolve these institutions of their complicity in the systematic disfunction we see in so many areas, but to focus exclusively on that part of the apprenticeship of sin would be counterproductive, in my opinion.

Rather, it is through gaining an understanding of the decision-making process and its relationship to the apprenticeship of sin, I believe enables those seeking to rectify this destruction will be able to effect real change, in their own lives as well as the lives of others. With that point in mind, let us now consider the influence of our political system on the apprenticeship of sin. Prior to my incarceration, I had the chance to get a small glimpse into how politics really works in this country.

A longtime friend and colleague named Todd Clark hired me to do some music production on a video he was producing for an event, an annual banquet hosted by a very large and powerful political action committee.

These political action committees, or PAC's, are organizations comprised of businesses, foundations, and individuals for the purpose of making their collective concerns known to and heard by legislators.

This particular PAC, the Business Industry Political Action Committee (or BIPAC) contains as its members and donors some of the largest, wealthiest, and most powerful organizations in existence today.

According to their website, "BIPAC provides the actionable intelligence, strategy, and creative direction so our members and partners can deploy cutting-edge campaigns designed to meet state and national goals that support the overall national mission of educating employee voters."

They detail some of their other activities, claiming "their political team monitors election-related developments at both the federal and state levels, and are the go-to resource when it comes to making sense of how the changing political landscape impacts the American business community."

They also state their "Political Affairs team will work with your company, association, or state business organization to help develop strategies and methods that will achieve your personal goals." BIPAC lists two funds as means by which they can affect its stated goals: the action fund and the prosperity fund.

Their website states "BIPAC's action fund is a non-connected political action committee that provides support to pro-prosperity elected officials and candidates," and "each election cycle BIPAC interviews and vets candidates for federal office who are seeking support and endorsements from the business community."

They claim that their "Prosperity Fund provides an avenue for corporate, political, and civil engagement that provides unparalleled return on investment."

This fund is "made up of leading members of the business community, stakeholders, and partners in the states dedicated to the mission of increasing the political effectiveness of America's private sector job providers."

They acknowledge they are an "elite group of individuals" that "not only (provide) the means to fund (their) custom state-based political affairs strategy, but also (act) as the engine behind the country's largest business grassroots network."

This particular banquet was to honor recipients of the Adam C. Smith award for excellence, and is given to members of the business and political communities for the work they do in furthering policies supported by BIPAC.

The first time I attended one of these events I felt like a fish out of water. After clearing the metal detectors at the Ronald Regan building, I entered the atrium where the banquet was being held. People were mingling around, socializing and networking as the sounds of a string trio played softly. There were trays of hors d' oeuvres carried by servers, who happened to be some of the only people in the room who looked like me. In fact, I may have seen two other people at the most who were there for the actual event that were black. Outside of my colleague, I didn't know anyone or even have an idea of what to talk about, so I suggested he and I go to the bar and get a drink. My colleague assured me I could relax, but I was as relaxed as I was going to get.

I wasn't exceptionally nervous per se; it's just I was in the presence of government officials and captains of industry, and at that moment I had no idea how that could be beneficial to anything else going on in my life.

I had a job at the time in addition to my illicit activities, and so I couldn't see the value in networking with the people that I was being exposed to.

My colleague did have a familiarity with quite a few people in the room - because I have known Todd for so long I forget sometimes that he is the beneficiary of white privilege as well, not because he espouses any of the views associated with it, but simply by virtue of the color of his skin.

Knowing my friend, I'm sure he hates to think about it that way, but on that day he was the validation for my presence among all of these powerful, white people, much like I would validate his presence if we were in "the hood".

I always joke with him that he looks like the police anyway, and as much as he and I attempt to exist in a world not based on these stereotypes I have to acknowledge reality.

When we got to the bar, we ran into a man named Tim Timpkin, whose family business is responsible for producing a large number of the drive axles made on cars in America.

Todd asked him to tell me the story of how the family business was started, and as I listened I remembered thinking how matter-of-fact he was about it all. He spoke of the history of his family's invention, one that would ultimately shape the future of the automotive industry, as if it were something common. I gained some valuable insight by attending that banquet. One of the first things I began to see was how important politics really is, when it comes to business and the conditions that most people deal with.

I remember that one of the award recipients recited an old quote, "Get into politics or get out of business." Its one thing to hear about the power and influence that exists among these types of organizations, but it was sobering to see all these powerful people together in one place, to walk among them and to interact with them.

After a while I became more comfortable, and I was surprised to see how down to earth some of these people actually were to talk to. I think now that I was amazed by how naturally these people wielded their tremendous influence, especially when I thought about the helplessness and despair that was present only a few blocks up the street from that event.

I considered that world and the people in the world that I was used to, and I began to wonder who spoke for them at events like these. I wondered who spoke for the people who elected the government officials that were present at that event, the people that were the consumers of all of the goods and services provided by the companies and corporations represented at that event.

It was in considering this stark contrast I began to understand how blind I really was before. Up until that point I filtered every situation, every outcome, and every conflict through the lens of racial equality. This event helped to open my eyes and understand what really mattered in America: capitalism. Above all, America moves and breathes capitalism; once I accepted that truth, I could change the way I viewed all that was around me.

I could see the deception of racial politics as a means to control a group of people, and begin to develop the independence I have learned in all the other areas of my life. No longer did I view myself as part and parcel of a group when it comes to protecting my interests; rather, I began to understand that, in order to function, I must function much like a corporate entity. My decisions are no longer influenced by political groupspeak and the "us-versus-them" created by this disfunctional system;

instead, I view all relationships, organizations, and entities through the language of capitalism.

I think in terms of assets and liabilities, revenues and expenses. It is in these terms I wish to discuss the world we now live in. This particular banquet I attended presented an award named after Adam C. Smith, author of the book *The Wealth of Nations and champion of laissez-faire economics.* At that time, I had no idea who he was or what he stood for, but I do remember Todd used one of his quotes in the video we produced: "political freedom without economic freedom is neither."

It wasn't until I came to prison I sought to gain a better understanding of the economic systems of the world and their relationship to politics. In his book, *How Much Do We Deserve? An Inquiry into Distributive Justice* by Richard S. Gilbert dives into the mindsets behind economic inequality. He describes the concept of utilitarianism along with laissez-faire economic policy as the "moral foundations for a capitalist economy."

He interprets the teachings of Adam Smith to be based on individuals seeking personal gain as the best method to bring about benefit for the common good.

He writes on the "invisible hand" concept attributed to Smith, which is the idea that something unseen somehow forms these individual efforts into the common good of free markets. This system is not without negative consequences, however.

Mr. Gilbert describes the inequality created as a zero-sum society, and he references Mr. Smith's view "(w)here ever there is property, there is great inequality. For one very rich man, there must be at least five hundred poor, and the affluence of the rich supposes the indigence of many." Gilbert goes on to address the ideas about the role of government under these principles.

He cites Milton Friedman, author of *Capitalism and Freedom* as an example of the progression of the free market doctrine. He contends that Friedman supports the competition of the free market as the deciding factor for goods and services that governments should limit their role in the free market except to ensure fairness.

I began to consider these ideas, in a way I had been unable to view them before. I thought about these large corporations and the influence they were able to exert over both the marketplace and the government. As a realist, I think it's pointless to sit around and complain about how broken the system is, if you aren't making any effort to fix it.

To protest against the way the world works is an exercise in futility, and although it is sometimes necessary to do in order to bring about change, I think it's always important to be realistic. The reality is no matter what else is going on, those with financial resources in a capitalist society will always be able to control policy. Since my childhood I understood this about the world, even if not in those terms. As a black man, there was always some injustice to protest; a lack of opportunity here or a slight over there.

While I would never try to diminish the importance of the struggle against inequality that was fought by those that came before me, I found myself at a crossroads in my thinking.

I had begun to consider what skills I bought to this free market, and how I could increase my standing in it. I think I inherently understood this for most of my life. Although the concept of free market was exposed to me through selling drugs, the principles of free market and its benefits are very much the same.

In the microeconomic environment of the so-called black community, there has always been a huge gap between those with financial resources and those without them.

Welfare programs and government aid, while undoubtedly beneficial to some, has never been a means to allow people to enjoy a quality of life beyond that which is handed to them. Programs such as section eight rental housing subsidies are strained, as demand continues to increase year after year and supply contracts are secured due to market demand.

Other such programs are the Temporary Assistance to Needy Families (TANF) "are below the poverty level in every state and in most states, below seventy-five percent of the poverty level" per Gilbert.

The Affordable Care Act (ACA), better known as Obamacare, has been the source of much controversy since becoming law. Many Americans gained access to healthcare for the first time; while many working families saw their insurance premiums skyrocket.

According to an article published in *IBD*, companies are now trying to avoid penalties by slashing employee hours and offering plans that are extremely expensive for most families. These plans usually have high deductibles, or eliminate coverage of hospitalization and surgery in order for customers to afford them. The article claims that "(f)or a full-time worker earning $17,500, paying $1,670 for bronze coverage qualifies as 'affordable'. That's a thousand dollars more than someone at the same income level would have to pay for an exchange plan that caps total out-of-pocket expenses at about five hundred-fifty dollars in 2016."

So what is the best method of dealing with these issues? Gilbert points out in his book "the free market has been the most effective anti-poverty mechanism ever. The sheer productive might of the American system has created such a huge economic pie that even those living on the crumbs are physically better off than people in the Third World."

This is the reality I choose to accept. I cannot deny statistics on inequality, and the vast sums of money controlled by a handful of people. But if I am to believe I am truly free, and if I desire to enjoy the freedoms of economic success available to me, then I can't expect the government to provide me with that which I am capable of creating myself. Consider the issue of immigration. According to the article "Stuck" in *Esquire magazine*, "(i)mmigrants are now twice as likely to start a new business as native-born Americans." I think that statistic alone is a referendum on the mindset prevalent in America, especially in the black community. I've certainly witnessed the drive and determination most immigrants possess. In fact, most small business owners in black neighborhoods are immigrants. I remember growing up; there was a corner store I used to frequent with my Aunt. Every time we went there, there was a different member of the family in there working in some capacity.

Years later, those same children who ran around the store as employees of the family business were now college graduates, in addition to being co-owners of an established family business. The same is true for the owners of several establishments where I spent my money, in neighborhoods all around the D.C. area.

If there is one common trait I have learned from immigrants who work or start a business in the U.S., it's that they have the willingness to sacrifice in order to get what they want.

They don't have the misguided concept that the government will do anything for them at all, other than give them an opportunity to create what they will of themselves. I used to work in the construction industry, and I saw this firsthand, from the scores of Salvadorian and Mexican immigrants willing to work long hours for less pay.

This is one of the most contentious issues in American politics today, as America tries to balance the financial stability of American jobs, the humanitarian concerns of those fleeing their country of origin, the security concerns of protecting the nation from those who wish to cause harm, the desire for top level talent trained in America but forced to leave when student visas expire, and those who seek to marry persons from other countries.

I'm always surprised at how simple people seem to think the solution is to this complicated issue. On one hand, I understand that a lax immigration policy puts immigrants into direct competition with people in my community, especially those who are seeking low-skilled jobs.

There was a time when most fast-food restaurants were staffed by young people seeking financial independence, but now it is not uncommon to see those same establishments staffed by immigrants.

This dynamic affects the labor market in communities already struggling to secure gainful employment for its citizens. I do believe there needs to be a path for those illegal immigrants already in the country to gain citizenship, however. Apart from any of the other issues, I think that it makes sense for tax purposes, if nothing else. I highly doubt our government will be able to find solutions to these issues any time soon, especially in the polarized political climate of today. This is one of the effects these PAC's have had on our nation's government.

After the Supreme Court ruling in *Citizens United v. Federal Election Commission* handed down in 2010 allowed huge sums of money to be poured into these PAC's, those with the financial resources to purchase media attention have used it to shape the political discussion as they see fit.

According to the *Esquire magazine* article "Billionaires Unleashed", in the 2016 (election) cycle, the Koch brothers alone will spend eight hundred million. Casino magnate Sheldon Adelson spent more than one hundred million in 2012 and will likely spend more." Congress has been significantly impacted by these tactics, in a number of different ways. By investing heavily in state congressional races, donors are able to influence and ultimately seat candidates in state legislatures. Then, state legislatures are able to control redistricting, which allows them to bunch voters into groups favorable to their party. This ultimately allows them to decide how votes are tallied for elections to Congress. According to the article, Republicans in Ohio now have twelve congressional seats compared to Democrats four. These policies have given Republicans a majority in the House of Representatives that is "near permanent" according to the article. They sum up the differing views on the issue this way, "(h)ere's your choice: status quo - they earned it, they can spend it however they want. Continue to allow individuals and corporations to donate unlimited amounts of money to candidates through super PAC's and keep pretending those super PAC's are independent of the presidential campaigns, or amend the Constitution. Ban unlimited spending by fat cats and corporations."

The article voices the opinion "oligarchs buying elections is the last thing a democracy sees before it dies."

This choice presented in that article is one I struggle with philosophically.

On one hand, I readily acknowledge those with financial resources will always control the direction of government. I do believe this power can't go unchecked, however.

While I firmly believe in extending full property rights to all individuals, I believe we cannot allow only the ideas to surface which have been sponsored by those with the means to do so.

But what do some of these differences look like, in terms of Republicans and Democrats?

In an article published in *National Review magazine* titled "Civil Rights Republicanism," Theodore R. Johnson addresses some of the challenges faced by many African-Americans and the variety of political views that they hold.

He begins with a story about how he was ignored by volunteers campaigning for Mitt Romney in 2012, presumably because he is a black man. He then goes on to point out that "nine in ten blacks routinely vote for the Democratic presidential nominee."

Indeed, black voters have history with the Democratic Party, beginning largely with support for President Roosevelt and the New Deal, and solidified in the 1960's with support for President Johnson's Great Society legislation.

But the Democratic Party had done very little for the so-called black community that makes it worthy of the unquestioned loyalty shown, in my opinion.

Rather, black people are blinded by attractive promises from candidates who then fail to deliver, and because some of the candidates look like them or mention their experiences, they are lulled into a false sense of meaningful representation.

Republican candidates may actually hold ideas and values that blacks find attractive, but because they are overshadowed by racial insensitivity and wanton disregard for civil rights issues, they disqualify themselves in a few short sound bites, before they ever address substantive issues.

As Johnson points out, "(o)nce civil rights protections are guaranteed, African Americans will feel free to vote in accordance with their varied economic and social interests. This simple truth is mostly obscured by the party's fundamental misunderstanding of black people and what motivates their voting decisions. Many Republicans have largely accepted, and even perpetuated, the false narrative that black Americans are beholden to the Democratic Party because it supports them with social-welfare programs and unearned benefits. Blacks' overwhelming support of Democratic candidates is assumed to be proof that the policy views of black voters are identical with those of the Democratic Party."

Johnson goes on to list several civil rights issues that the Republican Party should consider; voting rights in the wake of the Supreme Court's decision in *Shelby v. _ Holder*, disparate impact housing policies, and equal employment opportunities.

As I stated before, there has always been somewhat of a divide in the black community between those with financial resources and those without them. Johnson details these differences in the black community by pointing to research that shows the rising levels of inequality among blacks. He states, "African-Americans' buying power, a measure of disposable net income, is $1.1 trillion, and black household income is growing fast. Nearly one in five black households earns $75,000 or more."

As the product of two hard-working parents, I can attest to this divide. I've spoken at length about the struggles I had as a child in trying to reconcile my persona with the upward mobility created by two parents with middle class incomes. This culture war caused by socio-economic inequality is largely ignored, by both politicians and so-called black leaders alike.

As Hollywood has begun to cast African-Americans in more prominent roles that showcase affluent, intelligent characters, black people have the opportunity to see themselves in positions that more closely reflect the reality that hard-working, law-abiding people of color are in fact normal.

Although I have spent both terms of the first African-American president inside of federal prison, I'm glad my children can envision a world where this possibility not only exists, but has been accomplished.

This does not mean every policy created under his administration had been beneficial to the so-called black community though. African-Americans must not be confined by the concept of "linked fate", or the belief defined by University of Chicago professor Michael Dawson "one's success is contingent on the success of the group as a whole," as explained in Johnson's article. Rather, I believe that as more blacks continue to strive for individual achievement and become economically successful, they will develop the resources to create opportunity for others. This is what will create a true black community in my opinion - not only the shared experiences of discrimination, but economic empowerment that affords us real political representation.

Consider for a minute the issue of taxation in America. A large number of people I know are convinced that taxing both corporations and the rich more heavily is the solution to overcoming budget deficits in our country's entitlement programs.

They also believe by increasing the minimum wage, workers currently employed in low skilled jobs will become economically empowered.

In some ways, I do believe that corporations need to contribute more to both the country and its workforce, especially since American corporations have about $1.5 trillion sitting on their balance sheets.

However, I also don't believe that many of the proposed policies will bring about the results that many desire. The current corporate tax rate is thirty-five percent, compared to about a twenty-five percent average for countries competing for the revenue of these same companies. According to *the Esquire* article titled "America: These Are Your Choices," "since 2011, twelve U.S. companies have reincorporated as foreign entities to avoid paying U.S. corporate taxes, which are among the highest in the world."

The article takes the position that lowering the tax rate would keep jobs from going overseas and incentivize companies to repatriate two trillion worth of assets.

Cutting corporate taxes would also lower the cost of U.S. production, which would also make U.S. jobs more attractive. This is not a simple issue, and I understand that there are a lot of factors involved when considering tax policy. According to Gilbert, "federal corporate income tax has fallen from just over thirty percent of federal revenue in the 1940's to less than ten percent in 1990's while the federal individual income tax has gone from about forty percent in the 1940's to seventy-five percent in the 1990's."

Many suggest raising taxes on top earners, which currently at forty percent is up from thirty-five percent when George W. Bush left office and from about twenty-eight percent during Ronald Reagan's administration.

As for minimum wage, this too is a complex issue. In an editorial published in *Investor's Business Daily* newspaper (IBD) titled,

"How Minimum Wage is Used as a Tool In Arsenal of Racists",
Walter E. Williams describes the racist history tied to minimum
wage from its implementation in America under the *Davis-Bacon
act in 1931* as a method to exclude blacks from the workforce
who were the cheap labor of that time, from federally financed or
assisted construction projects, to its use in South African
apartheid in order to achieve the same.

This is not the premise under which it is currently implemented,
but rather as a tool that is supposed to provide a living wage to all
Americans. According to the editorial, two hundred ten
economists support a proposal by Sen. Bernie Sanders to
establish a fifteen dollars an hour minimum wage by 2020.
Gilbert supports the concept of living wage as well, suggesting
"any person who works full time and year-round should earn a
wage that is sufficient to support a family."

But Williams counters the living wage debate with this question,
"Is it likely an employer would find it in his interest to pay a
worker fifteen dollars an hour when that worker has skills that
enable him to produce only five dollars worth of value an hour to
the employer's output?"

Instead, Williams argues that raising the minimum wage
effectively "prices out" the least skilled in our economy, which
are usually the poor, the uneducated, and youth who lack
experience and maturity.

He goes on to argue that these policies will disproportionately
affect black youth, much in the same way that they did when
these policies were originally enacted in 1931.

As the father of three, including a daughter who as of this writing
has recently dipped her toe into the labor market, I fully
understand the concept of providing a living wage.

As a black man with two felonies who will be transitioning back
to the community, the reality is that although I have done all I can
to increase my skill set while incarcerated, I may be in a position

very soon that requires me to accept a minimum wage position, as a first step towards re-entering the labor market.

No matter how optimistic I am, I know as a felon and now a registered sex offender, this could very well be a reality for me. Yet I cannot ignore what I understand about how a minimum wage increase affects a balance sheet. As I said before, I choose to view all things from the perspective of a capitalist, as a path to success in this capitalist society.

In that regard, raising the minimum wage is effectively asking all companies to increase their operating expenses, which ultimately decreases profit margins for the company and the return on investment of its shareholders.

As much as people may note the inequalities in CFO pay and that of the employees underneath them; the truth is until the market responds to these issues in a way that affects a company's profits, these practices will continue.

CEOs have a fiduciary duty to shareholders, however, so the only way these policies of increasing operating costs outside of added regulations will happen is if the market responds.

In spite of any personal feelings I may have about the issue, I don't think this is a viable solution, especially in the face of a global economy that continues to expand through bi-partisan global trade deals that do little to protect American labor.

In no way do I consider myself an expert on any of these issues, but I feel the need to paint a clear picture of the political and economic conditions that exist from my current perspective.

I originally had no intention of delving into many of the subjects I encountered in my limited research, but I know it is necessary in the discussion of the apprenticeship of disfunction.

Far too often we examine political issues in a vacuum. We, as a country, get so caught up in the pageantry that is American politics, we lose sight of what I know as the seventh UU principle, respect for the interdependent web of existence of which we are a part.

We feel no connection to the people affected by these issues, or we allow our empathy to blind us from the reality of capitalism. This polarization is what fuels America as we now know it, and as I seek to move from the prison of today to the purpose of tomorrow, I find myself torn between two ideals.

I long for the social and communal morality expressed in my liberal theology, yet I know becoming more adept in the free market principles this country was founded on is the only way to find the freedoms I long to enjoy.

I believe the socialism versus libertarian debate is severely overinflated by the commercialized media. Almost every American would be against absolute practices of either side of these political spectrums, but the struggle continues to find balance between the capitalist versions of these two schools of thought.

History has shown us regulation alone is not the solution. Undoubtedly one of the best books I have ever read, especially regarding most of the issues addressed in this book, is Michelle Alexander's *The New Jim Crow*. She expands on so many of the subjects that are important to me, and that are relevant to the apprenticeship of sin. I could reference and make comment about almost every page of her book but I want to begin this part of my discussion by pointing out two issues. The first is the issue of jury selection and racial bias.

In her book, Alexander points out, "studies indicate that people become increasingly harsh when an alleged criminal is darker and more 'stereotypically black'; they are more lenient when the accused is lighter and appears more stereotypically white. This is true of jurors as well as law enforcement officers."

I think this further highlights the issue of race in this country. Somehow, the complexity and nuances of human behavior are not viewed in the same way for black people as they are for whites. I watched a documentary about life during prohibition. There were scores of older, white people on TV, talking about their open contempt for not only the laws of that time, but the principles behind it.

These were the same type of people who were often selected to sit on juries of black men, and more often than not, the sentiments expressed by the participants of that documentary never seem to find their way to the courtroom.

Usually, blacks stand little to no chance at seating jury members from their community, due to a list of laws that make it easy for prosecutors to exclude them. According to Alexander, "thirty-one states and the federal government subscribe to the practice of lifetime felon exclusion from juries. As a result, about thirty percent of black men are automatically banned from jury service for life." This is one of many areas that many black men find themselves rendered ineffective due to a felony conviction, but sadly it is not the only one.

Mrs. Alexander does a great job in her book explaining some of the finer points of these issues, including employment, discrimination, housing difficulties, voter disenfranchisement, and more.

One of the biggest issues that showcase the apprenticeship of disfunction is that of gun rights and violent crime. To put this in perspective, consider the group of people in Burns, Oregon, who decided to protest the conviction of one of their neighbors by taking up arms and occupying a federal natural wildlife reserve. I watched in awe as the group gave interviews with guns in hand, and fellow supporters paced in the background with all types of rifles strapped across their body.

I was quite certain this story would dominate the news for days to come, and that every network would be interrupting their regularly scheduled programming with images from the "breaking news" of SWAT teams and snipers moving into position. None of that happened, however. In fact, I didn't even hear much about the story over the next few days except for a few brief mentions during the cable news cycle, when it was reported that the local sheriff had been sent in to talk to the people and "calm things down."

As of this writing, law enforcement has regained control of the facility, after a traffic stop of some of those protesting ended in a shootout that left one of the men dead. Others have been arrested, after more than two weeks from when the protesters first took over the wildlife refuge.

None of the violent or physical confrontations between protesters and law enforcement was ever televised on national news. I think most people miss the hypocrisy of that response, both by law enforcement and the media. There was no talk of sending in the National Guard, no minute-by-minute aerial views of where these armed protesters were "holed up".

In contrast, citizens' participation in "Black Lives Matter" protests all across the country in the wake of multiple incidents between black men and violent police officers were consistently filmed.

Militarized police forces were brought in to "maintain order" almost immediately in most cases and reporters from all across the country documented almost every minute of it all with the fervor and intensity of a ring announcer at a boxing match.

Although none of the protesters openly carried firearms, the police who responded to these incidents were heavily armed.

Mrs. Alexander expands on the mindset behind the disfunction we see in the response to violence as well.

As she rightly points out, there has been a difference of opinion within the black community about both the causes of and solutions to many of these issues since the end of slavery.

As Alexander notes, many blacks experience what she refers to as a "dual frustration" around the issues of crime and law enforcement in their community.

So many people who mean well have no idea how to fix the problems within the community, but they are motivated by the basic human desire to feel safe. This need for safety, as I explained earlier, is a need surpassed only by a person's physiological needs.

It makes sense, then, that as the crack cocaine epidemic began to ravish the black community, many blacks begged law enforcement to "do something" about the violence that has now become commonplace in many communities.

The feeling of helplessness that many in the community feel is a powerful tool in the hands of those who seek power.

History has certainly shown that people are much more willing to sacrifice freedoms when they desire safety, whether that sense of safety and security is real or imagined.

This is one of the reasons why mass incarceration and get tough policies were supported by some blacks, even though they realized law enforcement was effectively dismantling the black community by incarcerating large numbers of its black men, they believed the sacrifice was worth it in order to end the violence.

In addition to that, many supported and still support the idea that failed morals is the ultimate issue at the root of the problem.

Mrs. Alexander speaks to this "moral uplift ideology" as having its roots in the Jim Crow era.

The idea is that blacks must behave in a manner seen as acceptable to white sensibilities, in order to bring about the racial equality they seek.

She writes that "(p)arents and school teachers counsel black children that, if they ever hope to escape this system and avoid prison time, they must be on their best behavior, raise their arms and spread their legs for the police without complaint, stay in failing schools, pull up their pants, and refuse all forms of illegal work and money making activity, even if jobs in the legal economy are impossible to find."

I think most people assume criminals don't believe in the law, or rather, that laws are necessary. Yet in my discussions with a lot of my fellow prisoners over the years, almost everyone agrees laws are a necessary part of any civilized society. As I said before, there are even rules and laws that prisoners create amongst themselves to govern conduct.

The problems lie in the application of the law. It is certainly obvious to most the law is unfairly biased against blacks, and the punishments being handed down have affected black men disproportionately.

We cannot, in the pursuit of a solution, forget about the economic factors involved in these issues. As Mrs. Alexander points out, African-Americans are all but obsolete in this global economy. Technology, modernization, and foreign labor have replaced the need for much of the low-skilled labor many communities across America have relied on for income.

Although this reality has affected communities of all races, African-Americans have been the slowest to adapt to the new economy.

This is what makes a lot of the violence in black communities acceptable to many of the perpetrators, because many of these men feel no real connection to that community.

They see no opportunity to own anything, to create anything for themselves. They quickly realize they are seen as unwanted, and their government and even their community see them not as an asset, but as liabilities.

They feel inspired by movements that profess "Black Lives Matter" but they don't see reality manifested day to day in their own community, amongst their own people. So how do we solve these issues?

As I have said several times in this book, I believe African-Americans must first learn to be better capitalists before we can address anything else.

As unfair or unjust that I believe current conditions are, until African-Americans are willing to use their enormous economic power not only to create opportunity for themselves and others in their communities, but also to put government officials in place that are paid to represent their interests, the system will continue on exactly the way it has been.

Recently there have been some bi-partisan efforts to remedy some of the injustices in the criminal justice system, and there has also been some legislation passed that appears on its surface to be a step in the right direction.

I'm not suggesting we can ever completely do away with crime, nor do I have any illusion that our society can ever be free of the imperfections in character that make us human. I do believe we can do better though.

Our collective approach must be proactive instead of reactive. The failed police tactics have been applied to the war on drugs has now begun to target sex trafficking as the "hot button" issue through the implementation of mandatory minimums and long prison sentences.

Although the calls from concerned citizens for law enforcement to "do something" are justified, the reality is we continue to pick at symptoms of a larger issue instead of dealing with the root cause. While I applaud any effort that seeks to change the current criminal justice model, steps must also be taken to ensure opportunities exist for prisoners when they are released. For instance, many people would be surprised at just how difficult it is to obtain and maintain a driver's license.

Heavy fines that local and state governments use as a source of revenue disproportionately affects the poor and the accrual of interest on these fines continue even if you are sent to prison. Despite the fact there is a high demand for commercial drivers in America, maintaining a driver's license has become increasingly harder, especially for blacks. Simply removing some of the many obstacles to maintaining a valid driver's license would expand the economic opportunity for a lot of men, especially returning from prison.

We must also create entrepreneurial opportunities for those in disadvantaged communities.

For instance, the current idea of halfway houses, which are supposed to serve to help people who are at the end of a sentence transition back into the community, could also serve as an incubator for those with aspirations of creating a business. Not only would this give them a chance to create something meaningful, it would also add value to the community. We must create a path for men like myself to become relevant to the financial and political fabric of this country.

We have to create success stories outside of those of athletes and entertainers, and the fairy tale that many from the inner city perceive President Barack Obama to be.

Until we consistently acknowledge that we see black men as assets and not as liabilities, we can never solve the apprenticeship of disfunction.

EPILOGUE

If nothing else materializes from this book, I have to say that it has been very therapeutic to write. There was a lot of self-doubt that crept into my head along the way, and I fought like hell to push past it to complete this part of my journey. I wondered if I was too honest or not honest enough, if my thoughts were too broad or too focused, or if people would even care about what I had to say.

On March 12, 2015 I lost my grandmother, Ella Rowe Greenfield, while I was locked behind prison walls. I'll never forget how that felt, not only to lose someone I was so close to, but to know that I had missed the last part of her life. I couldn't attend her funeral or take part in giving her the honor and respect that she had earned when it came time to bury her. I'm sure that feeling of loss will haunt me for years to come, but it also provided me with the extra push that I needed to finish my writing.

I can truly say today I understand my purpose much clearer than I ever have before, and I also understand how important it is to capture this moment of time from behind prison walls.

In his book, *From Murder to Forgiveness*, Azim Khamisa poses the question, "What if I became a foe: not of the boy who killed my son, but of the forces which led him to kill my son? What if I reached out as far as I possibly could, and devoted myself to fighting the plague of youth violence?"

While I applaud Mr. Khamisa's heartfelt sentiment, I pray that he and others like him will come to understand that you can't treat an underlying condition simply by treating the symptoms.

I remember the frustration I felt at his seminars not with him per se, but with the constraints placed on our conversation by the program and intended subject matter. I wasn't frustrated by what he was saying, but rather by what he wasn't saying.

Khamisa writes, "Between 1975 and 1980, I successfully invested in businesses in Seattle, Dallas, Atlanta, and San Diego." He reports that his "original thirty thousand dollars grew to $1.8 million." I remember jumping out of my chair and thinking we need to be discussing that! As painful and tragic that the violence that happened to Mr. Khamisa's son is, for the black men who have been exposed to this type of violence for most of their lives, this is sadly nothing new.

That doesn't mean that we can't empathize with that loss, but unless it serves as a pretext for a new solution it becomes difficult not to categorize as another side effect in the long list of those created by the apprenticeship of sin.

Robbing take out delivery people was so common at one point in the DC area that now many restaurants still refuse to deliver to certain neighborhoods.

But by creating better capitalists, who are able to better access the system in a meaningful way, we can begin to eradicate many of the conditions that create the apprenticeship of sin.

Our young people will be able to see a clear pathway to owning a piece of the community where they formerly caused so much destruction. Our young people, black people in particular, don't suffer from a lack of advice, they suffer from the lack of a real opportunity to apply what they are being told.

This is why I'm so passionate about the free market being the path through which I hope to make amends in the practice of restorative justice. But this is a path that I'll readily admit I can't travel on my own, not with a realistic expectation that I will be successful.

Hopefully I can look back one day on this moment with pride, the pride that comes from accomplishing even a fraction of the change that I have outlined in this book. I'm aware that statistically the odds are against me. Almost 30 percent of people released from prison are re-arrested within six months, and nearly 68 percent are re-arrested within three years.

Today, I choose to speak a new reality into existence. As I have already said, I don't care how well this book does in terms of sales, if it allows me the opportunity to meet people capable of helping me to accomplish my goals. It is with that in mind that I challenge you, the readers, to take action. I beg you to help me and those like me to find the economic and political freedom that we so desperately need. Invest in us, not with more empty advice and lip service of false support, but with real opportunity. I don't want a hand-out, just a hand up.

I offer you the unique opportunity to be a part of my success story. I even have a title already for part two of this series: The Apprenticeship of Success. I won't pretend that I have all of the answers though, and I am still working through some very real issues. I still have no idea how my personal life will end up, especially when it comes to my children.

Even though I'm confident that my relationship with my children is good despite the fact that I'm currently incarcerated, I can't pretend like the tumultuous relationship that I've had over the years with their mothers hasn't had any effect on them.

I also have doubts about if I'll be able to find women who are willing to have meaningful relationships with me under terms that I find acceptable, but all I can do is continue to be honest with people and let the chips fall where they may.

I'm at a place in life where I really know what I need from people who choose to be involved with me, and I would rather have some really good friends that I can be honest with instead of a relationship built on lies.

As much as I've grown, I still wrestle with thoughts and beliefs from my old way of life. Some of these beliefs I acknowledge that I need to let go of, and some of them I'm still on the fence about where I stand. I still very much believe in minding your own business. It seems that in this age of social media, what I call being nosy is now considered "cyber-sharing", but I still have a hard time accepting that it's acceptable for everybody to offer an opinion about how someone else chooses to live life.

But the whole mind your business mindset affects me in other ways as well including my willingness to call the police. I was apprenticed into the "stop snitchin'" movement that comes with the criminal lifestyle, and now that I desire to be a normal citizen again, there are some real issues to consider.

Let's suppose that my mother and I were out somewhere and someone robbed me at gunpoint, with no mask and in enough light to recognize their facial features, a short while later the police would apprehend a suspect and put together a line-up. I have no doubt that my mother or many of the other law-abiding citizens that I know would identify the perpetrator without hesitation, because that's what law-abiding citizens do. But what am I to do?

The rules of my former lifestyle dictate that I can't give any assistance whatsoever to the police, despite the fact that this man could have robbed or even harmed my mother or another member of my family. Under the rules of the apprenticeship the only acceptable recourse available to me is to seek justice in the streets. I've discussed this issue at length with different men who are or were incarcerated, but also seek to change from their former ways.

This is one of the many stumbling blocks that black men face in retiring from the apprenticeship of sin; the basic question that must be addressed is who deserves to go to prison? Most men would quickly answer rapists and child molesters without batting an eye. But let's suppose someone assaults a woman in your family or if someone breaks in your house while you are home. What do you do?

How do you protect your family and your loved ones? As felons, the laws are clear that we are not permitted to have any access to firearms, and there are plenty of men who are currently serving time for "constructive possession" of firearms that they didn't own. How are those who seek to retire from the apprenticeship of incarceration supposed to protect themselves from those who are still trapped in the hateful mindset present in their community?

How do we defend against those who have not let go of the destruction that we used to embrace? The law has made the options clear: possess a firearm and risk returning to prison, or become comfortable with calling the police and risk the dangers associated with your choice.

This presents several problems. First, calling the police for self-protection is by definition a reaction to an injury that has already occurred. Second, black men face a significant social stigma by agreeing to testify against another person in court, especially another black man.

It's easy for someone who doesn't face the reality of these challenges to dismiss them as trivial, but the reality of gun laws, law enforcement and distrust of the process, and the cultural resistance to change is ever-present for me and many others like me.

This is another reason why it is so important to have political representation that is sensitive to the challenges that the so-called black community faces. Michelle Alexander sums up these concerns beautifully, "(u)rging the urban poor - or anyone - to live up to their highest ideals and values is a good thing, as it demonstrates confidence in the ability of all people to stretch, grow and evolve.

Even in the most dire circumstances, we all have power and agency, the ability to choose what we think and how we respond to the circumstances of our lives. Moreover, we all have duties and responsibilities to each other, not the least of which is to do no harm. We ought not excuse violence or tolerate behavior that jeopardizes the safety and security of others, just as all people - no matter who they are or what they have done - ought to be regarded as having basic human rights to work, housing, education, and food, residents of all communities have a basic right to safety and security...the politics of responsibility is doomed to fail, not because there is something especially wrong with those locked in ghettos or prisons today, but because there is nothing special about them.

They are merely human. They will continue to make mistakes and break the law for reasons that may or may not be justified; and as long as they do so, this system of mass incarceration will continue to function well."

As far as religion is concerned, I've come to understand just how much of a mystery that God really is. I've journeyed through different religious experiences and explanations of who He is and how He works, but in the end I've decided to trust that He will tell me what I need to know. He always has.

I sent a sample of this book to the UUA's publishing house in an effort to get this published through them, but I was told that "for a variety of reasons it isn't quite right." I would love to know what those various reasons are, but it's all good. I still choose to make an attempt to navigate my spiritual journey through the principles that they profess, although I'm unsure how much involvement I'll have in the actual organization.

I do hope that they find a way to include men like me, men from communities like mine who have been scarred by the apprenticeship of sin, into both their conversations and their congregations. Hopefully I can be a part of that process.

I read an article the other day about an old man who is currently incarcerated here with me. This man has been incarcerated most of his life, and after spending a few years on the streets he decided to rob a bank in hopes of being caught and returning to prison for life. After spending most of his life in prison, this man felt more comfortable in prison than he did on the street.

I've met lots of men like him over the years, men who have been so consumed by the apprenticeship of sin that its consequences become a comfort zone.

In the article, the man talked about how easy it becomes to do time, and how the routine of prison becomes easy to navigate after a while. I considered all that he said, and I became nervously afraid at the thought of just how right that he is about that. It's a scary thing to realize how much you have in common with career criminals, men who have given up all hope of leaving the dark side and the apprenticeship of sin.

One of the saddest sights in prison is watching the vast number of men in their sixties, seventies, and even their eighties shuffling back and forth across the prison yard.

What's worse are those who still hold on to the ideals of the apprenticeship of sin, long after their bodies have become incapable of behaving in the manner that the dark side demands. It is during these moments that I'm thankful for my family and my parents. The story of the prodigal son is one of the most popular biblical parables, but every time that I've ever heard a sermon related to it, the focus is always on the actions of the son. My mother and father have, despite all that we've been through, done all that they could to raise me into the man that I was purposed to be. They provided me with the example that I now hope to provide to my own children. Their consistent, responsible behavior has been at times the only mitigating factor from the consequences of my recklessness.

Most importantly, no matter how many times I have demanded my share of the inheritance in order to pursue the apprenticeship of sin, they have always met me on the road home with an embrace and a kiss, and killed the fatted calf in celebration of my return. To them I say, I'm on my way home.

SELECTED BIBLIOGRAPHY

1) Market Digests Hillarynomics, Investor's Business Daily, Wed. Jan 13, 2016

2) How Minimum Wage is Used as Tool in Arsenal of Racists, Investor's Business Daily, Wed. Jan. 13, 2016, Walter E. Williams

3) How Much Do We Deserve? An Inquiry into Distributive justice, 2001, Richard S. Gilbert, Skinner House Books

4) Moral Purity, 2007, Rod and Staff Publishers, Inc. Aaron M. Shank

5) Catechism of the Catholic Church, 1994, United States Catholic Conference, Inc. Libreria Editrice Vaticana

6) Christian Doctrine, Shirley G. Guthrie, Westminster John Knox Press, Louisville, Ky., 1994

7) My Utmost for His Highest, 1935, Dodd, Mead & Company, Inc. Oswald Chambers

8) Message to the Blackman, 1965, Muhammad's Temple No. 2, Elijah Muhammad

9) Islam: Faith, Practice, and History, 2004, Ansariyan Publications, Sayyid Muhammad Rizvi

10) What Everyone Should Know About Islam and Muslims, 1996, Library of Islam, Suzanne Haneef

11) United States 2015 Sentencing Guidelines Manual

12) Lexis-Nexis, BNA Insights, 90 Criminal Law Reporters (BNA) 426, Drugs, Mary Price and James Felman, Jan. 4, 2012

13) Stuck, Esquire Magazine, Dec/Jan. 2015/16, Richard V. Reeves

14) The Confessions of R. Kelly, GQ Magazine, Feb 2016, Chris Heath

15) Understanding Psychology, 2008 McGraw-Hill, Robert S. Feldman

16) Unitarian Universalist Association of Congregations, 24 Farnsworth St., Boston MA 02210

17) Ferguson: Up to Our Necks, Meg Riley, UU World Magazine, Winter 2014

18) Darkening the Doorways, 2011, Dr. Mark Morrison-Reed, Skinner House Books

19) Secret-Keeping, Quest monthly, Erika Hewitt, January 2016 (1S)

20) Universalism in Practice, UU World Magazine, Nancy McDonald Ladd, Spring 2015

21) From Murder to Forgiveness, 2012, Balboa Press, Azim Khamisa

22) BIPAC, www.bipac.net, Business Industry Political Action Committee

23) Obamacare Mandate Worse Than Feared, Investor's Business Daily, Jan. 13, 2016, Jed Graham

24) Citizens United v. Federal Election Commission, 558 US, 150 S Ct, 175 L Ed 2d 753

25) Civil Rights Republicanism, National Review Magazine, Theodore R. Johnson, Nov. 2, 2015

26) America: These Are Your Choices, Esquire Magazine, Dec/Jan. 2015/16, Esquire

27) Magazine/Brookings Institution

28) The New Jim Crow, 2010, The New Press, Michelle Alexander

92892709R00178

Made in the USA
Columbia, SC
02 April 2018